COURAGEOUS
JOURNEY

COURAGEOUS JOURNEY

Walking the Lost Boys' Path from the Sudan to America

by

Ayuel Leek Deng, Beny Ngor Chol
and Barbara Youree

New Horizon Press
Far Hills, NJ

Requests for permissions should be addressed to:
New Horizon Press
P.O. Box 669
Far Hills, NJ 07931

Ayuel Leek Deng, Beny Ngor Chol and Barbara Youree,
Courageous Journey: Walking the Lost Boys' Path from the Sudan to America

Cover design: Robert Aulicino
Interior design: Susan M. Sanderson
All maps used in this book are courtesy of the CIA World Factbook unless otherwise noted.
Back cover image by P. Moumtzis courtesy of UNHCR

Library of Congress Control Number: 2008921807

ISBN 13: 978-0-88282-334-8
ISBN 10: 0-88282-334-5
New Horizon Press

Manufactured in the U.S.A.

2012 2011 2010 2009 2008 / 5 4 3 2 1

DEDICATION

This story is dedicated to those who sacrificed their lives in Sudan's civil war, those injured and mutilated by it and those displaced with no hope of returning to their homes. In a larger sense, we want it to bring hope to oppressed people everywhere who are in crisis—particularly children—looking for solutions as they remember the turmoil they endured. We pray that their dreams may become reality and the legacy of their suffering turn to happiness through that struggle. With faith in God, we hope that one day these people will find support and comfort by sharing stories of their painful journey as we have done in sharing ours.

—Ayuel Leek Deng and Beny Ngor Chol

AUTHORS' NOTE

These are the actual experiences and personal histories of Ayuel Leek Deng and Beny Ngor Chol, and this book reflects their opinions of the past, present and future. The personalities, events, actions and conversations portrayed within the story have been reconstructed from their memories, documents, letters, personal papers, press accounts and the memories of other participants. Events involving the characters happened as described; only minor details have been changed.

In an effort to safeguard the privacy of certain people, some locations, individuals' names and identifying characteristics have been changed. Some minor characters are composites.

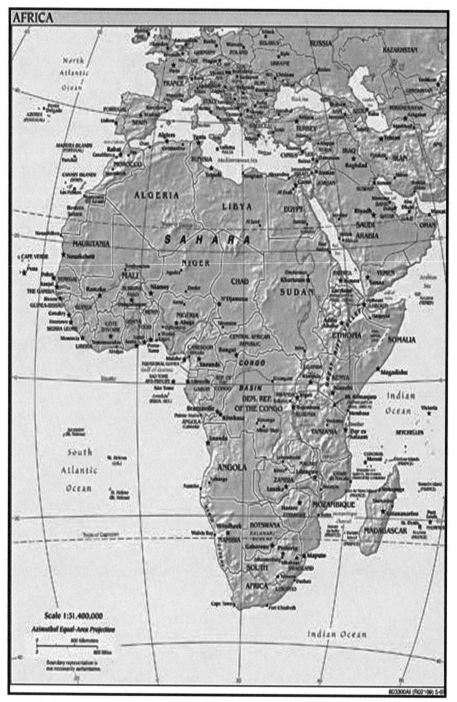

Map of Africa courtesy of the CIA World Factbook

TABLE OF CONTENTS

PREFACE

Sometimes we look through a single window at one of the world's many tragedies and are touched so deeply that we are forever changed. That happened to me when I met Ayuel Leek Deng and Beny Ngor Chol and heard their incredible story.

I knew Sudan was in Africa, but I had not been aware of the civil war between the North and the South, in which more than two million Sudanese had died and even more displaced. The war was still raging in 2001 when I first learned of the so-called Lost Boys of Sudan. Since I rarely miss a news cycle and am especially interested in global situations, I was shocked to learn that thousands of displaced children had walked for months across Sudan's barren land, menaced by starvation, disease, wild animals and shrapnel from their own government's helicopter fire. The world community made little effort to relieve their suffering. Though the peace accord was signed in 2005, a similar crisis has erupted in Darfur. Fortunately, this situation is receiving media coverage.

In 2001, when several of the Lost Boys—who had spent their childhoods in refugee camps—arrived in Kansas City, churches and community groups sought out mentors to help them adjust. I signed up. It soon became clear to me that these young men had goals in mind. Education was the first priority, followed by letting the world know about the plight of their country. They saw themselves as "seeds of a new Sudan." You will understand why as you read this book. Ayuel and Beny asked me to write their story to get their message out—*that there is a monumental crisis in Sudan. They and other refugees plan to do all they can, but their country also needs the resources of the rest of the world to help solve it.*

This book presents the struggles of Ayuel and Beny, which, in some measure, reflect the universal experiences of millions of others.

My aim is to personalize the consequences of worldwide conflicts by showing how Ayuel, Beny and their friends dealt not only with the physical challenges, but also with the spiritual dimension of anger, revenge, faith and forgiveness.

My portion of the proceeds will be donated to the Greater Kansas City Lost Boys Network, Inc., a foundation that offers support and financial assistance to Lost Boys across the area.

—Barbara Youree

ONE

GRIEF AND JOY

"Something's wrong over there," Ayuel said as he and Beny Ngor Chol walked down the dirt path toward the bulletin board in the refugee camp. "Wonder why all those people are headed to the riverbank."

"Maybe someone's going to make a speech," suggested Beny, yet unaware of the anxiety Ayuel was feeling about the gathering crowd. "It's probably too early for 'The List' to go up anyway. Come, let's see what's going on."

The two young men turned from the International Rescue Committee office where they were headed and quickened their steps toward the dry riverbed. Miles of mud and straw huts dotted the vast plateau near the equator, home to orphaned children and a fewer number of intact families—80,000 in all. In this desolate place in Kenya, Africa, only a few scrub trees survived—much like the fading hopes of the forgotten inhabitants.

Ayuel and Beny joined several people running toward the happening at the riverbank. The sound of pounding feet—unaccompanied by voices—lent an eerie foreboding to the stillness. A breeze swirled dust in the warm morning air. The screech of a single hawk drew Ayuel's eyes upward as he watched the raptor swoop low, flap its wings and soar again. Then, something else silhouetted against the emerging rays of sunlight. The excitement he'd felt about searching for his name on The List melted into horror. Beny saw it at the same time, and both young men stopped and stared.

There, suspended from a high limb of the tallest tree on the bank, hung a body, limp like a dead bird.

A flash of light, then another, recorded what had happened. *Why do they have to do that?* As the cameraman stepped back, two other workers from the International Rescue Committee came forward with a stepladder.

"Who is it—this time?" Ayuel whispered to another friend of his, who stood at the edge of the crowd. Ayuel, a sensitive young man with fine features, felt his mouth dry and his breath come in short jerks.

"Majok Bol. He's from Zone Two Minor."

And from the Bor region where I'm from. And Dinka too, like me. He remembered the tall, quiet boy with the charming smile.

As the two officers cut the rope and gently lowered the body, murmurs rose from the group of onlookers.

"Majok was our best soccer player…"

"Always a good sport."

"He was the smartest in our group," a boy said through quiet sobs.

But no one asked why. They knew. All of them had thought about it at one time or another. Suicides didn't happen often, but when they did, those who had passed their childhood here in the refugee camp were left traumatized.

As the men carried the body away, the crowd dispersed—some crying softly, others hissing angry words between their teeth, or just gazing blankly into their own hopeless futures.

Ayuel and Beny stood facing each other—shocked and devastated— not knowing what to say. Ayuel looked down at the spiral notebook he still carried in his hand. It contained the math notes he'd gotten up early that morning to study. *Why didn't I know?* His after-school social work included suicide counseling to those showing signs. No one had alerted him.

Now, he recalled the day that first posting had gone up. He saw Majok leaving just as he'd come to check for his own name. Majok had muttered something about it being hopeless to expect to see his name. Ayuel had tried to encourage him by saying there would be more listings and he was well-qualified. *Why didn't I take his comment more seriously?*

The sound of a stapler pounding the wooden bulletin board by the IRC office interrupted their sadness. Ayuel knew the posting meant ninety more names of lucky ones on The List. Since applying two years ago for refugee status in the United States of America, he had lived with the tension of hope. He knew some of the previously chosen ones who had already flown away to the western world, a fantasy place he could only read about—where ordinary people lived in enormous painted houses, drove big shiny cars, got fat from abundant food, and education was free for everyone.

The woman he loved and hoped to marry someday had left on the very first flight. She had gone to the United States. If ever he were chosen, he might be sent to Australia, the Netherlands, Canada or—if he were really lucky—the United States. Since that was a very big country, would he even be able to find her?

"You're going to see if your name's on it, aren't you?" Beny asked. Thoughtful and introspective, the event visibly distressed him, but he was also practical.

"Not yet," Ayuel responded. "Let's find out what they're talking about." IRC workers and several young men huddled together under the tree. A few wide-eyed younger children looked on.

As Beny and Ayuel approached, they recognized one young man who sobbed uncontrollably, standing just outside the huddle. The man had shared sleeping quarters with Majok. Ayuel put his hand on the man's shoulder. "I'm sorry. I'm so sorry."

"I heard Majok get up—about midnight—and leave our *tukul*. I just went back to sleep." The man wiped his eyes with his shirttail. "This morning I found the note—the note they are reading."

The huddle broke up and one of the IRC workers handed a piece of paper to Majok's roommate. "We'll need this back to make the report," the worker said. "We're sorry for your grief."

The roommate offered the note to Ayuel and Beny who silently read it together:

I don't know why my life seems so unpromising. Over all the years, today and tomorrow look the same. I lost my mother and father, my only sister, my brothers and recently my beloved younger brother. What kind of life is this? I am tired of this life and I am unable to continue this pain anymore.

★

Ayuel's emotions tore him in opposite directions. *How dare I hope to find my name on The List when I've just witnessed another's hope so miserably crushed?* Yet, he yearned to be chosen. Ayuel and Beny walked in silence toward the posted names. Both had risen to positions of leadership but Kakuma Refugee Camp in Kenya offered nothing more—no future to anticipate.

Ayuel had spent the past ten of his twenty years here, and four years before that in an Ethiopian camp, doing his best, never giving up. But to what end? If he returned to Sudan, his only means of survival would be to join the Sudanese People's Liberation Army and fight in his country's civil war. The cause was just. Colonel John Garang led his forces against the Arab-Islamic government that had declared *jihad* against the Black Christian and Animist South. The radical Muslims intended to enforce their harsh *sharia* laws, deny religious freedom and obliterate the villages over the newly discovered oil fields. But Ayuel, sick of the killing, had no desire to shoulder a gun.

Finding a job in Kenya was impossible—foreigners were not allowed to work here. According to rumor, only 3,800 out of the tens of thousands of refugees would ever find their names on The List of those chosen to go to the United States. Yet his heart pounded in anticipation.

Ayuel stood behind the knot of anxious youth and watched those at the board move out of the way. This was a silent ritual. Those who had searched long and hard for their names without success crept away with sagging shoulders and stony faces. Ayuel had done that many times. The few who found their names suppressed a smile, but the exuberance in their eyes belied their modesty. Ayuel inched closer, a step ahead of Beny. More hopefuls crowded behind them. He stretched his tall, slender frame, but the morning sun, bouncing off the white sheets of posted papers, made the names impossible to read from where he stood.

Ayuel took a deep breath and moved to the front. His eyes darted to the page headed "1992." That was the year he'd arrived at the camp as a starving, emaciated waif.

Ayuel Leek Deng.

There it was in black letters! His name. With a double blink, he looked again, bit his lip and slipped out of the way. He picked up his letter in the UNCHR office. It would give the details of where and when he would be going. Heading toward the straw and mud hut that he shared with three other young men, he dared not glance back to see Beny's fate. His friend would catch up with him.

Light has come to my darkness. Just as he allowed himself a broad grin, a hand slapped his back.

"Hey, I made it too."

After shaking hands and sharing a hug with his friend, Ayuel said, "Beny, you did? I'm so happy for you. When do you leave?"

"This Sunday," Beny said, waving his letter toward the blue sky. "I'm going to soar up there in an airplane and fly away from here to the utopia that is the United States of America." Coming back to Ayuel, he added, "I saw your name before I saw mine. I hope you leave the same time I do."

Ayuel unfolded his letter. He'd hardly looked at the details. "No, I don't leave until next month, August 5, but I go to the same orientation as you. That's good."

"Can you believe it? That starts at eight tomorrow morning."

Ayuel was laughing now. With no one close by he could show his joy. "I'll miss my math exam, but nothing else matters now." Ayuel clenched his notebook. The friends slapped each other's hands and rejoiced like children with extra food. Although he was only three months away from earning his high school diploma, Ayuel had been told that the paper from a refugee school would mean little in the United States. "Only what you have kept in your head will count," his teacher had said.

Having received special training, Ayuel counseled those with emotional or spiritual problems and helped new arrivals to the camp deal with their anger by expressing their emotions through drama. Beny, two years older than his friend, had finished his schooling the semester before and now worked on staff as Manager of the Community-Based Rehabilitation Program, helping the handicapped.

"Wonder what it will be like to look down from the airplane," Ayuel said. "From here, it always seems so tiny that it's hard to imagine people inside." His stomach grew tight and queasy just thinking about it.

"Guess we'll soon know."

*

That evening, after the one daily meal of a wheat flour and maize mush, Ayuel walked to a different area of the dry riverbed—far from the morning's tragedy. He needed time alone to deal with conflicting emotions that ranged from deep sorrow over Majok to exuberance about his new opportunity. No one else he knew in his zone had made the weekly list. He saw the pain in the eyes of those who congratulated him.

As he sat on the riverbank, he realized the future was too hazy and unreal to imagine. The past that he knew all too well flooded over him. He thought of the spilled blood of over two million of his fellow Sudanese people who still cried out for liberation of their country. The dead included his parents, his baby sisters and the countless children who had not survived the long walk to Ethiopia or here to Kenya. And then there are those who drowned crossing the Gilo River.

His two older brothers, Aleer and Deng, perhaps were among the lost. Aleer had made it to Kenya, but left to go to the university in Uganda. Ayuel had not heard from him in four years. He hadn't seen Deng since the bombing of their village in 1987. Could they have survived like him? Not knowing brought constant worry. And now there was Majok Bol, who had died from lack of hope.

I must honor all of them. I must find a new life, a better one in the United States of America. I must make a way for those left behind—still suffering and dying from the government's terrorism against its own people. I am a seed of the new Sudan.

TWO

SMALL TALK, BRUTAL EVENTS

Puffs of dust rose with the laughter and shrieks of children as they ran with bare feet on the hard Sudanese ground. Seven-year-old Ayuel and a group of his age-mates—Gutthier, Madau, Malual—were playing soccer with other village children, using a ball made of old strips of cloth bound together. Most wore only a pair of ragged shorts, but the younger boys were entirely naked. No need for clothes in this searing heat. Ayuel tripped his older brother Aleer as they ran toward the ball. Both missed, but his brother stumbled and fell. He quickly recovered, shoved Ayuel aside and kicked the ball into the semi-circle of dried brush that served as the goal.

"Not fair! He pushed me," Ayuel shouted. Although smaller and younger than Aleer by two years, he loved to win. The two brothers fought and competed at everything—except when their oldest brother Deng came home from boarding school in Bor. *That should be any day now*, Mama had said. His eyes glanced down the road every few minutes.

This time when he looked, Deng was actually coming toward them. Very tall and slim for a twelve-year-old, Deng wore khaki shorts, a plaid, short-sleeved buttoned shirt and sandals. With a backpack over one shoulder, he walked with the dignity of an important person. Ayuel's hero. The game was forgotten as all the children stood silently watching until Deng came close enough to speak. Aleer had just made the winning point, if it counted. But no one cared to argue now that Deng was here.

"Good morning to all of you."

With large grins, the boys answered, "Good morning, Deng Leek."

"I don't want to stop your game, but I need to talk to my brothers."

"We're competing with the other side of the village," Tor said, another one of Ayuel's age-mates. "I think we won, but..."

Not even the opposing team seemed to care.

Deng hugged both his brothers with an arm around each. Ayuel knew there would be gifts in the backpack. He waited politely. Deng swung the heavy pack to the ground, knelt beside it and reached into a small pocket on the side. Aleer squatted with both hands open to receive its contents— caramel candies—which he then passed around to all the boys.

"Thank you, Deng," each one said.

"Where will I find Mother?"

"She's hoeing sorghum," Aleer said.

"I'll take your bag to her *tukul*," Ayuel eagerly offered. Though the backpack was heavier than he'd thought, he lifted it to one shoulder and carried it just like Deng.

Ayuel's friends, Tor and Malual, walked beside him until they veered off to their separate homes. "See ya tomorrow," Tor said brightly, punching Ayuel on his shoulder.

"Sure, see you then."

Inside the circular mud and straw hut, Ayuel placed the bag reverently on a mat and dared to peek inside. *Yum! Mangoes and lemons. And schoolbooks.* He dared not reach in. Looking around his mother's *tukul,* he noticed a rag doll and other baby things lying on a small stool. He didn't like staying here with his mother and little sisters while Deng was away at school. Tonight the three boys would share their own hut.

Sometimes he visited his father's *tukul* when he came home on Sundays—but never spent the night there. When he stepped outside, Ayuel could see his mother and his father's three other wives coming in from the sorghum field. Deng and Aleer carried their mother's hoes. The other women clumped close together talking. Ayuel stood there, hands on hips, and remembered what his half-brother Gutthier told him when Deng had been selected for the boarding school: *My mother thinks it isn't right that Deng goes off to school while my older brothers work at the cattle camps.*

He'd accused Gutthier of being jealous.

"How could anyone think bad of Deng?" Gutthier had said. They never mentioned the subject again.

They both took pride in their father's position as district commissioner, judge and main leader of Duk's 8,000 people. Ayuel thought of his father now as he waited for his mother and brothers. The clan had built him a very fine office in the Sudanese style with a pointed thatch roof, and he served as the go-between from the Sudanese government in Khartoum to his people. Once a year, they gave him supplies to distribute: blankets, mosquito nets and food. The government in the North paid him enough money to buy cows, which represented Dinka wealth. He collected the taxes and, if there was a crime, he set up court under a large oak tree.

*

That night in the boys' *tukul*, Ayuel and Aleer hung on every word as Deng told of his adventures. Because of his high intelligence, the government had chosen him to go away to the boarding school where he studied Arabic, mathematics and geography. Tonight, he taught them some of his new knowledge and promised to draw a map of Africa for them tomorrow in the dust. Aleer went to the Arabic school in Duk and seemed to understand all this better than Ayuel.

In the village, Deng had always been the best wrestler. Everyone admired him for it. "At school it's a very important sport," he said.

"Do you win all the competitions?" Ayuel wanted to know.

"Well," he said, looking down and rearranging his crossed legs on the woven mat. "I win a lot of them. But others are very good too. Remember the wrestling match I took you to, Ayuelo?"

"Of course," Ayuel said. "How could I forget that? You showed me some good techniques."

The week passed quickly. Deng spent time alone with Aleer and then with Ayuel, according to the schedule of their chores. The last day of Deng's visit, Ayuel went for a long walk with him. Before they left the hut,

Deng said, "I have a present for you, Ayuelo." Whatever it was, Ayuel knew he would treasure it.

Deng reached into his backpack and pulled out a rolled-up cloth. "Here." He threw it at him, grinning broadly. "Just something I bought for you in Bor."

Ayuel caught and unrolled it. "A T-shirt!"

"Not just any old T-shirt."

Ayuel went outside to look at it more closely. "Is that a picture of Maradona?" He held it up and studied it. In the image, the famous soccer player from Argentina was kicking a soccer ball toward the goal.

"Yes, it's Maradona. He works hard and never gives up."

Ayuel slipped the T-shirt on over his bare chest. It hung to the bottom of his shorts. He felt proud. "I want to be just like you," he said.

"Be the best in your generation, among your age-mates. Be a champion. Don't ever give up," Deng said.

Ayuel felt a little taller and held his head high. The blazing sun dropped low in the sky as the two boys walked down the dusty path that led away from the compound of *tukuls*. Their shadows stretched out in front of them—one longer than the other. Grasshoppers jumped from the dry grass with each step. Deng seemed to have urgency in his voice as he spoke advice to his brother. Ayuel listened and remembered. Especially his repeated words: *Don't ever give up.*

*

The day after Deng returned to boarding school, Ayuel watched Aleer leave as part of a large group of nine to twelve-year-old boys from the village. They drove the huge herds of cattle, about one million in all, to better grazing grounds. They would be away several months. Because the long-horned animals were all important to the Dinka tribe, the boys had to protect them from lions and hyenas. Their owners drank the milk, mixed with blood siphoned from the living cows, and used the dried dung to make campfires. A man's wealth was measured by the number of cows he owned, and a bride's worth was calculated by how many cows she could bring to her family at marriage.

Ayuel knew that at the cattle camps the boys slept in huts, called *geth*, and sat around fires at night singing and telling stories. The supervising men would teach the boys Dinka ways. There would be fierce competitions: spear-throwing, wrestling and dancing. At cattle camp, a boy became a man. Ayuel could hardly wait to be old enough to take off on such important adventures. He longed to be on his own and make his own decisions.

Now with both brothers away, he was the oldest child at home and already had more responsibilities. He took over Aleer's old job of finding new grazing each day for the three cows kept close by. Early in the morning, he helped his mother milk the cows. Then, after drinking a big jug of milk, he would be gone until late in the afternoon. He always carried a sharpened spear with him for protection and a stick to prod the animals.

Except for the large plastic bottle of water he took along, he had nothing to drink or eat until evening. Again, he must sleep in the hut with his mother and sisters. He was too young to stay alone in the boys' hut because of the danger posed by wild animals.

Days became hotter as the rains diminished at the beginning of the month of *Kol*. Ayuel returned from his day's work, tired and thirsty. He tapped his cows with his long stick to make them go into the pen of upright poles tied together. They moved sluggishly, but obediently. He closed the gate and fastened it. Milking would be done again later in the evening. The new responsibility with the cattle made him feel proud, yet he felt fearful all alone out in the pastures, especially today.

His mother was grinding grains of millet with a mortar and pestle in front of the cooking hut. He wandered over and sat in the shade of the *tukul*. She smiled at him and handed him a calabash gourd of water from the well. She had been waiting for him. He drank until his stomach felt tight and uncomfortable. Beans for the evening meal simmered in a pot over the charcoal fire. A ripe melon lay on a stone slab next to fresh fish ready to broil. The baby slept contentedly on a straw mat under a mimosa tree while nearby his little sister, Achol, played idly with pebbles.

"I thought I heard guns today, Mama." Ayuel shaded his eyes and faced the huge orange ball of sun, filtered through the dust-filled air.

She pounded the grain harder. "What time was that, Ayuel?" She didn't change expression or look at him.

"It was about noon, I think, because there weren't any shadows." He didn't want to worry her, so he added, "But the guns sounded far away, and then I didn't hear them again." He knew something about the civil war with the North.

"Well, that is good." She stopped pounding and looked at him with a nervous smile. "Your father will be home soon. He wants to take you into Bor sometime—to the *souk,* the big market. We need to buy some things, and it will be fun for you to see all the different kinds of merchants and the items they sell."

She began pounding again, making the fine flour for bread. Ayuel watched her work. She wore a loose cotton dress that fell just below the knees. It was blue with some kind of large yellow flowers. A multicolored scarf was wrapped in a turban around her head. Even though she had given birth to five children, she had kept her beauty. Maybe that was because his father's position made their lives easier than others.

That November night in 1987, Ayuel said his prayers with his mother, as was the routine. He noticed her Christian prayer included a longer list of relatives, their village of Duk, the entire Bor region and Southern Sudan. He fell asleep in a T-shirt, but not the one with Maradona on it. He slept soundly and dreamed he was with Aleer in the cattle camp.

★

Ayuel awoke abruptly to his mother's shrill voice, "Ayuel, are you awake?" He heard loud banging noises that hurt his ears and he smelled smoke. Startled, he sat up and rubbed his eyes. In the total darkness, he felt dizzy and frightened.

"Quick, Ayuel!" his mother shouted. "We must go!" The baby was crying in her arms. Without thinking, he grabbed his *mutkukalei*—sandals made from a discarded tire. They ran outside and kept running. He flinched at the sound of a booming crash. Looking behind him, he saw an orange-red plume of fire leap into the dark skies.

Bombs!

Gunfire crackled behind them. Voices moaned, screamed, shouted. Children cried. Ayuel felt the heat of fire at his back. The stench of burning *tukuls* choked him. The flames broke the darkness. Silhouettes like black ghosts ran past in the eerie light.

His mother was running with the baby in one arm and pulling Achol with her other hand. Ayuel ran close beside them. The toddler struggled to keep up. Ayuel reached out to help her but a clump of thorn bushes briefly widened the gap separating them. He reached toward her again, his eyes darting frantically in an effort to keep her and his mother in his sight.

A grenade exploded between them with a deafening bang.

Ayuel jumped to the right. His mother with his sisters sprang to the left—and disappeared into the running crowds. His mouth and nose filled with hot dust and his eyes stung. He felt hot tears roll back into his hair and trickle into his ears. Like a baby bird pushed from the nest, he felt weak and frightened.

With bleared vision, he saw his friend Tor wobbling along, naked, the open flesh of his side torn in shreds, dripping blood.

"Ayue—lo…help…" His friend reached out a mangled hand, but Ayuel turned his eyes away. Fear drove him on. He knew inside it was wrong not to stop, but his feet kept running, pounding the earth as he clutched his *mutkukalei*. He nearly tripped on a body lying on the ground as he sped onward.

★

The distant civil war he'd heard the men of Duk talk about in hushed voices became real as Ayuel ran that night. All he felt was terror. Gunfire from helicopters killed many of the villagers as they fled in the darkness. The oldest and youngest fell behind from lack of strength. Those who could, kept running. They ran for miles without stopping. Though strong for a seven-year-old, Ayuel found it hard to keep up. He didn't want to be among those moaning on the ground.

In the light before dawn, Ayuel could see hundreds of people fleeing—all headed in the same direction. Like a stampede of elephants, the pounding rhythm filled the air and vibrated the earth beneath him. The cadence swept him along as if his feet had no will of their own. If he stopped, surely he would be trampled. He struggled for air to breathe.

The sounds became louder. He looked up and saw three planes passing low, the roar of their motors mixing with the noise on the ground. They swept on.

Then, there were deafening blasts.

Rolls of dark smoke plummeted skyward as the planes let loose their fire in the distance ahead. The crowd scattered and Ayuel tripped and fell over blackened pumpkin vines, still warm from the fires of the night before. No one trampled on him as most of the people had turned away from the ruins.

He looked out across a destroyed village where the rising sun cast shadows of broken trees. *Duk must look like this now.* A few partly blackened *tukuls* still stood. *Maybe ours didn't get burned.* A three-legged dog whimpered as it sniffed through the rubbish. Ayuel tried to block the awful smells with the back of his hand. A stiffened cow lay just inches away.

Terror gripped him. Beyond the cow lay a cut-off human arm, covered in clotted blood and buzzing flies. As more bodies and parts of dead people came into focus, his own screams startled him. He closed his eyes and sat still among the vines for a very long time, nearly passing out.

When he dared look again, a few people walked about, picking up anything useful. A group of older boys walked toward him, two he recognized from his village. He watched as they broke open a large pumpkin and laughed in shrill humorless voices. But just as he gathered courage to call out to them, they turned away and left him sitting alone.

Tears stung his eyes, but he got up from the gray ashes and found a ripe, half-burned pumpkin. He carried it until he was past the horror on the ground before breaking it over a rock. He took a few bites, letting the warm juice drip off his chin. When another wave of people rushed by, he followed, tucking the largest piece of fruit under his arm and stopping just long enough to pick up an empty calabash gourd. The pounding of feet sounded less urgent now. Thankful for that, he panted for breath and tried to keep up.

THREE

FLEEING TERROR

L ate in the afternoon, he could see trees ahead, outlined against the gray sky. The people were walking now. *Just a little longer. Keep going. We will stop among the trees.* No planes had flown over for a while. At last, he fell exhausted among the others in tall bushes and acacia trees. He heard someone say, "Here we will be hidden from the enemy planes."

Ayuel lay still several minutes. His heart raced as he gasped for breath and tried to push the images of the pumpkin patch with dead bodies from his mind. Rumors of water to drink spread among the crowd. The chunk of pumpkin had sustained him through the day, but now he needed to drink. He pulled himself up and followed the others to a pool of stagnant water. Like everyone, he knew it should be boiled but no one seemed to be thinking about protection of health. At this moment they thought only of saving their lives. Ayuel knelt, scooped the water with his hand and drank; then filled the filched calabash.

Everyone talked at once, asking the same questions: "Have you seen my mother?" "Have you seen Bol?" "Nhial?" "Do you know my brothers?" Ayuel recognized no one, but he pleaded, too. Where were his family and friends? Images of Tor and his little sister flashed across his mind.

He squatted down among strangers. Some didn't seem to be from Duk or even of the Dinka tribe. Where had they come from? He rubbed his sore and swollen feet. He had carried his sandals, gripped in his hand the whole way. *Mutkukalei.* The Arabic word meant "died and gone" because the tire rubber was known to outlive the wearer. Ayuel shook his head as he thought about the jokes he and his cousin Chuei often made about the funny name. He squeezed his eyes shut and saw his sandals sitting alone in the desert sand, *their owner dead and gone*; then he slipped them on.

A few people had picked up food from destroyed villages. Others had escaped with a bundle of supplies. One man had grabbed a pot, full of dried lentils and maize. Ayuel moved closer to him. Groups began to form around the "kings" with food.

Ayuel offered to gather firewood but the owner of the pot said, "We cannot build a fire at this time. The enemy may still be close and would see the smoke rising above the trees. Rest, now."

He lay back on the ground then quickly sat up, Acacia thorns stuck in his back. A stranger picked them out without saying a word. He moved to a better spot, carefully lay back down on dry grass and looked up through the trees at a hazy sky.

The shade felt cool after the day-long journey. Scavenger birds squawked overhead looking for corpses. *I want my mother. And my father. He was going to take me to Bor, to the* souk. *Did they bomb Aleer's cattle camp? What about Deng at school?* His thoughts swam in images, repeated, merged and faded as he closed his eyes. Confused and terrified over what had happened and not knowing why, he mumbled routine bedtime words: *"Our Father, which art in heaven, hallowed be thy name..."* Sleep soon mercifully overcame him.

★

Ayuel awoke to the sound of low voices and the smell of lentils cooking. For a moment he thought himself at home. He had overslept and his mother was starting the day's meal. Why hadn't his half-brothers and sisters awakened him to take the family cows out? He opened his eyes and stared up through sparse branches. The blue sky and heat meant mid-morning. He had slept a very long time.

He sat up and turned toward the giggling of children. They were queuing up with open mouths to get a few squirts of milk from a solitary cow. Ayuel jumped up and ran toward the woman doing the milking. Just as he opened his lips to shout *Mama*, she turned into an older woman who looked nothing at all like his mother. With a heavy sigh, he rubbed his eyes and got in line behind the other children for his turn at warm milk.

As the day wore on, no one seemed to be in charge, but somehow they all silently agreed to remain in the grove of trees during the day for safety. It was cooler there. Occasionally they heard gunfire and helicopters off in the distance. Other villages were being attacked. Families separated—hurt, burned, killed. People milled about looking for loved ones or slept. Ayuel did the same. Never had he felt so totally alone. No familiar face anywhere. No one to tell him what to do. *Everyone else must know at least one other person because they are all talking to each other.* He shivered in the heat, not understanding what had happened or why. Too young to think about tomorrow.

After a very long day, a small group of people moved out into a clearing. Ayuel followed. They were listening to a man who stood on a large rock and spoke loudly in the Dinka language. "We must travel to the east— toward Ethiopia."

Ethiopia? That's a far-away country. No one can walk there.

The rest of the three or four hundred people came out of the grove of trees and huddled close to the speaker, keeping quiet. The man waited, then repeated they must go to Ethiopia, but he didn't say why.

"Fill whatever containers you have with water," the man said. "We will walk at night and sleep by day. Be strong, for the weak will perish and…"

Quiet vanished as people rushed to the pool of water. Ayuel rushed too, but bigger boys pushed him back, and by the time he filled his calabash, the water was muddied. His mother had always warned him not to drink dirty water, but others were. So he did too.

★

The journey began in the dark of night. As they walked, Ayuel noticed groups forming—age-mates together, women with daughters, a few men and older boys. Where were *his* age-mates? Age-mates stayed together their whole lives, and now he would have no one to grow up with. He trailed behind a group of nine-year-olds and looked for Aleer. They paid no attention to him, but he imagined them as his group anyhow.

On the third morning, the crowd found refuge next to a trickling stream of water, sheltered by trees. Ayuel drank all he could hold, for it made him feel less hungry. He sat under a tree on the bank of the stream and washed his face, arms and legs with the water remaining in his calabash. He'd been taught to stay clean. At dusk he would refill it for the night's walk. As he tied the empty gourd around his waist with a vine, a boy from the group of nine-year-olds he had been following came and sat next to him. The boy clutched several strips of dried meat and handed Ayuel a few.

"What animal is it?"

"I don't know. Somebody gave it to me. It's food." The boy grinned at Ayuel.

He took it, ripped a bite off with his teeth and chewed on the stringy, tough meat for a while. "Thanks," he said.

After taking another bite, he looked up to find the boy had vanished. Slowly he got up to search out a place to sleep for the day. His legs ached and again he felt very alone and abandoned.

He walked along, looking down for a good spot without too many twigs until he became aware of someone coming straight toward him—a boy carrying a bundle of sticks. He glanced up and faced his cousin—same age, but more muscular, always the best soccer player. At last someone he knew. The boys ran and threw their arms around each other.

"Ayuelo!"

"Madau!"

Tears flowed. Sobs followed as all the anguish burst out. His cousin wore only a man's cotton shirt with buttons missing, and Ayuel was still in the T-shirt he'd slept in back when life was normal. They sat on the dry grass, hugging, each comforting the other. Somehow it seemed strange to Ayuel that Madau was out here, just a little boy, wandering about all alone. He felt that he, himself, had already become a man, living on his own these few days. Yet seeing his cousin made him aware that he, too, was but a small child.

"Where's your—your group?" the cousin asked when finally they sat apart, their sobs reduced to sniffles.

"Don't have one," Ayuel said simply. This was the first time he had cried since the bombing, and it left him exhausted. "I saw some boys I knew in a pumpkin field, but they ran away before I could talk to them." He wiped his face on the sleeve of his T-shirt.

"I'm with several of our age-mates. You know them. Your cousin Chuei…"

"I'd love to see Chuei. He's always saying something funny." Ayuel watched the smile fade from Madau's face.

"Not now. Chuei has trouble keeping up—and he cries a lot."

"What about Tor?" He remembered the last time he'd seen him—wounded—and hadn't stopped. Maybe he'd just imagined it.

"Someone said he died."

"Oh." Ayuel rubbed his eyes and took a deep breath. "Who else?"

"Your half-brother, 'Funny Ears,' and Malual Kuer. They just caught some little fish with a bucket and I went to get some firewood to cook them." The dropped sticks lay scattered around them. "You know how to make fire by rubbing sticks?"

"Sure. Done it lots of times."

"Come on."

The boys gathered up the firewood and Ayuel followed Madau through the crowds, eager to see his friends.

*

At last, Ayuel felt less lonely. He now belonged to a group of five seven-year-olds—his age-mates—who stuck together as part of a larger group of older boys, a few girls and two women. They looked for food, ate, hid, slept and walked together. Malual Kuer's father, who had been the pastor of the Christian church in Duk, had written songs based on Bible teachings. Sometimes they sang these as they went along.

Malual was his best friend. They'd never lacked for anything to talk about. Now, even more, as they walked side by side, they chatted constantly, which made the time go by. Before, he'd not played much with his half-brother, Gutthier. Their mothers resented each other since they were both married to his father. But now, their mothers were no more, so the boys became friends. Like the others, he teasingly called Gutthier "Funny Ears," because his ears stuck out. Gutthier was tall like most Dinkas and considered the most handsome among the age-mates in spite of his ears.

Every day, a few more joined their group while others left, all Dinkas from the region of Duk. Some, like his age-mates, he knew very well. They had played together in the village. Others had common acquaintances or knew about Ayuel's father, the chief and judge of Duk.

Each had a story to tell of the escape from his torched home—about those who died and the wounded left behind. Some said they'd found dead people whom they knew, laying on the ground. Thus, they believed all the people in that area must have been killed. A large group of boys had been found shot in one cattle camp, but Ayuel didn't know which camp his brother Aleer had gone to. Ayuel had seen a few dead bodies, but no one he knew. He thought about what his family would look like dead and squeezed his eyes tight to shut out the images.

Most of the talk centered on who had survived and who had not. Like all Dinka children, Ayuel had been taught the names of his relatives, living and dead, and how they were related to each other—even those he'd never met. It all made sense now, all those names that had seemed so tiresome when he'd recited them for his father. Now he said them to ask if anyone had seen or heard of them. He learned about several aunts, uncles and cousins who had been found dead. Someone had seen one of his father's half-brothers alive. Groups from his village began to travel near each other. Sometimes they mingled to ask about loved ones.

*

Three weeks passed. The hundreds became thousands walking across Sudan—a sea of people in columns moving east. No one seemed to know what happened to the man who had said to go to Ethiopia, but they still followed his orders to walk at night and sleep by day. Some boys carried bundles on their heads, unashamed to do as the women did. Food and water became scarce. There were always children crying, if not nearby, then in the distance.

At first when they passed through bombed villages, they'd found the dead, lying out on the ground. Now, as they crossed the desert, bodies lay under an arrangement of dried weeds and small branches—apparently an attempt at burial. And these corpses were the people who had gone ahead of them. Walking just like them. The awful stench of death was everywhere.

Arguments broke out continually, followed by shouting and fist fights. Mostly the Dinkas fought with the Nuers, who had always been enemies. Equatorians clashed with both of the other clans. Those who didn't fight whined and complained. For Ayuel, weary from hunger, thirst and fatigue, a sense of hopelessness set in.

Many of the grown-ups began to say, "I can't do it. I would rather die here." Those words scared Ayuel for he knew that meant they were giving up. In Dinka culture, you must stay strong. You must take care of your body so you will have strength. *But how can you take care of yourself with nothing? And with no one to tell you what to do?*

One evening, as they prepared for the night's walk, Ayuel and his age-mates watched in disbelief as the women formed new groups and started walking back the way they had come, toward the setting sun, not toward Ethiopia. *Back to the burned villages?* There had never been many men along, but most of those remaining left with the women. Ayuel had heard stories that the men were first to be shot in the attacks. *They may have killed my father at his office in town,* he thought. He tried not to think about how that would happen.

As they stood watching the adults leave, Malual Kuer turned to Ayuel and recited a common proverb they all knew: "To quit is a shame on future generations." Others around them nodded agreement or repeated it in low voices.

Ayuel remembered what the religious leaders had said in teaching from the Holy Bible: "God punishes the children and their children for the sin of the fathers to the third and fourth generation." *Surely it is wrong for the grown-ups to leave us children to find our own way. We will be punished for their wrong,* he thought, but said nothing.

Most of the girls, in keeping with tradition, chose to go with their mothers or with women they knew. A few of the boys hung onto their sisters or mothers and quietly pleaded with them not to give up. Not to leave them to walk alone.

The abandoned children stood in silence as the setting sun dropped out of sight, leaving streaks of red across the western sky. The outlines of their grown-ups diminished and disappeared into the dusk. With the rest of the boys Ayuel turned and walked into the gathering darkness.

★

The two women and all but one girl had left Ayuel's group. Other boys joined. The reshaped group numbered seventeen, all of them Dinkas from the Duk region. To keep peace, they avoided children from other tribes and regions. One of the older boys had a cooking pot, which would be put to good use from time to time.

Ayuel and his four age-mates—Gutthier, Madau, Malual Kuer and Chuei, who had grown up together—stayed. Everyone accepted Donayok—another cousin of Ayuel and the oldest at fourteen—as their leader, though they all looked after one another. Six boys were between eleven and thirteen, the others younger. And the only girl, Akon, was ten, a cousin of both Gutthier and Ayuel. Though she was as tough and strong as the boys, they all kept a protective eye on their "sister."

Almost daily now, Ayuel found cousins and other relatives among the different groups or heard news of the dead ones, but no word of his parents or blood brothers and sisters.

In the evenings, just before the walk began, Ayuel could hear the Animists practicing their religion, dancing and chanting prayers to the spirits. His people had left the traditional beliefs two generations ago, when his grandfather converted to Christianity, but he hoped the spirits of trees, rocks and sky would help them all.

One night seemed especially tedious. Ayuel tried to pray to God as he had been taught by his mother and also in their Episcopal church, but his mind could not form the words. His stomach felt hard as he put his hand to it—swollen from lack of food. *Don't ever give up.* His brother Deng's words throbbed in his head—his advice from their last day together. How could he keep going? What good was it?

There was little talk among the group of seventeen now. Every bit of energy must be saved to move one foot after the other and not fall. Some in other groups had dropped and not gotten up. Death happened daily, but so far none of the seventeen had gone down. Chuei was keeping up or sometimes Donayok would carry him on his back. Chuei, the jokester, never said anything funny anymore.

Cold came with night. Poisonous scorpions and cobras hid in the darkness, ready to strike and kill. Ayuel could hear them, or thought he did. Terrified of dying, he tried to keep alert at all times. The evening before he had seen a girl not too far away screaming from a snake bite. He hoped someone helped her, but knew she probably died. He had walked on and hugged his skinny shoulders with chilled, bony fingers in an effort to bring warmth.

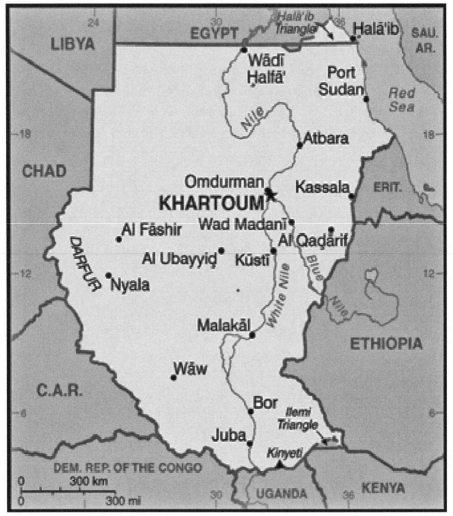

Map of Sudan, courtesy of the CIA World Factbook

FOUR

FEAR LURKS

They were crossing a large field now. If life were normal, it would be called a beautiful place—open with waving grass. A fine area to play soccer or have wrestling matches. A few scattered trees stood out against the gray sky of early morning. Soon they could rest, but he knew sleep would not come easily. During the day, mosquitoes came to draw blood and leave terrible sickness. Burning heat would replace the cold. Bad dreams and lurking dangers would torment him.

The dawn sky began to turn a rosy pink and Ayuel could see a grove of trees ahead. *Just a few more steps.*

Suddenly, seven or eight soldiers in drab-green uniforms, carrying long guns, emerged from the trees. *I'm dead now*, Ayuel thought and stopped as did everyone else. Maybe they were being kidnapped so they could be taught how to fight in the war. He didn't want to kill anyone.

As they all watched, the soldiers halted and laid down their guns. The tall officer in front stepped forward and raised both arms. He had several things tied around his waist—a black box and some bags—and a belt of bullets across his chest. He took a short metal stick with a black ball on top out of the bag. Ayuel watched as he held the ball in front of his mouth.

"I come in peace," he said. It sounded like God speaking—very loud and important. The words echoed from the trees at the right of the field: *I come in peace.*

The crowd of thousands moved closer—merging the groups tightly together. Ayuel's seventeen were near the front and could see the man clearly. The children stood like statues, stunned. When Donayok sat down, the rest of his group wearily followed, sitting cross-legged and leaning forward. They all respected him as leader and mentor.

"That stick makes his voice sound like that," Madau said and poked his elbow in Ayuel's ribs. Ayuel noticed his cousin's muscular frame had withered like the others.

"How does it do that?"

"Shush."

"My name is Chol Aruei," the officer said to the stick. "We have been sent here by John Garang to guide you."

"Who's John Ga-rang?" Ayuel could hardly say the words, his mouth was so dry.

"I don't know. Listen."

"Colonel John Garang, as many of you know, is the leader of the Sudanese People's Liberation Army, the SPLA. He is leading the fight against the Islamic Fundamentalist government in Khartoum—in the North—so we may again worship whatever gods we choose and not be forced to follow Islam's *sharia* laws with their harsh punishments, like cutting off hands and stoning."

Ayuel remembered hearing his father talk to men in the village about *sharia*. He knew it was something bad, but the officer's big words meant little to him.

"Only Muslims, Arab fundamentalist Muslims, can hold government positions now. And a company called Chevron has found oil under our land. That is why the North has bombed our villages. They want to impose a strict Islamic government and they want our oil, but we are fighting back!" The officer turned to talk with the other soldiers in a low voice, not using the stick.

The Arabs have killed my father, because he had a government job, Ayuel guessed. *He was a good father and a good commissioner.* Anger surged up for a moment, then mixed with the sadness he always felt, but he remained still and listened, trying to understand.

"They don't look starved like us," Gutthier said. His ears stuck out more prominently in his starving condition. No one called him "Funny Ears" now.

"But I don't think they have any food with them," Madau said, always one to thoughtfully consider a situation.

"Chol Aruei is very handsome in his uniform," Malual Kuer said. "I'd like to be a soldier."

"Not me. Hush." Ayuel was now fascinated by this new turn of events. Maybe he was going to live after all. And wouldn't be captured, either.

The officer held the stick in front of his face again. "Colonel Garang cares about you. He says you are the hope for rebuilding Sudan after the war, after we have won back our rights and our way of life. I care about you also. That is why these soldiers and I have agreed to make this journey with you." The officer paused and looked out over the crowd of children. "And also, I believe two of my young brothers are here among you. If so... ?"

Two boys not much older than Ayuel got up and walked to him. Officer Chol knelt down and hugged them, an arm around each. When he stood up, the boys leaned against him, grinning. The officer wiped his bare arm across his eyes and sniffed. The funny stick made the sniff especially loud, and everyone knew he'd cried. The age-mates giggled.

"I—I'm here to help you," he said. "I couldn't bring food for all of you—there must be about 4,000 children here. There are thousands more ahead of you and thousands more being chased from their homes behind you. With our guns, we will try to protect you from the Arabs.

"You are right to travel east, but you are too far north to reach the refugee camps in Ethiopia. I will lead you through the bush. There will be water soon. And probably some wild fruit. We will shoot any animals we find, and the different groups can cook them." His voice was gentle and kind.

"Why would they bomb us for oil?" whispered Gutthier. "I never saw any oil in Duk."

"My mother uses oil when she cooks the maize." Chuei grinned and put his hand over his mouth. It sounded like a mock confession, as if her cooking had caused all the misery.

Ayuel laughed and pushed his cousin. The old Chuei was back with his funny sayings, but Chuei suddenly turned angry and pulled away. He dropped his face into his hands and sobbed.

★

In the bush they found water and berries. The group of seventeen cooked a small antelope—shot by the soldiers—over a fire. In their cooking pot, they boiled roots and leaves, which together with the meat made a real feast. There was enough to satisfy all seventeen with leftovers for another meal.

As they sat licking their fingers, Ayuel said, "Officer Chol is very smart. I think he speaks the truth. Do you think Ethiopia is on the other side of this forest?"

"Nah, but I think we will be there in two or three days," Malual Kuer said as he sucked on a bone. "Then we will have milk to drink, bread and maize to eat, chicken and rice. Maybe mangoes."

The sun became hot. Ayuel lay down next to his friends in the shade, his heart full of hope and a better kind of hurt in his stomach. Wrapped in a newfound security, he fell into deep slumber, muttering, "Abba Father, I am thankful…"

★

Ethiopia was not on the other side of the forest, nor two or three days away. Nothing but barren land stretched for miles and miles. After another two weeks, there was no food of any kind. Nor water.

Officer Chol called the assembly together using his *microphone*—the name the boys had learned for the talking stick. "My brothers and sisters, you are brave and courageous. You must never give up. You can and will survive anything. Anything, trust me. When we come to trees or bushes, pick and eat the leaves. Carry leaves and bark with you to eat later, for, as you can see, this is desert land with very few plants.

"We are just now leaving the larger region of Bor to start a long journey east. It is not a short distance to Ethiopia. It will take us two, maybe three months to get there. You will be safe in Ethiopia, and there will be enough to eat for everyone. Be strong."

But Ayuel was not strong. Madau, his cousin, and Malual Kuer, made him walk between them, his arms across their shoulders for support. His knees refused to stay straight to support him, and the heat made him dizzy. Ayuel felt ashamed of his weakness, but he would not give up. He knew Madau and Malual were using up their energy to help him.

When they came to some scraggly plants, his friends picked leaves for him. No one knew if they were poisonous or not. Who could tell by moonlight? But they needed to eat. So they nibbled the half-dried leaves that stuck to the inside of their mouths. The strong taste was unpleasant and lingered a long time.

"We need leaves with moisture in them," Donayok, their fourteen-year-old leader, said. He squatted down beside the younger ones, sniffed the dry leaves and pitched them away.

No one answered him. Of course they needed moisture.

Toward morning, as they walked, the ground was not so dry. Tall grass came up to the boys' knees. Here and there grew a few green vines. Ayuel's friends laid him down gently in the dry grass. He could hear his own breathing rattle in his chest. He closed his eyes and rested.

"Here, chew on this," said Malual, who sat beside him and offered the leaves from the vines. They weren't dry, but they could be poisonous. Ayuel chewed slowly, drifting in and out of sleep.

"Madau and Gutthier have gone to find more leaves—and water might not be too far…"

Malual's voice faded away and Ayuel slept.

By noon, the sun was too hot to lie out in the open to sleep, so they continued the journey. Ayuel felt a little better and could walk by placing his hands on his friends shoulders.

When evening came they discovered a jungle up ahead. They ate some of the lush leaves and drank from puddles of swamp water. The long, thick vines that hung from the trees were scary in the dim twilight. Ayuel thought some might be snakes, from the way they moved.

The screeching of hawks warned of danger. There were also sounds that the boys did not recognize—strange bird and animal calls. The seventeen held hands as they wove their way single file through the tangled mass of tall grass vines and sharp rocks on the ground.

Ayuel had trouble keeping his *mutkukalei* on his feet, but he was glad he'd brought them. Some of the others muffled cries of pain from stepping barefoot on the rocks.

All light quickly faded in the thick jungle but the crowd kept tramping—thousands of feet marching through the undergrowth. Ayuel felt pursued by the beat, even though he was part of it.

A low growl not too far away stopped the children. They stood silently listening. Ayuel's heart pounded in his throat. He dared not even breathe deeply. The growl came again, louder, more like a roar. The seventeen stood frozen in total darkness. Only far away the rustling of marchers continued.

Another loud roar. Angry now.

A pause. Then the shrill cry of children: "Oh, eeyo, oh, ee-yo, no-oh!" More low growls. Crunching sounds. Then silence.

The group sat huddled together in the grass for a long time, not risking talk.

In the distance, they could hear the howling of different animals, like dogs, only more terrible.

"Hyenas," whispered Donayok.

The howls became louder—and closer. Again screams of children. Snarls. Thrashing about. Screams. More snarls. Quiet.

Ayuel and his friends shivered in the darkness, startled by every bird screech and every rustle in the grass. With thousands of people crouched in the jungle, no one could be sure if movements were by human or beast. They dared not close their eyes—though it was impossible to see anything. Squatted close together, terrified, they waited through the long night, hoping to be alive in the morning.

★

"Ayuelo, get up." Gutthier, his half-brother, was gently shaking his arm and whispering in his ear. Pale light filtered through the trees, and waking birds chirped innocently. Ayuel could hear voices over where the terrible night noises had come from.

"What? What?" Ayuel said too loudly. He had fallen asleep on Gutthier's shoulder for a few minutes just before dawn. Startled, he felt sick and vomited the green leaves he'd eaten the evening before. "What's going on?"

"Let's go see."

The boys pushed their way through the thick vines to a place where lines of people filed past, some lingering, but mostly they shook their heads and went on. Some cried, others talked softly.

Ayuel and his friends stretched their necks to get a look. Bloody bones of six or seven children lay among shreds of clothing in the grass. Flies buzzed.

"Lions."

"And hyenas over here."

The seventeen chose not to go look at the second place.

Some of the SPLA soldiers were standing nearby. One said, "We're sorry. We are here to protect you... we... There just aren't enough of us." He turned his head away.

Officer Chol said, "We must walk through the jungle by day so we can see the dangers. We'll lie still at night. He shook his head and blew his nose on his shirttail. "We can get out quicker going this way. Follow me." He turned and began walking, his two young brothers trailing close behind him. The officer took a little black box from his belt and held it close to his ear.

"What's in that little box?" asked Madau, always the curious one.

"I think it's a radio," Ayuel said. "My father has one at his office." *If he has an office—if he's alive.*

"He listens to BBC," Malual said.

"What's that?" Ayuel wanted to talk about anything except what they had just seen.

"All I know is, it's not in the Dinka language."

"Then it must not be important."

The boys shrugged their shoulders and followed the officer.

The children soon learned, as gossip spread, that wild animals had attacked many throughout the camp that night, leaving similar bloody scenes. As the daytime heat rose, it became difficult to breathe the humid air. Ayuel felt faint, but he held to vines and scrub trees to pull himself along through the thick underbrush. More than once they came across a shallow pool. Each time Ayuel untied his calabash from around his waist and drank the stagnant water.

By the third nightfall, they were out of the thickest part of the jungle with no more nearby attacks. "We must walk until we come to safe cover," the soldier with them said. After struggling through the vines all day, the children wanted to lie down, but the soldier told them it wasn't safe yet. Not only the animals posed a danger, but also some had died in the jungle from eating too many of the wrong kind of leaves.

"Let's stay here just a little while," said Akon, the only girl among the seventeen. "I'm so tired." She sat down and then fell over and lay still. Images of his little sister sleeping, curled up safely on her mat, crossed Ayuel's mind.

He stood over her a couple of minutes. Her bare feet, scratched and caked with dried blood, stuck out from under her soiled cotton dress. "There are wild animals here. Remember? They will chew you up like they did the children the other night. Come on." Though weak himself, he took her arm and pulled her up.

*

Six weeks had passed since the beginning of their journey to Ethiopia, and again they were completely without water and without food. With no shelter in the desert, they now must walk by day and sleep in the open at night. Like sticks, the legs and arms of the children seemed stuck to their bodies, skin pulled tight over ribs and swollen stomachs, sagging elsewhere. Hair that their mothers had kept neatly cropped now stood in clumps with patches of orange. Those who still could moved slowly, moaning in agony.

Every now and then a child fell, writhed and groaned in the dirt until laying forever silent. Some gave up and laid down quietly to wait for death. With no time for sacred burial, friends of the dead piled dry brush over the bodies as they had seen earlier. Such makeshift graves lay everywhere, some exposing decaying flesh and bone, all covered with buzzing flies. The scorching sun bore down on the naked and near-naked bodies of the living. Unrelenting. No refuge anywhere from the heat and stench of death.

In desperation, Officer Chol shot his gun into the air and screamed this prayer: "Oh God, don't do this to these children! Please, God!" His cries seemed to fall on deaf ears of the Almighty.

Ayuel dropped to the ground under a tree whose bare branches gave no shade. He moved his lips to say *I can't go on*, but his mouth and tongue were too dry and swollen to utter even one word. The sun blinded his eyes and the caked earth burned his skin. Death clutched at his neck trying to choke off his life. He curled his toes inside his *mutkukalei*. Some child would find his "dead and gone" sandals and pull them from his lifeless feet.

As he lay there on his side, Malual Kuer knelt on the hot ground beside him and put his hand under the side of Ayuel's face. Ayuel could see that his best friend's eyes were sunken into his skull, like his own must be. He let his eyelids drop shut, content to give up.

He could feel the vibration of someone running toward him, but he didn't turn his head. "I heard he was down." The voice belonged to their leader, Donayok. "I came as soon as I could."

"He's not well," Malual said.

"You must live," Donayok whispered. He untied the calabash from around Ayuel's waist. "You must pee in this... and drink it."

Ayuel's forehead wrinkled, even in his weakness. *How disgusting!*

"I've done it. Others are doing it," he urged.

Ayuel tried, but his body was too dehydrated to urinate.

Others walked past him, moaning and crying. A boy gave one long lament, then toppled over dead only a few feet behind him. He could hear the rustling sounds of dried brush, quickly gathered to cover a fallen comrade. Ayuel didn't want to be buried like that. Donayok knelt beside him and waited. Akon, the girl, stopped a few moments, then respectfully moved on.

Ayuel tried again. This time a few drops of urine came—perhaps a spoonful.

"Here, sit up," the leader said. He helped him lift the calabash to his dry lips.

He drank it.

The bitter taste lingered in his mouth. Then, miraculously, clouds moved across the sky, blocking the searing heat of the sun and providing shade.

"God is with us," whispered Malual, the minister's son. "You can go on now." He helped Ayuel to stand on wobbly legs. Donayok hoisted him onto his back. Instead of dying, Ayuel traveled five more miles that day, sometimes walking, sometimes on the back of the good leader—until an oasis appeared in the distance.

FIVE

LAKE OF DEATH

As Ayuel limped along supported by Donayok and Malual Kuer, he could see trees in the distance moving in the waves of heat. He blinked with dry eyelids over dry eyeballs. Relief at last. Green leaves to eat and probably water.

Water! As they came closer, they could see shimmering—a small lake, calm and clear. Boys began running toward it and threw themselves in. The water splashed unusually high and vigorously. Something seemed amiss.

Then Ayuel could see why: Hippopotamuses and crocodiles infested the pool. More boys rushed blindly into the lake of death. Ayuel and his group stood on weak legs in horror, unable to move. To help the unfortunates would mean the certain end of any rescuer. For a half-hour or more, they heard screams of pain and fright. The life-saving water now churned with blood and mud. Bodies of those killed floated in the mire. Those merely hurt crawled to the shade of trees where older boys tied rags around their wounds.

Now that the crocodiles had their fill, they sunned themselves at the water's edge. The hippopotamuses seemed vindicated, lunged out of the water and lumbered on. The stink was like that of dead fish. Ayuel dared not drink, but he sat down at the edge of the pool in the cool mud. His body sobbed at the sight of death but his eyes lacked the moisture for tears. He scooped up some mud and patted it on his tongue.

When planes had roared overhead a few days before, the thousands separated into smaller bands of hundreds, hoping many targets would be harder to hit. Ayuel, still weak, walked under his own power with his sixteen friends. No protective SPLA soldier was anywhere in sight.

In the distance ahead, Ayuel could see smoke curling up next to a grove of trees. Donayok raised his hand to stop the group. "Something's burning," he said.

"Could be coming from an enemy attack," Madau said who walked beside Ayuel.

"Or someone cooking food," offered Ayuel. The only other group nearby was traveling between them and the trees.

Suddenly shots pierced the morning air. Ayuel clasped his hands over his ears. More shots. They watched as bodies fell to the ground in the group ahead.

"We're being massacred!" shouted Madau as he dropped to his stomach. The others followed suit.

"Lie still," commanded Donayok. "If we run, they will shoot us in the back."

As Ayuel lay frightened, the aroma of cooking meat mixed with the dust under his nose. The familiar feelings of hunger replaced the constant gnawing pains of starvation. *I'd like to eat something before I die.* He could feel his heart pounding in his ears. Daring to look up, he watched as the "dead" on the ground up ahead slowly rose and came back to life. "Look." He shoved Chuei's arm. "Look, they're getting up."

Men in uniform stepped out of the woods with guns pointing skyward. Shots rang out again but no one fell.

"I think we're saved," Donayok said, springing up. "They aren't shooting at anyone. Let's go see." The seventeen ran and joined those who had sprung back to life. As they came closer, Ayuel could see a few military men but most were boy soldiers in ill-fitting uniforms, toting guns as tall as themselves.

One of the officers shouted, "What tribe are you?"

"Mostly Dinka," Donayok yelled back.

"So are we!" called a boy not more than eight years old. "Come eat with us. We're soldiers of the SPLA."

"*Oyeah! Oyeah!* Great is the Sudanese People's Liberation Army!" the boys shouted as they rushed toward the campfire.

The SPLA group had just slaughtered an elephant and was cooking strips of meat speared to sticks over the fire. A uniformed boy handed Ayuel a stick with sizzling meat. "Eat slowly and not too much," he said. "As starved as you are, too much food can kill you." Ayuel noticed these boys were not as skinny as they were.

"Thanks," Ayuel said, looking the stranger in the eye, grateful to be alive as well as to receive food. Since the meat still sizzled, he held it in front of his face and breathed in the smoke and good smell. Meat had not been part of his regular diet back in the village of Duk. He remembered the festivals when a bull was slaughtered in a religious ritual.

He sat down in a circle with Madau, Malual Kuer, Gutthier and Chuei. They all had received a portion too. "Remember the wedding of your sister's friend?" Ayuel said to Madau as he pulled off a small bite with his fingers. He popped it in his mouth and licked his fingers. Still too hot.

"Sure. They butchered a bull and danced around it—an Animist sacrifice. It was the groom's family that worshiped spirits. I wonder if that couple is still alive—and my sister and her husband." With a sigh, Madau bit into his portion of food.

"This doesn't taste much like beef," Chuei said. "Ever eat elephant before?"

"No," Ayuel said, chewing slowly. "Don't eat so fast, Chuei." He worried about his cousin who used to make jokes. Now he looked the worst of any of them, with his sunken eyes and bloated stomach.

As they sat and gnawed the last strings of meat from the bones, a group of older Dinka boys in uniform emerged from the bush, dragging parts of another slain elephant.

"Look," a boy soldier sitting next to Ayuel called out. "I see our brothers are back from the hunt."

"There are more elephants waiting for us at a watering hole," one of the uniformed hunters announced proudly as he let go of his burden. He shaded his eyes and looked out over the crowd of new arrivals that had swollen to nearly two hundred. He turned to his fellow soldiers and said, "Looks like many guests have come to our feast. Cook this and we will return with more." The eager young hunters waved bloody spears and disappeared into the thicket.

Ayuel and his group, along with others, stayed in the camp several days, filling their stomachs, drinking from the watering hole and swapping stories. Some boys, at the officers' urging, joined the Sudanese People's Liberation Army to become boy soldiers so they could eat well and carry guns. But the seventeen all decided to go on to Ethiopia, where their Officer Chol had assured them that food, clothing and shelter awaited them. When they took their leave, each child carried a bundle of dried elephant strips, enough to last several days.

★

By the end of the month, the thousands again traveled together and converged on the town of Pibor, home to the Murle tribe. Since the area had been spared bombs from the Khartoum government, grass huts stretched for miles. Made of mud and straw with pointed thatched roofs, they resembled the *tukuls* of Duk. Skinny Dinka children wandered among the healthy Murles.

"They look even worse than us," Gutthier said.

"We're just used to looking at each other," Ayuel said. He could almost imagine himself back home as he looked out over the multiple compounds, pole fences lashed together with reeds and women stooped over large black cooking pots or pounding maize into flour. Fields of sorghum and herds of cattle edged the village. A wave of homesickness washed over him, but this was not home.

He and Gutthier stopped in front of a woman cooking maize in a pot over a charcoal fire. They stood and watched, their hands clasped behind them. "Please, Mama," Ayuel said, for Dinka children traditionally called all women *mama.*

The woman looked up and wrinkled her brow into a frown. "I can't feed the whole world, you know," she said, dipping the cooked maize into a large pottery bowl. "We are overrun with hungry Dinka offspring. But I'm sorry your villages got destroyed." She glanced about in all directions. "Don't tell where you got this," she said as she handed them the bowl.

The boys scooped up small bites from the common bowl, then handfuls, being careful not to appear greedy. The mush felt smooth and warm in Ayuel's mouth and tasted just like what his own mama used to make.

"Now, go on and don't come around again," the woman said, placing her hands on her hips. Her words were gruff, but her voice sounded kind.

After licking their hands clean, Ayuel said, "Thanks, Mama, and may the spirits bless you." He assumed that, like most Murles, she was of the Animist religion that worshiped nature spirits. Gutthier nodded agreement to Ayuel's words. The two turned and ran.

As always, when the boys came across a new band of Dinkas, they asked about their relatives and friends. Everyone here seemed to come from the Dinka region of Jongli, but not from Duk. After Ayuel and Gutthier drank their fill from the village well, they sat down under a nearby tree and waited for anyone they knew to pass by. The seventeen had agreed to meet by the well at sunset, and the sun already hung low in the western sky.

Their friends, in twos and threes, gathered to stand or sit in the vicinity. Madau and Malual, chewing on boiled cassava roots someone had given them, strolled by, then turned in recognition.

"Hello," Gutthier said. "Do you have any news? See anyone we know?"

"No, but we talked to an SPLA officer from Duk," Malual said, taking another bite of the boiled root. "He didn't know anyone we knew."

Ayuel and Gutthier shook their heads in discouragement.

"But," continued Malual, his voice lighter, "This officer asked if we had heard anything about Chief Leek Deng. Of course, anyone from Duk would know your father..."

Ayuel and Gutthier jumped to their feet, as the chief was father of both boys.

"Where is he?"

"Where did you talk to him?"

"I'll show you," Malual said. "But don't have too much hope."

The half-brothers left Madau at the well and followed Malual Kuer past pole fences, a dried-up vegetable patch and several dwelling compounds until they came to a large open-air market, a *souk*. Several men sat on benches out in front, engaged in conversation.

"There he is," Malual said as he pointed to the uniformed SPLA officer, standing with one foot on the end of a bench, waving his arm as he talked.

"I can't just walk up to him and interrupt their discussion," Ayuel said timidly. "He's an officer."

The three boys stood in silence.

The officer turned his head, glanced at them and then resumed his conversation. The boys faced the setting sun and could not see the man distinctly.

Finally the officer took a second look and walked toward them. His face fell as he stopped in front of them. "Oh, sorry," he said, "I thought for a moment I knew…" He looked at Ayuel, then Gutthier, but spoke to Malual, "You're the one I talked to before."

"Yes, sir. I am Malual Kuer."

"But, you," he said, pointing to Ayuel. "You look a lot like a nephew… but, no, he was bigger. And you with the big ears resemble another nephew… named Gutthier, but…" He turned and walked back toward the *souk*.

Ayuel recognized their uncle's voice even though he couldn't see his face clearly with the sun behind him. "I'm Ayuel Leek, Chief Leek Deng's son," he called out. "And this is really Gutthier."

His uncle turned and ran to them. "Ayuel and Gutthier, you poor children!" He encircled them both with his arms and lifted them up. "You're…alive," he said in a choked voice. "Is anyone else in your family…?"

Ayuel hugged his arms around his uncle's neck and whispered, "I don't know."

His uncle set them down and patted their heads. "Are you going to Ethiopia?"

"We are all trying to, Uncle. I'm not sure we will ever get there," Gutthier said.

"We are not far from Ethiopia now. That's where my group is headed also. Why don't you—and your friend here, too—travel with me?"

The boys all looked at each other. Malual frowned at the offer.

"We'll think about it, Uncle," Ayuel said.

"I hear there's a refugee camp set up there for us. They would probably let you stay in the officer's shelter with me and my son." Their uncle squatted down to look the boys in the eye. "To survive, you must be strong."

"I know." Ayuel looked up to him with hope. "So you don't know if... if my father is alive?"

Tears streamed down his uncle's face. "We've lost so many. I don't know about my brother. I ask everyone."

"But, your cousin, my son, is here with me. We are staying with a family who has been very good to us." The uncle made no attempt to wipe the tears running freely down his face and dripping on his uniform. "Oh, God, you boys are so thin. You shall have milk to drink. Follow me."

*

Since the wave of travelers with his uncle had arrived first, the villagers welcomed them, but now, even in the large settlement of Pibor, there was not room for thousands more. So the new arrivals were told to move out the evening of the second day. Ayuel and Gutthier spent that time with their uncle and cousin in a friendly compound. Since Malual Kuer had chosen to return to their group for the night, Ayuel asked him to tell the others to wait for them at the well before leaving.

The next afternoon Ayuel's uncle walked back with them. He begged them one more time to stay and travel with him. "But, Ayuel and Gutthier, we are your close relatives," he pleaded. "Your mothers and father would want me to watch over you. Besides, I'm an officer and you will be safer with me."

Ayuel wrapped his arms around his uncle's waist and leaned his head against him. That did make him feel good and safe. He loved his uncle, but he thought of his cousin Chuei who was becoming weaker by the day; his friend, Malual Kuer, who had stayed with him that awful day—the first time he drank his own urine, and Donayok, the good Samaritan, who had put him on his own back and carried him, probably saving his life. Their leader certainly would never abandon the group.

"I'll find you again in Ethiopia," Ayuel finally said and wiped his eyes on the tatters of his T-shirt sleeve.

Gutthier agreed with his half-brother and spoke convincingly. "The seventeen of us decided to stay together and not give up until we all got there. We must go with them. We have responsibilities, Uncle."

"So that's your decision—okay. I understand your loyalty. Loyalty is a good thing."

They walked the rest of the way to the well in silence. Their entire group was waiting and stood up out of respect for the officer. Without tears Ayuel and Gutthier shook their uncle's hand.

"See you at the camp in Ethiopia," their uncle said. Ayuel looked up at him and smiled. Their uncle patted both heads, turned and walked back into the village.

"You could have stayed with him, couldn't you?" Akon said. "I know I would've."

"Could've," Gutthier said.

"Yeah."

' After a few minutes, Donayok said, "We must prepare for the night's journey. While it's still light, let's go bathe in the river and wash our clothes. That's what everyone is doing." The group followed him down to the narrow stream that flowed near the town. There they splashed and played with shrieks of laughter—like normal children—until nightfall.

Ayuel and his group then filled their containers with water and joined the thousands that made up their wave of migrants. When they were all well out of Pibor, Officer Chol took out his microphone and assured all of them: "The Ethiopian border is not too many days away. There we will find food, shelter and security. And all of you can go to school."

Thus, with renewed energy, refreshed in body and soul, Ayuel and his chosen family picked up their meager belongings and headed toward the "promised land."

SIX

INCHING FORWARD

The last leg of the journey took much longer than Ayuel or anyone expected—three weeks of endless plodding. Mercifully, a great downpour of rain provided water. The only other excitement came one night when a herd of zebras suddenly burst through the crowd as they walked. The racing animals knocked down several children nearby, leaving them with cuts and bruises, but no one was killed. Again, the seventeen miraculously escaped injury.

The larger group had diminished to around 3000 and split into three groups to follow different routes. At last, Ayuel's band arrived mid-morning at the town of Pochalla, near the Gilo River. On the other side lay Ethiopia. Ayuel noticed two men on the bank, each tying up a wooden boat, apparently used to ferry passengers across the river. He and his friends watched as Officer Chol approached them.

"Peace to you, my good men," Officer Chol said. "As you can see, I have many starving children here who need to cross the Gilo to find refuge in Ethiopia."

The men grinned and rubbed their palms together.

"We have no money, but the God Almighty will bless you greatly for your kindness…"

The men's faces fell as they resumed tying up the boats. "We have a business here," snarled one of the men. "There is no god but Allah, and he blesses us by sending paying customers."

So they're Muslims, thought Ayuel, *but black like us.*

The boys all watched Officer Chol as he slowly removed his rifle from the sling on his back, then cocked the hammer. "I demand that you provide transportation for these innocent children to cross," he said in a calm but firm voice.

"We have nothing to do with either side in this war," said the man who had spoken before, as he yanked a tight knot in the rope.

Officer Chol shot once into the air and stepped closer to the men.

"We have no choice," the spokesman hissed between his teeth at his partner. "They have us." The silent man shrugged his shoulders and slowly began to untie the ropes.

"Get in!" the spokesman yelled at the boys standing nearest. Five boys gingerly crept into the boat, fitting comfortably on the planks around the sides. The man laughed, but not with humor. "We can stuff a few more in. It'll take a week at the normal load." He grabbed the arms of a couple of children and shoved them toward the boat. "Add two more to these. Move along. Save me my place to row," he hollered.

His partner followed his lead and counted off nine more passengers, including an SPLA soldier, to climb into the other boat.

After the two boats had left the shore, Officer Chol turned to his followers on the bank and spoke over his microphone, "We're almost there. You are the survivors. We won't have far to go to the refugee camp after we get across. We will be safe from the Arab government there, as they don't dare invade another country. Have faith, be strong a little longer."

The throngs of people sat down in their various groups, scattered over a wide area next to the village. The seventeen filled their containers with water from the river and found shade under a baobab tree. Ayuel sat between Gutthier and Malual, his heart full of hope. *Life will be better now, no more attacks by the government or wild animals, no more hunger or thirst. And something to wear besides this worn-out, dirty T-shirt.*

"Somehow I feel like I'm home now," he said to his friends.

"Me too," Malual Kuer said. "Except there is no mother to fix food for me."

Ayuel missed his family. But for the first time since that horrible night of bombing, he felt a tinge of happiness. All seventeen in his group had stayed together and survived.

"Look," Madau said, pointing toward the village. "Look at all those women coming this way. They seem to be carrying food—maybe for us."

"Someone said the Anuak tribe lives here," Donayok pointed out. "At least the Dinkas are at peace with them."

The local women spread out as they came closer, each bringing some food to a single group. One woman approached the seventeen and sat a large bowl of boiled maize on the ground. Ayuel accepted a loaf of millet bread from her hand. She said something in the Anuak language that he didn't understand, but her smile spoke the intended message. Again she smiled when they all said, "Thank you, Mama," in Dinka, even though she did not know their words.

Ayuel pulled off a bite of bread and passed the loaf to the next child. Without fighting or shoving, each dipped the bread into the maize. Still warm from cooking, it tasted and felt on their tongues so much better than raw leaves. They finished by scooping their hands into the meal and licking them. One of the soldiers came by while they ate and told them to divide into groups of nine. He said he would tell them when it was time for them to go to the boats.

Finally, they passed the bowl for one last swipe apiece. Afterward they all lay in the dry grass and slept. When evening came, the usual time to begin walking, they went to the river to watch the last crossing of the boats before morning.

"I think there are more than nine in that boat," Malual said, pointing. It was too far out in the river to count the people, but it appeared weighed down. They watched the boat on the shore as the owner packed in the children.

Ayuel counted them. "There are eleven. That's too many," he said. "They don't want to take us across because we can't pay."

"Look how low they are in the water," Chuei said. "Maybe they want to drown us."

"I don't think so," Ayuel said. "The owner would drown, too. Have courage, Chuei. We'll all get to Ethiopia. God has brought us this far."

Early the next morning, Officer Chol woke the seventeen. "You are the first to cross this morning. Go over and wait by the boats. I made the two men stay here all night so they wouldn't desert us."

"Where are those men?" asked Gutthier.

"The guard soldier took them to get breakfast tea. We owe them at least that much."

"I think they overloaded the boats yesterday, sir," Ayuel said.

"Yes, I know," Officer Chol said. "I told them nine was the limit, only eight if there was an adult or a large boy. We'll watch more closely today."

The children didn't have to wait long in the warm, foggy morning. When the men arrived, still looking angry, the seventeen divided into two groups. "I'll go with you," said Officer Chol, taking a spot next to Ayuel and placing a smaller boy on his lap. Akon, his cousin, sat down on his other side. "That will leave one soldier to come with the last group at the end of the day."

The owner gave a low growl but said nothing.

Ayuel felt pleasure in the crossing, dangling his hand in the swift-moving water. Emotionally he was sailing into a bright future, where life might again be normal. He remembered that Officer Chol had said everyone could even go to school. Akon followed his lead and trailed her hand in the water too.

"Look over there, Ayuelo. Aren't those crocodiles?" Ayuel could see the heads skimming above the surface near the bank. Akon's voice sounded frightened.

"But, we are moving away from them, Akon. I don't think we have to worry." He knew she had to be thinking what he was. "Those crocodiles in the oasis pool probably attacked because they thought we were going after them. The river is big and they should have lots of fish to eat."

She smiled and seemed satisfied.

When they landed, Ayuel and his friends went scrounging for food, as they had eaten nothing since the maize the previous morning. The river ran too swift for fishing. With no village on the Ethiopian side, they resorted once again to leaves and grass. Officer Chol told them not to go far as they would head toward the refugee camp as soon as all got across.

Toward the evening, they sat along the bank watching the boats.

"This should be the last crossing," Officer Chol said. "I don't see anyone on the other shore. That was quick." He shaded his eyes, looking out over the river toward the setting sun. As he walked along the bank, encouraging the children, he told them: "Our lives will all be better soon— food, schools and hospitals."

As the last boats neared the middle of the river, Ayuel said to Donayok, "I think they are overloaded again."

"The sun's in my eyes, so I can't count the people. But the boat on the left looks tilted and very low in the water," said the fourteen-year-old. "I'm going to tell Officer Chol." He walked in the direction of the officer, still keeping an eye on the river.

Ayuel thought the boats seemed much farther apart than usual and moved more slowly. The soldier weighted down the corner of the boat on the left. As they all stood watching, it suddenly tipped and sank, spilling its occupants into the swirling waters. After only a few shouts for help, most of the passengers went under. Some of the boys and the soldier fought the swift river in an attempt to swim, but one by one, they too went under. All were lost.

As the people on the bank stood in shock, not believing their eyes, the other boat pulled in. "Did you see that?" a boy cried as he got out and pointed to the boat that had resurfaced upside down. "My brother was on it! My brother and my sister! They crammed fifteen people in that one. Fourteen in ours." He began to wail as did others.

"Where's the owner?" shouted Officer Chol, anger in his voice.

"They both deserted us as soon as they packed us in," said one of the older boys. "Neither one of the men got in the boats."

"They ran," said another. "Since we were already in, and there was no room for them anyhow, we took off. I had the paddle. They made us all get on. He said they weren't going to make any more free crossings."

Officer Chol cursed. Then sat down and cried.

Ayuel's heart sank. His future now seemed no brighter than what they'd experienced the past two and a half months. Some of his cousins had just been sucked into the churning river and drowned before his eyes. He went over and stood by Akon.

"Those crocodiles," she whispered.

Ayuel shuddered as he shared her thought. For a long time they stared at the river, until the overturned boat and a few scattered bodies floated out of sight.

★

Two days after crossing the Gilo, Ayuel and his group heard a faint rumbling in the distance, but with the constant tramping of feet around them, it was difficult to identify. As they listened intently, the rumbling became more like low bellowing.

"Sounds like a cattle camp up ahead," Madau said. "The cows are refusing to move on."

"We could all use some milk," Donayok said, who was carrying Chuei on his back. "Especially this one."

"Hey, Chuei," Ayuel said, taking his cousin's limp hand. "I'll get milk for you in my calabash." Ayuel ached inside to see the former jokester breathing so hard through his mouth and staring back at him with large sunken eyes. *He doesn't look so good.*

Ayuel watched as the crowd up front crested a knoll, picked up speed and dropped out of sight on the other side. The moaning of cattle grew louder. *They will take all the milk before we get there.*

Malual Kuer ran ahead to the knoll and shouted back to his friends, "Those are people! Not cows. Thousands of them, even more than us. We're here! We're at the Ethiopian camp!"

The group picked up their pace to get a glimpse of the camp—their reward for months of misery.

"We made it!" shouted Gutthier.

Similar shouts echoed throughout the throng.

"None of our group died," Akon said as she caught up with Ayuel and flashed him a weak smile.

An emotion of victory flooded over Ayuel—like winning a very long race. "None of us ever gave up, did we, Akon? God was with us!" he said shaking a small fist in the air as others were doing.

The seventeen bunched closer to one another, wishing to enter the camp together. Visions of everything Officer Chol had promised swirled in Ayuel's head.

"I don't see any tents," Malual said. "I heard my father say one time that refugee camps have tents—and hospitals and schools." He slowed down a bit as if resisting what might lie ahead.

Indeed, when they merged with the milling thousands, no one met them with food, water or clean clothing. *Nothing.* A huge soggy and sandy field stretched as far as the eye could see. They noticed a few adults here, mostly women with listless babies in their arms and toddlers clinging to their skirts. Children stood with blank expressions or groaned and sobbed. At their feet lay the dead and dying. Flies moved like a living blanket over the corpses and buzzed in the hot and humid morning air. Mosquitoes rose from muddy puddles and spread stings over the exposed flesh of the new arrivals, leaving beads of blood. *The stink is the worst of the whole trip*, thought Ayuel, as he dipped his calabash into a shallow pool of water. "I guess it rained here last night," he said.

Donayok sat Chuei down on a patch of trampled grass. Ayuel held the calabash to Chuei's lips. He took one sip, then shook his head. "Maybe some more later," Ayuel said. Then he drank the rest himself.

*

Ayuel woke early the next morning pressed between Gutthier and Malual Kuer. The group had made a small clump of thorn bushes their "home." He sat up and rubbed his eyes, then the hard ball of his stomach and the sagging flesh on his boney arms. He looked at his very closest friend, Malual, and thought he was probably the healthiest of all of them. *If anyone lives through this, it will be Malual.*

"Hey," Malual said as he opened his eyes. "What's going on? Have you heard anything?"

"Nothing," whispered Ayuel. "I didn't sleep at all last night. Well, maybe a little this morning." They had both scouted around the day before, looking for Officer Chol or his soldiers, but no one knew about them. No one seemed to be in authority. "Some people say they've been here for days. Maybe this isn't the camp and we're all lost."

"A man told me yesterday that the town of Panyido is just over there."

Malual pointed to some thin lines of smoke coming from morning cooking fires. "This is supposed to be Camp Panyido. The man said you could find scraps of food in their garbage dumps."

"I'm going to go look around, see what I can find out," Ayuel said.

★

Ayuel returned in late morning, his hands full of fish bones and bits of bread he found in the dumps. Malual, Madau and a couple of others from their group were pitching a ball made from rags.

"Want to play catch?" asked Madau.

"Not now. I've brought you some food."

The boys quickly devoured the scraps and resumed their game. Ayuel joined in, but stopped suddenly and asked, "Where's Chuei? I want to check on him."

"Asleep over there by the thorn bushes."

"Hey, Chuei," Malual said, "Wake up. Let's play ball."

"Let me sleep," Chuei mumbled. "I don't feel like talking."

Ayuel shook his shoulder gently.

"Is that you, Mama?" Chuei said with his eyes closed. "Are you bringing me sorghum cakes?" His voice sounded happy, but his words didn't make sense.

Donayok came over and knelt beside him. Without saying anything he gently turned Chuei's face toward them.

"What's wrong with him?" said the boy who held the rag ball.

Donayok pulled Chuei's eyelids over his eyes. "He's dead."

★

Ayuel grieved over the loss of his cousin Chuei. All day he sat by the thorn bushes next to his cousin's body. The others came and went. Some stayed awhile. Before he'd lost his family, Ayuel never thought about any of them dying. He'd obeyed his father and his mother. He fought with Aleer and tried to be like Deng. When he took the cows out to pastureland, he never thought about coming back and not finding his family. Life was normal and would go on being normal. Of course, he loved them, but they would always be there. Today he missed them terribly. Worse than ever.

But with Chuei and the others—he knew death hung over their heads.

It was all around them. The bonds among them had grown deep and strong. Even the pleading of his uncle hadn't been able pull him away from his group of seventeen. Somehow by taking care of each other, they had made it all this long way to Ethiopia without losing a single one. Now Chuei had been torn from them. He felt as if his own heart had been ripped from his chest.

Akon came and sat beside him. She stayed a long time with tears trickling down her cheeks. Finally, she said, "I think we should bury him."

"We have nothing to dig with," Ayuel said without looking at her.

"We can cover him with brush so he isn't exposed...." she offered.

Gutthier, Malual, Madau and some of the others helped break off the brittle thorn-bush branches and make a big mound over their friend. Afterward, Donayok said a prayer and they sang a Dinka hymn about God, the Shepherd of Life and Death, that Malual's father, the church pastor, had written. Then, with hands bleeding from the thorns, they left their friend and went to look for another spot to call home.

★

As the group wandered through the masses, they noticed several people running in one direction. They stretched their necks to see what was happening and saw three trucks creeping into the crowd. When the trucks stopped, the boys approached and saw a man climb on top of the cab of the front vehicle.

"That's Officer Chol!" Madau said with excitement in his voice. "No, I guess not. It's someone else, but he has a microphone like his."

The man holding the microphone was neatly dressed in a camouflage uniform. His loud voice echoed over the crowds: "Everyone stand back. Please stand back." About a dozen men with him pulled out their rifles and surrounded the trucks to make sure everyone obeyed.

"I represent the government of Ethiopia. This maize is a generous gift from the people of Panyido to you. The people brought us whatever they could spare. It is just enough for each group to have one meal. Bring whatever containers you have and we will fill them." People started clamoring, pushing and yelling.

A gunshot rang out and scared the crowd into silence.

"Now, hear me out," said the government man. "One person from each group of about twenty, line up over here on the right. Then take your food and your group far to the other side. Don't, I repeat, don't eat the grain raw, and don't eat too much. Chew slowly. The Panyido River is just beyond those trees, so you can get water and boil the grain until it is soft. And don't come back for more. When these trucks are empty, we will go for the rest that the townspeople have collected so everyone can have one portion. There's enough..."

The crowd drowned out the officer's voice as they queued up to the trucks. Donayok sent half his group to fill their containers with water and the others to find firewood. He chose for himself the hardest task of standing in line with their one cooking pot to receive the grain. Even though the river was a mile away, they all knew walking was easier than standing in the hot sun. There would be shade by the water.

★

Fortunately for the sixteen, their grain lasted for two meals. A few days later, the government of Ethiopia brought in several trucks of maize and gave each group an allotment, enough for a week, with one small meal a day.

Children who had survived long periods without food now began to die from eating more than they were used to. Their thin bodies couldn't adjust to processing the grain. The flies, filth and stench became unbearable. With thousands of people packed close together in the relentless heat by day and cold by night, they became too weak to make the long trek outside of camp to relieve themselves or to carry away the dead. With the absence of even minimal sanitation and the lack of clean water, large numbers of people became ill with diarrhea, followed by violent vomiting.

Two Ethiopian government men came back in less than a week with an empty truck. Without bothering to get out, one of them talked over a microphone. "We are trying as best we can to get health workers here, but it will be a while. Be patient." Groans went up from the assembly. "You must clean up the space around you and boil the water you drink. Cholera has broken out here." Shrieks mingled with the moans. Everyone knew about the vicious and deadly disease. "Take the dead bodies outside the camp, but don't take them near the river." The truck turned and sped away.

Ayuel's group carefully followed the rules now. Like the others, they had become lax, because it took so much of their energy to do anything. But even with all their care, another boy from the group died during the night.

SEVEN

GRIEF AND WELCOMES

A few days later, Ayuel and his best friend, Malual Kuer, went down by the Panyido River for firewood to cook the day's meal. After bathing and collecting a nice bundle of sticks, they sat on the bank to rest. The water's edge swarmed with masses of people in and out of the river but the two boys kept to themselves. Certainly they would boil the drinking water they had brought back.

While they leaned against tree trunks, Malual began singing a Dinka song his father had written during the famine a few years back:

> Lord, we know that we have wronged you many times.
> We know that we just believe in words, but not in spirit.
> So, Lord of the whole world, if You weren't there,
> We would have no seed left during this famine.
> So, Lord, come and bless us,
> Give us rain so that our cattle can feed on grass.
> Give us food to eat so that our souls can live.
> Ooh, Lord help us!

When Malual stopped singing, he said, "God is punishing us."

"Why? Why do you say that?" Ayuel said. He looked at his friend and could tell his words were serious. He seemed to have a strange glow on his face.

"Look at us. We are so young, just children. We don't have mothers and fathers, sisters or brothers. We don't have spears to hunt animals. Today we cook the last little bit of food we have. So what kind of people are we? Why is God punishing us?"

"I cannot answer that." Ayuel threw a pebble into the river and watched the circles grow wide where it sank. He tried to find some reasons for Malual. "Maybe because our fathers or grandfathers were not good. They did something bad. Perhaps God is punishing us because our fathers did something against the Lord. That could be why He's punishing the children of Sudan."

"You know the scripture," Malual said. "It says God is a jealous god. He carries revenge on the children for the sins of the fathers to the third and fourth generations."

The boys picked up the sticks for firewood and headed back to the camp. On the way, Malual complained of stomach pains. Then he told Ayuel he was having bloody diarrhea.

"My mother used to boil roots to make a tea that helped that," Ayuel said. So they dug roots with their hands and took them back and made tea.

"We have no knowledge of these roots, whether they can be used for medicine or not," Malual said. "They might be poison." He wouldn't drink the liquid, but lay down and held his stomach.

Malual Kuer, the strongest in the group, became weaker and sicker by the hour. Ayuel sat beside him, giving him water and trying to get him to eat. They talked no more of God's punishment.

On the morning of the second day, Ayuel held Malual's head in his lap and fanned away the flies. *We're age-mates. We're supposed to grow up together. Please, Malual, don't leave me. Please, God, don't let him.* Tears dripped off his chin and fell on his friend's neck. He wiped them off with the tail of his T-shirt. As he looked into Malual's face, he saw that strange glow again.

"I'll ask God about it," Malual whispered. He closed his eyes and was gone.

★

Lord, we know that we have wronged you...Lord, come and bless us.

Malual's voice rang in Ayuel's head. He remembered first meeting Malual when he'd followed that angelic voice through the village. Since that day, they had remained close friends. Sometimes Ayuel sang the words aloud as a way of mourning for his friend—his age-mate, his soul-mate. Yet the song was always there from the moment he rose to the moment until he lay down at night. *So give us food to eat so that our souls can live.* Sometimes just a line repeated itself over and over. Other times, he would sing the whole song as a prayer.

One morning after the worst of the cholera had subsided, the fourteen sat around drinking what they loosely called tea—water left from boiled leaves. Gutthier turned to his friends and said, "So... this is worse than when we walked every night. We could keep walking then because we thought we were going to a good place. But now we are here, and it's not a good place."

"I heard yesterday that there are other camps in Ethiopia," Donayok said, sipping his tea from a gourd shell. "Dimma and Itang. Close by there is Markas. Maybe we came to the wrong one."

"I hear they teach you to shoot guns in Markas and the food is better," Madau said.

Ayuel remembered that Malual had once said he would like to be a soldier.

"I think Markas is not far from here," Madau said, "I'd rather walk than sit around this smelly place all day. Who wants to go?"

Before they could make a decision, a commotion broke out around a vehicle that apparently had just pulled into camp. Since the meager food supply had arrived yesterday, this must be something else. A man's voice boomed over the microphone. What was he saying? "Listen, listen," Donayok said, motioning for them to hush.

The officer was standing on what they later learned was a jeep. "Tomorrow is a very important day in our lives. A congressman from the United States of America is coming here to visit you. The whole world will then know what terrible things are happening to the children of Sudan and in the refugee camps here in Ethiopia. They will want to help us. It is not right for you to endure this tragedy."

Several people started shouting, "No, no! It's not right!"

"What is a congressman?" Ayuel asked. "And where did he say he was from?"

"Unite something," Madau said. "There are some Nuer boys here from Unity. That's the town with an oil company where the government killed everybody in a raid. I hope that's not where he's from."

"We will want to welcome the congressman," said the official. "So I am going to teach you some English words. This is what the words look like." Two men held up a huge banner attached to long poles at each end.

Ayuel had seen Arabic words before, but this didn't look anything like that. A wave of excitement came over him. He was going to learn something.

"This is the first word right here." The officer pointed to some marks at the left on the banner.

"I can read that," said a boy, whom Ayuel had never seen before. He read off the words rapidly and then repeated them in Dinka. He grinned at his own accomplishment.

Amazed, Ayuel said, "How do you know how to read English?"

"Just do." He rattled off a bunch of unintelligible words.

Ayuel was duly impressed, but said, "Let's listen to the officer."

"This says *welcome*." The officer moved his stick to the next group of marks. "Does this look like the first word?"

A chorus of voices shouted, "Yes."

"Right. Now repeat after me: Wel-come, wel-come."

"*Wel-come, wel-come.*"

After teaching them to say *American congressman*, the man said, "Now some time tomorrow the congressman from the United States of America will be here. When the men hold up this banner, we will all shout out the English words you have learned. Now go practice saying these words to each other: *Welcome, welcome, American Congressman.*"

The boy who seemed to know English turned to Ayuel and offered his hand, "My name's Emmanuel Jal."

Ayuel shook his hand and introduced himself. "Am I saying it right?" He repeated the words they had just learned.

"Almost. It's like this." The boy practiced with him a few times until a bunch of his friends came by. "See you later, Ayuel."

The next day, Ayuel—as well as the whole camp—watched with curiosity as long metal poles with some boxes atop rose at the place where the trucks usually stopped. Late in the afternoon some extremely bright lights shone from the boxes. Like the sun, they were too bright to look at directly. Donayok put Ayuel up on his shoulders so he could tell the others what was going on.

"They're setting up a shade for the congressman, sort of a shelter with four wooden poles and a roof. Now a whole line of vehicles is coming toward the lights," he reported. "But only one is a truck. The others are low with tops on them. I see people inside."

"They're called cars," Donayok said with a laugh. "I've seen them in Bor."

"Well, there is one that is very, very long with lots of windows. It has little flags on each side and it's black and shiny. They've stopped by the lights and the shelter now. Two men are getting out of the long one—the long *car*. They look very strange, wearing funny clothes with sleeves that come down to their hands. Their skin is pale, much lighter than any Arab."

"They're *khawaja*, white people," someone said.

"Now what are they doing?" asked Madau and pulled eagerly on Ayuel's foot that hung over Donayok's shoulder.

"Someone is pointing something big—I don't think it's a gun—right at the two pale men, the *khawaja*."

"That's a TV camera," an older boy from another group said. "They can make pictures that move with it."

How can pictures move? That's not possible.

"Some of our men are setting up a tall desk, like a church pulpit, under the shade."

"Here comes the banner!" shouted Madau.

From his high perch on Donayok's shoulders, Ayuel scanned the crowd for Emmanuel Jal, but never saw him.

As two men held up the banner, a man from the Ethiopian government jumped into the back of the truck with a microphone. Pointing to the banner, he began the chant: *"Wel-come, wel-come!"*

"Welcome, welcome! American Congressman," yelled the crowd over and over, not so much to welcome the congressman, but to show off their new

knowledge.

"Very good," said the man at the microphone. "Okay, okay. That's enough. We do heartily welcome the congressman who has come all the way from the United States of America to talk to you." He handed the microphone to one of the white men and clapped enthusiastically along with the crowd. The government man said the name of the congressman but it sounded so strange that Ayuel and his friends couldn't remember it.

"Let's move over where we can see better," suggested Gutthier. Ayuel slid down from Donayok's shoulders, and they found a spot in the middle of the assembly. The crowd grew silent and sat down to hear what the man would say.

The congressman got out of the long car and stood under the shade behind the pulpit. He spoke a few words over the microphone in a strange language that Ayuel guessed was English like "welcome." Then the Ethiopian man repeated them in Dinka, for that was what most in the camp spoke.

"Thank you for your very kind welcome," the congressman said. "I am happy to be with you this evening. The government of the United States of America has heard of the terrible situation here, and I have come to see for myself. It is, indeed, worse than I ever imagined." He took out a white cloth and wiped his face.

"I have let the United Nations know about you. Shortly they will send you food, clothing, soap, tents and blankets for cold nights." The assembly of thousands roared with applause. "Then we will set up medical clinics and burial grounds. You will have schools and teachers." More applause.

The congressman talked on for a very long time. Much of what he said Ayuel and his friends didn't understand, but they understood what meant the most. Their lives were going to be better. The whole world would help them.

One week later, a convoy of trucks brought food and clothing. They brought shovels and machines to bury the dead. Ayuel made a rag ball from his torn and ragged T-shirt. It would be good for playing pitch. His new one had been worn by someone before and had words on it, but it smelled clean and felt soft against his dry skin. His new shorts wouldn't stay up over his thin body so he tied a vine through the loops, but he kept his old *mutkukalei* on his feet. They had served him well.

Life became better. Aid workers from various countries came to help the sick. Men with razors came to shave off the children's orange and brittle, lice-filled hair. More bags of clothing arrived, marked "U.S.A.". Each group received a chunk of soap for bathing and washing out their cooking pots, containers for storing grain and a bucket for carrying water. Now, in addition to maize, the food rations included beans, oil, sorghum and wheat flour. In the wooded area near the river, the boys often found mangoes and other wild fruits.

A few days later the people were ordered to form several lines, each in front of an official of some kind. After standing long hours in the hot sun, Ayuel arrived in front of a man who squatted down to question him.

"What is your full name?" he asked. "And you are from which clan?"

"Ayuel Leek. Dinka, sir."

"How old are you?"

"I think, sir, I am still seven."

"Do you have a mother or father, sister or brother in Camp Panyido?"

"No, sir."

"To your knowledge, do you know if anyone else in your immediate family is living?"

"I don't know, sir. I hope so."

"Name any half-brothers and sisters, cousins and any relatives that are here in camp."

Ayuel mentioned every relative he'd met on the journey, including his uncle, the SPLA officer, even though he'd never found him in the camp. Of course, he mentioned Gutthier and Madau.

"Ever been to school?"

"No, sir."

"Next."

The fourteen had become separated from one another when the assembly rushed to get in the lines. Now, near the end of the day, they gathered at their new home at the foot of a dead acacia tree. One of the boys had found a woman's shawl, which they stretched out from the tree branches and attached the ends to two poles. This made a shade for a few children at a time.

Since Gutthier and Madau had been first to finish the questioning, they brought water from the river for everyone. When Ayuel arrived, he fell exhausted under the shelter. After a while, he sat up and slowly drank the boiled and cooled water from Gutthier's plastic bottle. "We don't have any more food, do we?"

"No," Madau said. "We finished our supplies last evening. Let's go gather some tree leaves. This old acacia tree probably died because people ate all the leaves."

"I'm too tired from standing so long," Ayuel said. He lay down and closed his eyes, but could hear the rest of his group gather and talk about the day's experience. He recognized each voice and automatically counted off the names as he had done so many times in an effort to keep track of everyone. He drifted off to sleep and when he opened his eyes, it was nearly dark.

"We're all here except Akon," Donayok said with strain in his voice. "Did anyone see her today?"

Ayuel sat up, wide awake. "I haven't seen her since we boiled the tea this morning. Maybe we should go search for her."

"No. She knows where to come," Madau said. "I saw her in another line, talking to some other girls. They're her cousins on her father's side. Her mother and mine are sisters, so we are cousins, but on our mothers' side." The explanation was not unusual for a Dinka child who learned to recite the relationships of his relatives at a very young age.

Just then, Akon appeared with two taller girls, one on each side. The boys all stood up, "We were worried…" Donayok said.

"Here, I brought you some bread," she said and handed out some dried scraps, obviously from the dump. She smiled broadly, showing real happiness. Ayuel thought she had invited the girls, whom he recognized as Akon's cousins, to join their group. That would be great; they needed some mother types.

"These are my cousins," Akon announced and then choked up, unable to speak.

One of the girls said, "We found Akon this morning in the lines. Our mother is still with us. And our little brother, about your age." She pointed to Ayuel.

"Our father was shot. Right in front of us," the other girl said without showing emotion. "Akon is going to live with us."

The boys remained standing in stunned silence. No one had just left since forming the group of seventeen. Akon had always been a comfort to Ayuel. "I'm happy you have a family," he finally said. "But we can still see you every day."

"Where is your family's base?" asked Madau. "I'm glad you will have a mother."

"Didn't you hear?" Akon said as she wiped tears with the tail of the new T-shirt that she wore over a flowered skirt. "They are putting all the families on the far side of the field. I have to go now. It's getting dark."

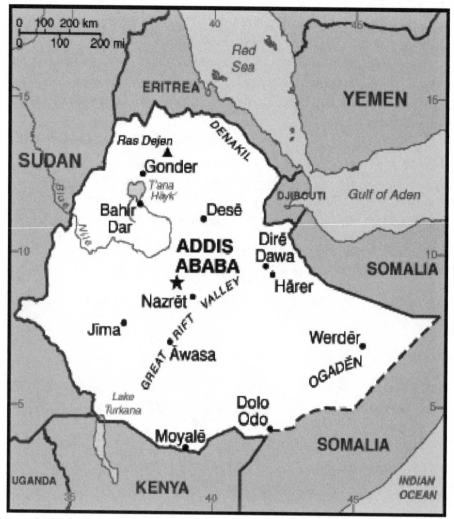

Map of Ethiopia, courtesy of the CIA World Factbook

EIGHT

HUNGER'S LESSONS

The thirteen remaining boys still had each other to depend on. They missed Akon's gentle ways but they were glad for her. The officials began moving the families the next morning, separating them from the orphan boys. All the girls, they discovered, were being placed with families.

"Akon is really lucky to find her aunt," Madau said. "Most of the orphan girls will just be put with strangers."

"Let's go see if we can find her and greet her aunt," suggested Ayuel. "I want to see her one more time. She really looked happy." *Maybe Gutthier and I should have gone with our uncle when we had the chance. He offered to take Malual, too. Maybe I made a bad decision. Staying didn't keep him and Chuei from dying.*

He and Gutthier searched for their cousin Akon every day, but never found her. The officials would not allow them to mingle with the families who had already been identified.

It took five or six days to relocate the families on the other side of the camp. Some boys tried to sneak in with them, but the officials checked every name and orphaned males were turned back. Ayuel again felt abandoned by adults, even though he knew none of them. He thought of the time the women and girls had turned back to their burned villages rather than walk to Ethiopia.

The next few weeks passed slowly. Food remained sparse. The boys watched the points of tents rise up in the far corner of the field. A rope stretched across, dividing the two societies—orphaned boys from families with mothers, sisters and brothers, and sometimes fathers. Soon a high pole fence replaced the rope. *We must be less important, less valuable,* they concluded. The thirteen took comfort in remaining together. They too, were a family.

The Ethiopian officials vanished just as the SPLA soldiers had disappeared when the boys arrived. Men in uniform wearing light blue caps appeared. Instead of the one microphone, these men talked over two huge microphones shaped like bells that sat on top of their trucks. The person speaking hid in the truck cab so no one could see him. But his voice came out loud and clear.

"Good morning, boys," the hidden voice said. "We are here from the United Nations. Now that we have the families and girls settled, we are going to make life better for you, too. As you know, there are several different clans and tribes here. We must all get along. Already we've seen fights break out—Dinkas against Nuers, Equatorians against Dinkas, boys from one town fighting against another town. The remedy for this, the U.N. has decided, is to form new "families" of about thirty to fifty boys each that we are calling villages, mixing up the clans, separating relatives and forcing all to live together in harmony. This, we believe, will prevent gangs from forming. Then several villages will be put together to form twelve larger groups."

"This is the end of our little family," Madau said. "I don't like their idea one bit."

"I don't either," Ayuel said as he sat surrounded by his friends and listened to the voice coming from the bells. *I'll be alone again with a bunch of strangers.* "But what can we do? At least we have a little food here, and they have promised us schools."

"You can still visit your friends," the voice said in a softer tone. "But you are in this camp to keep from being hurt anymore by the war in your country. We don't want small wars to break out here." After the low grumbling of the assembly faded, the voice continued. "From now on the supplies will be distributed to the new groups, which we will be forming immediately.

"Please, get in one of the lines in front of these officials to find out which group and which village you are in. Let's do this in an orderly fashion. Move out of the way when…" The voice droned on, but Ayuel had stopped listening. "At least we can still see each other," he whispered to Madau.

Since Madau was his cousin and Gutthier his half-brother, Ayuel knew they would not be put together. He tried to be brave and accept the new rule, but it left him feeling lonely. That night, lying between two strangers, he dreamed of coming home with the cows. His mama welcomed him with a smile and said how proud she was of him. He played soccer with his brother Aleer and with Malual and Tor, their voices full of laughter and their bodies brimming with good health.

★

"So what's your new group and village like?" Ayuel asked as he walked along the edge of camp at dusk with Gutthier and Madau. They were in Group Ten. It felt good to be with his old friends rather than the strangers he'd been assigned to live with.

"I don't talk to the people in in my village. They're mostly Nuers and a few Equatorians. The Dinkas are all older," said Madau who, by nature, was prone to keep quiet.

"Wish we could've all stayed together," Ayuel said. "There're about fifty in Village One, or my 'family' as they call it. It's not at all like our family of seventeen." He slapped at mosquitoes attacking his arms.

"And we're about the only ones left that get together," Madau said. "I did see Donayok the other day. He's the head leader of Group One in charge of over 1,000 boys. He supervises all his village leaders and has his own *tukul* and boys who work for him."

"They couldn't have found a better or fairer leader," Ayuel said. "We should go see him sometime. Leaders get extra food."

"Yeah, and he would share. I never see anyone else. Wonder how Akon is doing with her aunt and cousins."

"Better than us."

"Like I said, I don't talk in my village, but I listen to what people say," continued Madau, picking up on his earlier comment. "The Dinkas were saying—and they're the only ones I understand—that when the United

Nations people first got here, they counted about 33,000 of us. Then 12,000 died of cholera or starved to death."

"Or from eating too much, too fast," added Ayuel. "Or from diarrhea." He thought of Malual Kuer.

"They took away the families and girls. Now there are about 16,000 of us boys in the twelve groups," continued Madau.

"I still think maybe we should've gone to one of the other camps, Markas or Itang," Madau said. "Maybe we could stay together there."

"We could just keep going—right now, tonight."

"I've heard Itang is north of here. I don't want to go to the Markas training camp and be a soldier," Ayuel said, considering the possibility.

"Well, there's the North Star." Gutthier pointed to the first faint star to show in the evening sky. The boys kept walking in that direction without making a decision. "What else do the Dinkas say?"

"That we are going to start building *tukuls* to sleep in—like back in Duk."

"Are we really going to go to Itang?"

More stars began to brighten and hang low as darkness fell.

"We don't have food with us, and we could run into hostile gangs or...."

The howl of a hyena in the distance cut off their conversation. The three friends turned and ran back to their separate new families.

*

As Ayuel got to know the others in his compound, he spent less and less time with his old friends. He soon realized the boys from the Nuer tribes were not as terrible as he'd been led to believe. The members in his new family felt as lonely as he did.

In a couple of weeks, the United Nations assigned a man to each designated group to teach the boys how to build huts in the style of the ones they'd known in Sudan. Like the other boys, Ayuel dug holes and stuck sapling poles deep in the ground, then plastered the sides with wet clay mixed with straw. The older boys framed the roof with poles that came to a high ridge in the middle. Ayuel helped bundle the thick thatch to place on top. The boys worked through the morning and evening hours building their compound—a sleeping *tukul* for every fifteen boys with three rows of beds, another building for the kitchen, and one to store supplies after delivery. Ayuel enjoyed the work, and it made him feel proud of his new compound. In the hottest part of the day, the boys rested.

One morning, as the buildings neared completion, a U.N. official called the assembly together to hear an announcement over the loud speakers. Thousands of boys crowded together in small clumps, sitting in the open area of trampled dry grass. The official introduced the new schoolmaster Maker Thiang and praised him as "an educated man from Sudan who speaks English as well as Dinka, Arabic and Swahili." Maker Thiang stood in the back of a truck, holding a regular microphone.

"Good morning, young men of Sudan," he said. "Today is a very important day in your lives. Today you all will become students in the schools we are forming. You will learn numbers, geography, science and the history of Africa." He paused. "Not all today, of course."

The crowd roared with laughter over the joke, then applauded the new schools. They could like this schoolmaster.

"And you will learn to speak, read and write English." More applause.

"We now have, however, only a few teachers so your classes will be very large. Some of you, I've learned, have had one year or more of schooling, so I am asking you to help one day a week with the beginners. If you are at least eleven years old and have been to school, please see me before going to your classes. Everyone will start in First Class because you will be learning English, a new language for all of you."

Ayuel turned to Madau and whispered, *"Welcome, welcome."*

"American congressman," his cousin added with a giggle.

"Until we have more teachers, you may choose which school to join. They will all be the same. Just try to go to the smallest class you can find." The schoolmaster then pointed out the locations of the teachers.

With joy in his heart Ayuel, along with Gutthier, Madau and new friends from both of their villages, chose an area in the shade of a baobab tree. As Ayuel was leaving the assembly, he noticed Donayok among the older boys reporting to Maker Thiang. He waved and his former leader waved back. *Donayok was a good leader. I always thought he was intelligent, but*

I never knew he went to school.

The boys reported, along with about 800 other students, to a young man whom they found perched on a lower limb of the baobab, waiting. At first, the boys pushed and jostled for a spot in the shade, but when the teacher spoke, they sat down quietly and reverently, packed close together. The teacher had no microphone, but he spoke in Dinka with a very loud voice: "I am Joseph from the region of Juba. I studied in Bor, but when I was twelve years old, a missionary took me to London, England, for a year where I learned to speak English."

"Where's London, *English?*" whispered Ayuel.

"No idea." Gutthier shook his head and grinned.

"It's where BBC comes from on the radio," said an older boy behind his hand.

"Our first lesson is about English letters," said the teacher. "Repeat after me: A, B, C."

★

In the beginning, all the lessons consisted of repeating after the teacher. Ayuel found it hard to learn in such a large class. Sometimes he would miss important parts of Joseph's explanations. When he came back to his compound, the boys all talked about the lesson, but there were always disagreements over what the teacher had said. The Nuers and Dinkas argued. Some began to lose interest in learning.

According to the new U.N. rules, jobs rotated within the village families. Back in their homes, these boys hadn't been expected to do women's work, so they were learning these skills for the first time. Some pounded grain into flour, using a hollowed-out log and a club to crush the grain. Others kept the compound clean and ready for inspection by the caretakers.

The four boys assigned each day to do the cooking couldn't attend class, because their extra duties took the entire day. They had to walk a mile to the river, carry back two buckets of water each, gather firewood and boil the grain or beans. After building the fire, they would take turns stirring the contents of the big black three-legged pots almost continuously so the food wouldn't burn.

Sometimes, if wheat had been issued and pounded into flour, they made a sort of flat bread that could be cooked on a metal slab over the fire. The caretakers, who were both men and women from the family camp, came around to check to see if the food was correctly prepared. When the others returned from school, the cooks rang a bell and dipped the food into wide shallow bowls. The forty-seven boys in Village One were divided into sub-villages that ate in shifts beginning at five o'clock in the evening. Those who were sick or malnourished could eat earlier. Everyone in a shift had to be present and accounted for before someone said a Christian prayer and they all could begin eating. Each boy carried his own wooden spoon in his pocket, but everyone shared a common bowl.

Ayuel didn't mind being on cooking duty, but when those who'd been in class tried to explain the new lessons, he became more confused than ever. He never seemed to know what the right way was to do something or who had the correct information. As he sat alone one evening, Gabriel, one of his cousins and age-mates from Duk, came out and sat down next to him in the shade of their sleeping quarters. Neither had listed the other as a known relative in the camp, for indeed they hadn't known at the time they'd been asked. Discovering each other in the same village brought happiness to both.

"Can you say all the ABCs?" Gabriel asked.

"Sure," Ayuel said with pride. This was one thing that came easily for him and didn't require much understanding. He reeled off all the letters, only pausing once at "Q". "Now, you say them."

"I always get stuck on K," Gabriel said sheepishly. "I know it ends with W, X, Y, Z, but I don't know what's between."

"I can teach you," Ayuel said. "We'll have helpers tomorrow, and if we can say it all, they will teach us how to write the letters in the dust."

*

Every day, the boys listened to their teacher, Joseph, as he read from a book. Sometimes he held up large cards with words for the students to say aloud in unison. Then they copied the words in the dust, writing with a stick or a finger. At first, Ayuel thought of going to school and writing in the dirt as a game. It took his mind off the sorrow he carried always in his heart.

But when Joseph started beating children about the head and

shoulders with a long stick if they couldn't make the letters right, he became discouraged. *When Deng came home from Bor, I loved hearing about what he'd learned in the boarding school.* Except on days when the helpers came, this school made little sense. *Why should I learn this hard language that nobody talks?*

Twice he and his friends chose to go to a different school, but that made learning even more confusing as the teachers all taught different words. So they returned to Joseph. The teachers never checked to see who went where. They all carried disciplining sticks. None had been trained as teachers. They were mostly Sudanese refugees themselves who had a few years of schooling.

For weeks, he said "Good morning, Teacher" along with the others with no idea of its meaning, only that the words were English. He asked around but no one else seemed to know either. One day as the class broke up, the boys sang out the usual, "Goodbye, Teacher. We are going home." A boy beside Ayuel turned and waved at the teacher and sang out the same words in Dinka.

"Is that what it means?" Ayuel asked.

"Yeah. And in the morning this is what we say." He yelled the words in Dinka toward the teacher. "That will make him mad." They both ran, fearing Joseph would come after them with the long stick.

"How do you know all this?" Ayuel asked when they slowed down.

"I have—I used to have a big brother who went to school and he told me that is what they always said."

The boys headed straight for their village. Since, as usual, their one daily meal awaited them, they didn't loiter or play games. Rarely did anyone arrive late and cause the others to wait.

As they sat in a circle finishing their bowls of beans and maize mush, Gabriel asked, "What did that sentence we learned today mean?"

"Don't know," Ayuel said. "But to me, the words in the first part sound in Dinka like: *I hit your mom's eye…*"

"*… and she became blind…*" another boy added.

"*… from sound,*" finished Ayuel.

The boys roared with laughter, jumped up and danced to the rhythm of the words. They sang the new sentence over and over, substituting the Dinka words for the English that sounded similar. This became a means of learning many of the sentences and eventually they would find out the true English meaning for most of them.

NINE

FINDING A BROTHER, MAKING A NEW FRIEND

One day after several weeks of school, Ayuel and Gabriel stopped to watch with fascination as a crew of U.N. workers stirred water and dirt in a large tub until it formed the right consistency for clay. Scooping the mixture onto the ground, they molded it with wooden paddles into several rows, each higher than the one before, like stair steps. When they began to mix up another batch, Gabriel asked, "What could they possibly be making?"

"Don't know," Ayuel said, "but we can't be late for the meal. We'll come back later."

When the boys arrived with spoons in hand, everyone was already talking about the strange objects being built across the campground. No one seemed to know what was going on until, after the prayer, an older boy said, "Listen, everyone, I asked one of the U.N. workers about it. Want to know?"

"Tell us! Tell us!"

"Well... they are making school buildings for us."

The boys sat in stunned silence. Ayuel had no understanding of what a school building was supposed to look like, but these things certainly appeared strange to him. After a few moments, the boys threw in their ideas.

"Maybe the teachers are going to sit on top of these mounds."

"Or they're for a new game. Maybe we run up them and jump off."

In class the next day, Joseph explained that the new classes would have only sixty students each instead of 800. "You will sit on these rows of dried mud. Each row is a little higher than the one before so everyone can see the teacher. You will go to the school you are assigned and always sit in the same place. That way the teacher will know your names and who is there. The children from the family section will come over for the classes."

"*Girls* too?" whispered Gabriel.

"I guess," Ayuel said, trying to imagine what that would be like. *Very nice,* he thought.

As the days passed, the boys watched walls go up around the seating and thatched roofs added on top. One day as they stopped to check the progress, Gabriel turned to Ayuel and remarked, "I was helping lift heavy beams like that when we were building the large houses we now live in. Because I'm tall, I stood on a pile of logs to put the roof up."

"Like those men are doing? I helped mix the straw and mud and set the wall poles in place. Kinda fun, really."

"Well, it was until I slipped and fell. I guess I passed out. I've had trouble breathing ever since."

"Did you go to the clinic?" Ayuel frowned. He thought Gabriel's injury sounded serious.

"Yeah. They said I didn't have to work for a week. They gave me some pills, but I never feel like I used to playing soccer."

*

One day weeks later, excitement buzzed throughout the camp. This was the first day of class in their new schools. Ayuel and Gabriel, as well as most of Village One, were assigned First Class in the same school. A few had been promoted to Second Class and received half a broken pencil and half a notebook to write in. First Class students would still write with a stick on the ground. They chatted in high voices and giggled with glee as they skipped or ran to get in line, all in clean clothes and with freshly washed faces.

Ayuel wore a sun-dried pair of khaki shorts and a pale yellow, buttoned shirt. His eagerness didn't take his mind completely off the emptiness in his stomach. He thought about how he used to drink all the milk he wanted in the morning before going to tend the cows.

From all over the camp, the 16,000 boys walked in columns toward their assigned schools. Shorter lines emerged from behind the pole fence — including girls in multi-colored skirts. When Ayuel and his friends arrived at the entrance of their assigned school, they stopped in solemn silence. A bit of dread mixed with their enthusiasm. Would this teacher be meaner than Joseph? *I can't hide behind others as easy in a class of sixty. What if...?*

"Welcome, students," said the teacher, appearing in the doorway.

Ayuel recognized the handsome young man he had seen in the Group Six store just yesterday, reading the words aloud on the supplies. "They're sending us food with expired dates on them," the man had said to his companion. "Not that it does any good to know that." He'd laughed in a fun sort of way and shrugged his shoulders. Ayuel had wondered what *expired* meant.

As the boys filed in, they each said in English, "Good morning, Teacher."

"Choose your places," the man said. "You will always sit in that place unless I decide to move you." The higher seats in the back had already filled up, so Ayuel took a place next to the center aisle on the third row.

Ayuel looked around in awe. He breathed in the new smell of dried grass between the poles that formed the sides, leaving a wide space at the top of the wall for light and air. The four poles down the center, stripped bare of bark, smelled of green wood. They held up the thatched roof, keeping out the sun. *But not a single girl in the class.*

When each had found a place on the hardened mud seats, the teacher said, "My name is Kiir Ayuel. I come from Gokrial in Bar el Gazal. When I call your name, please raise your hand and say your full name, beginning in English with, 'My name is'." He held a notebook and wrote something in it after each boy introduced himself. When it became Ayuel's turn, and he announced his name, Mr. Kiir stopped and asked, "And where are you from, *Ayuel* Leek?"

Ayuel had already noticed that they both bore the same name, but he felt uncomfortable being singled out on the first day. He knew a Dinka child takes the first name of his father as his last name. His father Chief Leek Deng had given both names—in inverse order—to his oldest brother, Deng Leek.

"I'm Dinka from Duk, near Bor, sir."

"O-oh," said Mr. Kiir, raising his eyebrows. "I too am Dinka. We might both come from the same historical background, called Ayuel-dit. Do you know your family's generations?"

"Most of them, Mr. Kiir, but I don't know about the Ayuel-dit."

"We'll talk about that sometime," the teacher said and moved on to the next student.

The teacher's notice of him now gave Ayuel a warm feeling.

Mr. Kiir then turned to a large board attached to the front wall. "This is a chalkboard." He took a short white stick and wrote the letters CHALK-BOARD. He held up the white stick and said "chalk." Thus began the first lesson in the new school.

★

A few weeks later, after the meal, with his stomach comfortably full, Ayuel made a routine trek to the river to wash his clothes. The water's edge churned with boys squealing and splashing each other. He watched a few minutes and noticed how flesh had gradually grown back over the children's bones, plumping out the sagging skin—especially around their eyes. They moved with more energy. He felt it in himself.

After taking off his clothes, he squatted beside the river and thought about how much he enjoyed wearing clean clothes again and sleeping on a bed that he had built himself with grapevines to hold the mattress. But images of his family kept creeping in. As he dipped his clothes in the water and rubbed them with a bar of soap, his thoughts wandered from one loss to another. *What happened to my brother Deng at his school in Bor? And Aleer at the cattle camp? My parents and sisters?* He'd searched, without luck, for his uncle and cousin in Panyido. *Did they not make it?* In fact, he'd seen no SPLA soldiers here, not even Officer Chol. He tried to shake from his mind the anguish he felt for his close friend Malual and his cousin Chuei.

With a final rinse to his two shirts and one pair of shorts, he wrung them out and spread them over a thorn bush in the sun as he remembered his mother doing. Back home, this would not be a task for an eight-year-old boy. Nor would he pound the grain or do the cooking. *At home, there was always enough food for two meals a day, fruits and vegetables. I played with my friends and wasn't afraid.* After wiping his eyes with the heel of his hand, he jumped into the water. When he came up, Gutthier was walking briskly toward him. His half-brother's broad smile lightened his heart.

"Ayuelo!" he called, out of breath. "Ayuelo, I have good news."

Ayuel got out and pulled on his wet shorts. His bare chest tightened. He'd come to think of *news* as bad, even in spite of the word *good* next to it. "Hey, 'Funny Ears,' I haven't seen you in a while. How's your new school?" he said in a nervous effort to quiet his anxiety.

"Who cares about school? You won't believe what I have to tell you."

"So tell me."

"Your brother Aleer is right here in Camp Panyido!"

Ayuel opened his mouth but words choked in his throat. Tears rolled down his cheeks.

"Come on," urged Gutthier. "Aleer is waiting for you in Group Eight, Village Two. He had to finish a task or he'd have come with me."

Ayuel snatched up his shirts so no one would steal them. The clothes would dry by the time they walked the mile back to camp. "Are you—are you sure you saw Aleer?" he asked sniffling.

"Saw him? We talked," Gutthier said. They were running now. "He said that he and some other boys from the cattle camp joined up with a wave of walkers…"

"You're sure it was Aleer, my brother?"

"Like you, he's my half-brother. Of course, I'm sure."

They slowed to a fast walk, neither one strong enough yet to run the entire distance back to camp.

When they neared Group Eight, Village Two, Ayuel saw Aleer standing by the pole fence. He'd grown a littler taller in the year they'd been apart. Thinner, too. He dropped his laundry and the brothers raced toward each other, arms outstretched. After hugging, Aleer punched his younger brother's shoulder like old times. Both remained speechless for several seconds.

"Ayuelo, I can't believe it's really you."

"Why?"

"That was a very hard walk for a small child." With his hands on Ayuel's bare shoulders he looked deeply into his brother's eyes. "How did you manage such a long journey?"

A smile spread across Ayuel's face. He remembered how the two had always competed at everything. "Because, I too am a man."

*

Ayuel and Aleer saw each other every day now. They often met after the meal to talk about memories of family and community life back in Duk. They recalled how they'd loved to catch fish in the river near their compound, and their mother would cook them. So good!

"We had festivals at least once a month, with singing and traditional dancing," recalled Aleer.

"And the wrestling matches. Remember how Deng always used to win against his age-mates?" Ayuel said.

Aleer also recalled that their parents would beat them with a stick that they kept in a hidden place, for the least thing they did wrong. "Our parents were overly strict, I think."

"Just like some of the teachers here," Ayuel said. "I guess I've only thought about the good times because we've had so much bad."

One evening, Aleer came to Ayuel's lodging and brought a T-shirt he'd outgrown. "Here, see if this fits you," he said as he pitched it to him. They both sat on Ayuel's neatly made bed. The rains had begun and a half dozen boys were talking or practicing math problems on the hard dirt floor.

Ayuel caught the shirt and pulled it on, then sniffed the front of it. He laughed. "You didn't even wash it. Remember Deng brought me a T-shirt from Bor with Maradona on it?"

"Yeah. That visit was the last time I saw Deng. He brought me a tablet of paper and a whole pencil. Because I'd been to the Arabic school in Duk, I wrote my name for him. I think he was proud of me. If I can remember, it was like this." Aleer picked up one of Ayuel's writing sticks and carved out his name in Arabic on the damp floor.

"That doesn't look at all like English, and you wrote it backward. Mr. Kiir says we are going to learn real Arabic sometime. He said what we call

Arabic Juba is just a jumble of words from several languages so we can talk to the Nuers and everybody."

"You like Mr. Kiir, don't you?"

"I guess. He's like a friend. We may even be related to him because his last name is Ayuel, but he can't figure out how. The other day he was showing us what the world was like. He held up a soccer ball that he'd drawn countries on. Africa is on the front and the United States is on the back. I asked him after class where Argentina was. That's where Maradona, that soccer player, is from."

"I know. It's in South America, I think."

"Yeah, he showed me on the ball. Right below the United States." Ayuel sat quietly looking out at the rain. "I miss Deng."

"Father was so proud of Deng for going to school. He wanted him to get a good education so he could follow him in his position as commissioner and judge."

"You think we are getting a good education here?"

"I don't know, Ayuelo. Deng had books he could read and tablets to write on."

"Do you think Father would be proud of us for going to school?"

"No doubt about that."

★

Ten-year-old Aleer kept a close check on his younger brother's welfare. He brought a piece of metal he'd sharpened into a razor to keep Ayuel's hair close-cropped and made sure he always brushed his teeth after the meal. He showed Ayuel how to make brushes by splitting the end of a green twig into fine bristles as their mother used to do.

One afternoon, Ayuel was playing the drawing game with some boys from his village. Each would draw an animal with a stick in the dust and then call on an outside judge to rate the quality of each picture—excellent, good, fair, bad. Then finally, the judge would look again at those he'd labeled "excellent" and choose a winner. The boys had just learned the English names for giraffe, elephant, hyena, zebra and even hippopotamus. Ayuel was working on the spots of his giraffe when Aleer and another boy walked up. He heard his brother's voice behind him say, "Beny, do you know Ayuel? He's my brother."

Ayuel jumped up and turned to face the two. "His name is Beny Ngor Chol," said Aleer. "And his Christian name is Abraham. He got it last Sunday when they baptized about a hundred people in the Episcopal church."

"Yeah, I was there. Are you the Abraham they called for several times to come up?"

"Well, they just told me my new name before the ceremony and I didn't realize they were calling *me*." Beny laughed and extended his hand.

"My Christian name's James. Got it when I was a baby, but no one here calls me that, so I wouldn't know either," said Ayuel. Somehow, he felt an instant tie to this boy who looked him in the eye and could laugh at himself.

"Beny walked even farther than we did—all the way from Unity on the border between North and South," Aleer said.

"I've heard of that place. How long did it take you?"

"Three or four months," Beny said. "I don't know exactly."

Ayuel glanced back and saw the judge put an "E" for excellent under his giraffe. He loved to win, whatever the competition. Sometimes, he did win at this game. But at the moment, he was more interested in his brother's new friend. "So did you just get here in Panyido?" He was surprised that Beny looked so good for that many months of walking.

"No, no. Some SPLA officers brought two hundred of us over here a couple of weeks ago from the other camp in Itang. That just took two nights of walking." Ayuel could see sadness in Beny's eyes. "I was there nearly a year, but there's no school. And too many people. Lots of handicapped—amputees from the war. You know, in the war they hack off people's legs, arms or just a hand or foot."

Ayuel cringed. He was glad he and his friends hadn't gone to Itang. "So, it's better here?"

"Yeah. Aleer's been showing me around and explaining how things work."

"We're age-mates and in the same village," said Aleer. "His bed is even next to mine. We…"

Clapping and cheering went up from the boys in the drawing contest. Two pictures had tied as winners: an elephant and a running zebra. "Guess I lost out," Ayuel said, contributing his applause.

"Better luck next time," said Aleer, hiding a teasing smirk behind his hand. "Well, we'll see you later."

"Sure," Ayuel said, embarrassed that he hadn't won—especially in front of his brother and his new friend Beny.

★

"Are you two going to play in the big soccer tournament?" asked Ayuel as he sat with Aleer and Beny under a tree by the soccer field. They had just finished a scrimmage game and the other boys had gone to the river for a swim.

"Sure. We were both chosen—out of 989—to play for Group Eight," Beny said. "We're the only ones from the Village Two team to get on. But a very good friend of mine, Samuel Kiir, who came here with me from Itang—I want you to meet him—was chosen from Village Four in our group. We're not the team's best players, though. They've mixed up the different ages. You playing for Group Six?"

"Yeah, but I'm not so good."

"Oh, they let eight-year-olds play?" said Aleer, bumping against his shoulder in mock ridicule. Then, being more generous, he added, "You were always better than your friends back in Duk—well, except for Madau and Gabriel. And you made a point today, Little Brother. Bet you're just saying that to make us think you'll be easy to beat."

"I'm just glad to play," Ayuel said. "Madau will be first-string goalie for Group Ten. The Tournament players all get T-shirts for their team, all the same color."

"I know. That's like professional teams," Beny said. "We'll get the special shoes and socks tomorrow. I've never worn socks."

"That's why we get them early so we can get used to them. But we can't wear the shirts before the games. Who's sending them? Do you know?" asked Aleer.

"Some big company in England, I think."

"But not the one that gave us the net and balls."

"Guess someone in the world knows about us," Beny said. He wistfully added, "Wish we could have cows to give us milk to drink."

"Soccer and even milk can't make up for the bad things." Ayuel tossed the newly issued soccer ball in the air and caught it. "But it's more fun playing with a real ball." He lay down in the cool grass with his head resting on the ball. He looked up at the deep blue sky showing through the tree branches and turned to the subject always on his mind. "Beny, was your home village bombed? You've never said."

TEN

VIVID MEMORIES

Beny sat with his arms clasped about his knees and stared out over the soccer field. "No, Panrieng wasn't bombed."

"What happened that you left?" said Aleer as he stretched out on his stomach, head in hands.

"There was an attack. But before I tell you about that—well, I'll never forget my last conversation with my mother," Beny said, his eyes sparkling with amusement. "That day I couldn't decide whether to go with Uncle Acuil Chol who had invited me to go into our town of Panrieng. He'd said if I went with him, he would buy me a shirt.

"But my father had asked me to go with him to see my older brother Lueth at the cattle camp. I wanted to see my brother and all the thousands of cattle. Maybe drink lots of milk. I was only nine and wanted to do both. I asked my mother what I should do.

"She answered by telling me the story of Cholmong, the well-known big eater among the Dinkas. Both his grown daughter and his son, who lived in opposite directions, had invited him for a special celebration. He knew his daughter was a wonderful cook, and she would prepare special foods and drinks. He also knew his son would slaughter several bulls and there would be lots of meat to eat. 'Like you, he couldn't decide,' my mama said. She told me how Cholmong started out down a single path that would lead to either house, but then the road split. He started down the way to his daughter's, then came back and went toward his son's place. He kept repeating this all day. At last he sat down at the fork in the road. By that time all the other guests were coming home. They stopped to tell him about all the wonderful food and how sorry they were he couldn't be there.

"'So don't be like Cholmong,' she told me. 'Make a decision or you may miss doing both the things you want.'"

Ayuel and Aleer laughed with him at the story. "So what did you decide?" Ayuel asked.

Becoming serious, Beny said, "I chose to go with my father. After we got there that night, I was asleep in a *geu*—one of those small, circular shelters they have in cattle camps."

"I know what they are," said Aleer. "I was in a cattle camp too."

Beny closed his eyes and buried his face in his hands. When he looked up, he seemed to leave his friends behind as he recalled vivid memories. "We had gone to visit my older brother Lueth. He was twenty-nine. We brought him food and things from home. He was sleeping in another *geu*. I don't know what happened to him. My cousin, Ngor, was with my father and me in the shelter.

"I awoke to horrible sounds of people yelling and screaming. Cattle were bellowing in awful ways like I'd never heard before. Lots of guns were shooting. We all ran outside. So much confusion, I can't remember everything. It was dark except I could see the fire from guns. Bullets whizzed right past me. I saw men on horseback, shooting the cows and the people. We ran from the trucks and the people firing guns. I ran as fast as I could and got lost from my father and my cousin."

Ayuel whispered to himself, "I lost my mother and sisters when a grenade exploded between us."

"Fire was all around. The *geth* were blazing up. Smoke got in my eyes and nose, but I kept running. Someone grabbed at my hand. I pulled away until I saw it was Ngor. Then we ran together. We headed for the road that led back to our village near Panrieng, in Unity State. There were thousands and thousands of people and cattle in the camp. I don't know why they did this to us.

"We ran up the road toward our village, back to where our families lived. I was just nine years old and I remember thinking how upset my mama would be when I came running back without my father. We had gone only a little way when we met Dinka people rushing toward us. 'You can't pass,' someone yelled at us. 'They're blocking the road with trucks and shooting everyone. The villages are all burned.' Then I saw the trucks with soldiers shooting at the people. It was still dark except for the fires. They shot the man who had warned us.

"The dry season had just begun, but flood waters from rainy times still stood on the low side of the road. Ngor and I waded through the waters and hid in the jungle on the other side for a few days. Thousands of people hid there. Trucks couldn't get in through all the tangled trees and vines, so we were safe. We drank water from puddles and found some fruit, but we were hungry and wanted to go home. Most of the people passed on through the jungle, but Ngor and I were afraid of getting lost. We wanted to stay near the road to Panrieng."

"Any wild animals in the jungle?" Ayuel asked, thinking about the children who had been eaten by lions and hyenas on his journey.

"With that many people, I guess we scared the animals off," Beny said. "Except the snakes. We were standing in mud under a tree when I looked up and saw a cobra twisting around a branch above my head. Cousin Ngor whispered to me to not stare up because the cobra saliva could drip in my eye and make me blind. Of course, it could jump down and kill us, too, but he said to just look out for the enemy. So I did and forgot all about death hanging above me.

"I remember most that terrible, awful day—the day we crept out of the jungle, back into the water to get to the road. Just as we were coming out of the shallow water next to the road, we saw people marching toward us in front of trucks and men on horseback, shooting guns. It was early morning, and as they got closer, we could see mostly women in front and a few children. If a woman stepped off the road, they shot her.

"About fifteen of us got back in the water—it came up to my waist. An old woman stood beside me. She said, 'You children, stay hidden behind those bushes sticking up out of the water. Don't move and don't make a sound. I am old and my life is near the end. You are young and might live through this, but I don't want to die in this water.' She walked out right onto the road just as the bad men got there. They shot her and her body fell back into the water and floated. A wounded man had been sitting in the water a long time, trying to keep his head up, but as the day went on and the sun beat down on us, he swelled up and finally died. We couldn't help him.

"Ngor and I stood in the bloodied water, holding hands, from early morning until late afternoon. Mosquitoes covered our bodies from the waist up. They stung our eyes and got in our mouths and noses. Leeches grabbed onto us under the water. We couldn't pull off the leeches or swat the mosquitoes. We dared not move. Another boy stood near by. We kept glancing at each other, but we couldn't say anything. I knew he was suffering like me. We talked with our eyes.

"We had to stay perfectly still or the bad people would see and shoot us. Some children died from the mosquito bites. It smelled awful. We didn't move all day and the men never saw Ngor and me. In the daylight, I noticed the men were black like us, but they seemed to be speaking Arabic and shouting something about Allah. I thought only Arabs were Muslims.

"We watched all kinds of torture and killings just a few feet away on the road or on the raised ground on the other side. One band of people would go by. There would be a short break, but never long enough to get back to the jungle. Then more would come, marching captured women in front. The men had axes. We watched as they chopped people up—men, women and children. And left their bodies on the ground or threw them in the water in front of us.

"I saw my neighbor lady who lived right next to my family. I wanted to call out to her, but, of course, I couldn't. She carried her small child in her arms. I saw her stumble and almost fall with the child. Then a man grabbed the little girl out of her arms. The mother wailed and tried to snatch her back, but the man took the child by her legs and swung her against her mother. The child screamed once or twice, but the man kept beating her against the mother again and again while two other men held the woman's arms behind her. He beat the child against her mother—until she died. Then the men laughed."

Ayuel and Aleer sat stunned at the horror they'd just heard. Both had also witnessed horrible things, but right now they shared the anguish of their friend.

"We'll get even with those cruel men someday," Ayuel said through clenched teeth.

"When we are older, we'll take revenge on all these people who have hurt us for no reason," said Aleer, his face turning red with anger. All three boys got up and headed back toward their villages. Ayuel carried the soccer ball to return to his school.

"Our men tried to fight these people with spears and only shields to protect them. But it did no good against guns. We don't know who these evil people are or why they wanted to kill us. God will punish them and I am ready to help," Beny said. "I want to do to them what they did to us." His voice became tense with bitterness.

"So do you know if all your family was killed? Have you heard about them?" asked Aleer.

"Nothing. Not a word," Beny said, "After the sun set that day we thought we would be safe back in the jungle, but they ambushed us and we ran through tall grass and water for hours. We hid again behind bushes. I recognized the boy hidden beside me as the one I had seen standing in the awful water all day. Now that we could talk, he told us his name was Samuel Kiir. He had seen his uncle killed right before his eyes. His mother died the day before the attack from an illness. In his grief, his father couldn't run very fast and was shot. We became close friends because we shared the tragedy.

"Samuel and my cousin Ngor walked all the way across Sudan with me—for months through swamps and deserts. Lots of very bad things happened. A little while after we got to Itang, Ngor died—of diarrhea."

★

For the boys at the camp, anger began to eat away the sadness. When their only goal had been to stay alive by not giving up, they thought little about the reasons for the horror they'd endured. Now provided with schools, shelter and rations of food at the camp, the desire for revenge and the feeling of helplessness to do anything about it brought intense frustration. Soccer became a good outlet. Kicking the ball felt good—like kicking the enemy.

On the evening of the final game of the Panyido Tournament, thousands of spectators gathered to stand around the edges of the field and watch the two best teams compete in the finals for the coveted golden cup trophy—the *kasi*. Group Eight, with Beny, Aleer and Samuel Kiir, in their new green jerseys faced Group Ten, decked out in yellow. Madau, the most athletic of the friends, opposed them as the goalie. Each team could count on about a thousand from their group to cheer them on. The boys in the other ten groups picked their loyalties according to the players they knew on the teams. That made it hard for Ayuel—whose Group Six had lost earlier—to choose between supporting either Madau or his brother. Aleer, as well as Beny on that team, won out.

In the last minutes of the game, Group Ten led one to nil. Ayuel ran along the touchlines, following the players. "Go Group Eight! Pick your spot, Aleer," he shouted. His brother dribbled the ball with his foot, keeping it close.

"Stop him! Stop him!" the other team's supporters chanted.

Aleer made a quick turn, threw the defenders off guard and kicked the ball up the wing to Samuel who bounced it off his head to Beny. Beny kicked a low hard shot that whipped past Madau into the back of the net, tying up the score one to one. The crowds went wild.

Gutthier, Gabriel and Ayuel danced in a circle, cheering in hoarse voices.

"They're going to win!"

"Just a few more minutes!"

"You can do it. Group Eight's the best!"

Quiet settled over the crowd while the players lined up for the kickoff. With the ball back in play, the crowds resumed their chants as the teams raced back and forth with renewed energy.

Suddenly, a player in green failed to intercept and the ball flew across the field to a Group Ten player who headed it past the goalie and into the upper-right corner of the net. The referee's shrill whistle ended the game. Shouts and groans went up from the crowd. Group Eight had lost.

Some boys with buckets of water rushed out on the field to offer drinks and shower their friends. The crowd broke out in singing and dancing.

"Sorry to let you guys down," said Aleer when he found his brother and friends. He dripped with sweat and the shower of water. His broad grin denied defeat.

"No, you and Beny and Samuel were great," Ayuel, who still wore his blue Group Six uniform, said. "We lost our second game of the tournament."

"Wasn't your fault," Beny said. He accepted a bucket of water from a stranger and drank deeply before the boy poured it over his head. "Oh, the water feels so-o good." He gulped and turned back to Ayuel. "You made some great defensive moves in your game and intercepted the ball from an older opponent."

"Yeah."

"How did it feel to kick in that goal?" asked Gutthier, slapping Beny on the back.

Beny's face lit up and he clinched both fists, "Like I was kicking the face of one of those cruel guys with axes."

Samuel walked up, dripping with water. He and Beny slapped hands. Ayuel had met Beny's friend before the Tournament. "Good job, Samuel," he said.

"Attention, everyone." The voice of Maker Thiang, the schoolmaster, came over the microphone. "Will the two teams, Group Ten and Group Eight, please come to this end of the field." Some older boys beat drums as the players lined up in front of the goal. The sun had gone down and light began to fade. Two of the caretakers lit torches on the ends of poles and stuck them in the ground behind the teams.

"Congratulations to Group Ten, the first place winners of the 1989 Panyido Soccer Tournament," said Maker over the microphone. "You did a great job. I declare you the camp's best team. It is my distinct pleasure and honor to award you this golden *kasi*."

Madau, the goalkeeper, stepped forward and took the cup. Fire from the torches reflected on the trophy, enhancing its importance. The crowd applauded. Ayuel shouted, "Great job, Madau!" Certainly he was proud of his athletic friend, even though he had cheered for the other team.

Group Eight, who had stood back, now came forward and shook the hands of all the winners, murmuring congratulatory words.

"And now—to our second place winners who played a good game also..." The schoolmaster brought out another *kasi,* not quite as large but one that also glistened in the firelight. "Congratulations." More applause.

Ayuel fought his way through the masses of boys to get a close look at the cup. "It's beautiful," he whispered when he got near enough to the *kasi* being passed around among the Group Eight team.

"You hold it," Beny said.

"'Second-place award.'" Ayuel held the cup by both handles and slowly read the English words printed on the base. He ran his hand gently over the smooth surface. "'Panyido Soccer Tour-na-ment, 1989.' Wow!"

A sense of power seemed to surge through the crowd. Competition had been fierce, but the energy didn't come from winning. Everyone had been part of the Tournament, whether on a team or not. Celebration, with all the teams mixing together, continued well into the night with singing, dancing and impromptu soccer games. Homemade torches appeared and led lines of twisting dancers around the field. Ayuel, Beny and their friends missed none of it.

Finally, as they headed back to their compounds by moonlight, laughing and hoarse from shouting, Ayuel said, "Somehow I think we gave a blow to the enemy tonight. And by enemy I don't mean the other team."

"A small kick, at least," Beny said.

*

Near the end of the first year of schooling Ayuel and the others were making progress in their learning. Competition took on many forms.

"You don't spell *geography* with an 'f,'" Ayuel said as some boys sat in a circle on the ground, playing the spelling game.

"Sounds like it does," said Gabriel, who had just taken his turn and written the letter in the dust. "Go check the dictionary—someone."

"I'll get it," offered Ayuel and ran off to the nearby school building to borrow the book. Beny had begun the round by starting a word with "g." The next person and the ones following each wrote a letter. If the letter didn't fit the emerging word, the player lost one of his ten points. After the word had been completed, the next person had to pronounce it and give the meaning.

"Here it is. Mr. Kiir said to keep it until we finished the game." Ayuel sat down with the dictionary between himself and Beny. Together they leafed through it until they found the right page. "Here it is: g-e-o-g-r-a-p... You lose a point."

The following two players gleefully finished the last two letters. Aleer, next in the circle, pronounced the word correctly. He then glanced around the circle, deliberately pausing, and said with confidence, "About countries, oceans, hills and things like that."

"No," Ayuel said, slowly reading from the dictionary. "It's 'a sci-ence that deals with the phy-si-cal fea-tures of the earth.'"

"Same thing," said Aleer.

The boys voted to give Aleer the point. However, Ayuel remained proud of reading the whole English sentence, even if he didn't know what "physical features" meant.

★

Now that girls were mingled in the camps the boys all became curious. In Dinka culture, it was forbidden to speak to a girl who wasn't your relative until you had been introduced. That was usually arranged by the two families or simply by a child relative. A boy might tentatively approach a girl, smile at her from time to time and finally, if she seemed friendly, muster the courage to say "hi."

Yet here in the camp, there was never a moment of privacy, and one never knew if a brother or cousin might be around to defend the girl's honor. Ayuel and Gutthier enjoyed the prestige of speaking to Akon, who had been in their group of seventeen. At eleven, three years older than Ayuel, she had become quite attractive to boys. Gutthier's mother and Akon's mother were sisters—Ayuel was her cousin, also.

One day as Ayuel and Gutthier were on their way to the river, they saw Akon returning with a bucket of water on her head. A group of four or five boys followed behind her, talking.

"Hi, Akon, how are you today?" Gutthier said loudly to impress the pursuing boys.

"Hello, Akon," Ayuel said. "How are your classes going?" He put out his hand.

Akon, while still holding to the bucket on her head with one hand, extended the other to her cousins. She smiled and said loudly, "I am very fine, thank you, and my classes are going well." Then she lowered her voice and added, "But the boys back there are bothering me. I don't like what they are saying."

Only too happy to help, Gutthier said in a mock-angry voice as he doubled up his fist, "Why are you talking to our sister?"

"Don't you know we are her brothers and we'll defend her?" Ayuel added.

The boys shrugged their shoulders and one said, "So what? We don't care. This girl was acting rude to us."

"Well," Gutthier said, "If we ever see you boys bothering her again, you will face a problem."

The gang turned away without a fight, giggling as they went.

"Thank you," Akon said sweetly to her cousins.

As the boys continued to the river, Gutthier said, "There's this girl I really like—I don't know her name—and I want to say 'hi' to her, but she's never alone. I've watched her play volleyball on the soccer field, but she doesn't even know I'm around. Will you help me out, Ayuelo?"

*

Ayuel was more than happy to help his half-brother. This would give him a chance to speak to a girl, too. Gutthier was the bolder of the two. He was handsome, popular and known for his charming ways—and his ears were no longer so prominent. As soon as classes were dismissed, they planned to run to her school and then walk near her.

After they had done this several times without speaking, Gutthier decided the day had finally come to actually say "hi."

Mr. Kiir had finished the lessons but all the classes had to wait until the bell was rung before leaving. Ayuel looked across the room to Gutthier who raised his eyebrows and grinned. Ayuel nodded. At the sound of the bell, they took off running toward the school of the admired girl.

As planned, they followed her from class, then moved in front of her and pretended to speak classic Arabic, which neither of them knew. They gestured as they spoke, glancing back to see if she was watching. She lowered her eyes and seemed to ignore them.

"Hi," Gutthier said. No response. "Hey, girl, we are talking to you. Are you deaf?" Ayuel frowned, feeling perhaps Gutthier's approach was not the best.

The girl began to walk faster, looking straight ahead.

Gutthier and Ayuel trailed behind her until she slipped through the pole gate to the family quarters. They peeked between the poles of the fence and watched until she disappeared behind a grouping of *tukuls*.

"I think you lost out," Ayuel said with a smirk.

"Not at all. Just wait until tomorrow."

When tomorrow came, Ayuel feigned fatigue and said he would wait at his *tukul* to hear how things turned out.

Some time later, Gutthier appeared in the doorway while Ayuel was doing his homework. Grass clung to his rumpled hair, scratches and dirt covered one side of his face and a torn pocket dangled from his shirt.

"Did your girlfriend do all that?" Ayuel asked, laughing.

"Very funny. She has two big brothers to protect her," Gutthier grumbled. "I'm through with girls!"

ELEVEN

"SEEDS OF THE NEW SUDAN"

Ayuel carried two heavy buckets of water from the Panyido River as he approached his compound in late afternoon. It had been an ordinary day, like any other when he was on cooking duty. He'd been glad to miss sitting in a classroom all day. Mr. Kiir's *tukul* was next to his in the compound, and, since they had become friends, he knew his teacher would give him a private lesson if he asked. However, the excitement he heard when he arrived was anything but ordinary. Something big had happened.

He set the buckets down and asked a small clump of boys that included his cousin Gabriel, "What's going on?"

"Oh, you weren't in school to hear the big announcement," said one of the boys. "There's no school tomorrow and ..."

"A very important person is coming to talk to us. What's his name?" Gabriel turned to another boy.

"Dr. John Garang."

"He's not a doctor like at the hospital though."

"He's the head of the SPLA," Ayuel said, joining in the excitement.

"Right, the head of the whole Sudanese People's Liberation Army," emphasized Gabriel. "If we win this war, our teacher said, he will be the next president of all of Sudan. And we can go home and live in peace."

Ayuel could hardly wait to talk to Aleer and Beny and hear what they knew. Since he was on the cooking committee, he would be in the last shift to eat. Another group would clean up. Others on the committee dipped out a third of the maize mush into the common bowl, then set it off the fire so Ayuel could make a sweet drink that they called "tea."

In the last delivery of food there had been a rare bag of sugar. With a small amount of water in the pot, Ayuel dumped in some sugar and stirred it until it browned. Then he added more water and brought it to a simmer. The first shift would drink it after the mush, accompanied by flatbread—also an unusual treat. Then, Ayuel would make another pot of tea for the next shift.

Just as he finished handing out the first serving, one of their caretakers arrived, a young Ethiopian woman from the family camp. Most of the caretakers were Sudanese refugees themselves, but, as she had no family, the woman was allowed to stay in the camp as a worker. Ayuel felt nervous when he looked up and saw her. Usually very strict, she would find any detail he had done wrong. His mind had been on John Garang's visit rather than his duties.

"Peace, Ayuel. Can you spare a cup of tea for a tired caretaker?" She smiled and held out the cup she had brought for this very purpose.

"Of course, Mama. Village One makes the best tea in Panyido." He filled her cup from the dipper. "I guess you've heard the news?"

"About John Garang? Of course. The Ethiopians think he is a great man, too. That's why we let his troops train here and allow the refugee camps on our soil. This will be a very important day in your life, Ayuel. Listen closely to what this man has to say."

"Yes, Mama, I will."

"Good tea," she said and, just as she turned to leave, added, "And a very clean kitchen."

★

Ayuel and Gabriel found Beny and Aleer sitting in the shade of the pole fence outside Village Two in Group Eight. "What did your teacher tell you about tomorrow?" asked Gabriel after the exchange of greetings. He and Ayuel sat down facing their friends.

"Mr. Mayen said Dr. Garang will be here in Panyido for two days," Beny said. "We don't know what he will talk to us about tomorrow. Maybe he wants us to be SPLA soldiers. But the next day he is going to visit our classes. We must study hard so we will know the answers and show Dr. Garang what we are learning."

"I'd better talk to Mr. Kiir tonight to see what I've missed," Ayuel said. "He always calls on me with the hard questions. I really don't want to be a soldier."

"He's called doctor," said Aleer, "because he studied in the United States of America, someplace called..."

"Iowa," Beny said. "And he got military training in a place called Georgia. He's a very educated man. We don't know where he is coming here from."

"Does he live here in Ethiopia?" asked Gabriel. "There are SPLA training camps here."

"We don't know."

"I remember that soldier, Officer Chol, who led us on the journey, said John Garang cared about us," Ayuel said.

"I heard that too from officers with us," said Aleer. "That is so strange that we both had so many of the same experiences. Wish we could have found each other then."

"The whole camp is to meet here tomorrow outside our school building at eight o'clock in the morning," Beny said. "I think our Group Eight was chosen because we always win the awards for cleanest compound and best personal hygiene."

"Right," said Aleer. "And our Village Two got a box of biscuits for winning last time. I'll go get one of them for you."

★

Ayuel couldn't sleep that night. He kept thinking about what the caretaker lady had said, *This will be the most important day in your life.* He could feel it, but he didn't know why. His life didn't seem very important here. Ever since Mr. Kiir had taken an interest in him, he enjoyed learning, and it wasn't so frustrating as in Joseph's class where he was always afraid of the big stick.

He really saw no purpose in school with his family all dead—except Aleer—and his village gone. How could he ever gain enough cows to live in dignity? Or cows to pay a bride's parents so he could marry? And he the son of a Dinka chief—the tribe that used to be the wealthiest. The war seemed to go on with no end in sight. They heard about the battles, more people killed, more villages burned; cease-fires, more battles, more of the same. Refugees came in all the time but not the masses like at first.

He got up early and gently shook Gabriel who slept two beds over.

"Wake up. This is the important day."

"Ummm."

"Come on. I saved some water in the bucket from last night. Let's get ready for Dr. John Garang."

Gabriel rolled out of bed. The boys pulled the blankets up over their beds and smoothed them out. They went outside and splashed water on their faces, got dressed and cut their nails with the razor Aleer had made for them from a scrap of metal. By then the other boys were getting ready, talking with enthusiastic voices instead of the usual grumbling.

"Wish we could sit with Beny and Aleer," Ayuel said. "But we have to stay with Group Six."

"That's so the caretakers can make sure we behave," Gabriel said. "Let's go."

The caretakers stood at the doorway with their long sticks. "Come along, boys, follow us," said the lady who had been so kind to Ayuel the evening before. Her stern voice was back.

Boys from Group Six walked in lines toward the Group Eight school building. Other groups, more than a thousand in each, were coming from different directions. Ayuel watched the children—especially the girls—from the family quarters file past. He stretched his neck to see the preparations being made outside the school. A small wooden platform had been erected for the speaker.

Some caretakers were setting up a canopy over it, four poles with a thatched roof, much like the one for the American congressman who had talked to them over a year ago. A single microphone topped a stick at the front of the stage. A caretaker's voice came over it. "Please sit down with your group in your assigned location. Dr. John Garang will be here shortly. No talking."

How can we not talk on the most important day of our lives? Dr. Garang did not arrive shortly. For hours, the boys sat in the sun as the temperature rose. Different volunteers came to the microphone to lead the audience in school songs that helped the time to pass. One of the most popular had been composed by a boy in camp, Kiir Chol. Ayuel had sung it many times without thinking much about the words:

> *I need to be well cared for,*
> *I need to be well educated,*
> *I am the hope of my people.*
> *I am the leader of tomorrow.*
> *Tomorrow is my time to be well educated,*
> *My time to be a good leader!*

"I don't think he's coming," Gabriel whispered behind his hand to Ayuel. A whack on the head from a caretaker ended that conversation. Another caretaker came to the microphone and said, "We have just received word that Dr. Garang is on his way. When he gets here, we will shout 'Welcome, Dr. John Garang.' Now let's hear it!"

"Welcome, Dr. John Garang." The crowd chanted the words several times then applauded.

More songs were sung. The crowd's enthusiasm began to wane. Ayuel felt hot, tired and disappointed. The caretakers patrolled up and down between the groups, swishing their sticks in front of them and occasionally striking a restless boy. He could see Beny and Aleer, sitting at the edge of Group Eight, but dared not wave at them.

Around noon five small cars crawled into the camp and parked next to the school building. Enthusiasm returned instantly as shouts of "welcome" rose spontaneously from the crowd. The first three cars were open with no tops, so it was easy to see the men inside. The occupants of these cars got out and formed a line across the front of the cars, standing at attention. They were Ethiopians and carried long guns. Apparently the most important man was not among them.

Two men in camouflage, also carrying guns, stepped from the front doors of the fourth car, an enclosed one, and opened the back doors. Two men in military uniforms came out without guns. They looked important so a few of the boys shouted "Welcome." The Camp Chairman, Mr. Pieng, quickly grabbed the microphone and said, "Not yet. Wait just a minute and I will tell you when." The crowd immediately grew silent as everyone loved and respected Mr. Pieng.

The men in military uniforms stood behind the platform while the guards went to open the other enclosed car. A man in civilian clothes stepped out, followed by three more guards. Mr. Pieng made a motion for the crowd to stand.

A large man with a short beard, dressed in a military uniform, emerged from the last car. The boys went wild, waving their hands in the air and shouting.

"Welcome, Dr. John Garang! Welcome Dr. John Garang!"

The great man bowed slightly to acknowledge their welcome. It took several minutes for the shouting to diminish, for the caretakers with their long disciplining sticks had disappeared into the crowd.

"I'm seeing Dr. John Garang with my own eyes," Ayuel said to Gabriel.

"He's very impressive, isn't he?"

The SPLA leader took his place beside the other two gentlemen behind the stage.

Mr. Pieng came to the microphone. "You may sit down now." The boys immediately obeyed and became very quiet. "We are all happy that Dr. John Garang has come…"

The boys shouted again at the man's name and waved their arms in the air.

"We are very glad, Dr. Garang, that you have come today. Welcome to all three of you. I will now introduce them to you. Mr. Salva Kiir is Dr. Garang's Chief of Staff." The man waved to the crowd who responded with shouts of welcome. "And Mr. William Nyoun, Dr. Garang's chief deputy." The Deputy waved, and received welcoming shouts also.

"And, of course, the man we all love and revere, our hero, the leader of the SPLA, Dr. John Garang de Mabior…"

The crowd jumped up, waved their arms in the air, stomped their feet and shouted over and over, "Welcome, Dr. Garang!"—until Mr. Pieng motioned them to stop.

"Our first speaker this afternoon is Mr. Salva."

A tall, slender man stepped to the microphone and said a few words in classic Arabic. The man in civilian clothes, who stood beside him, leaned the microphone toward himself and repeated the words in the Dinka language. Even the other tribes had come to understand much of the dominant speech of the camp.

"We are happy to be with you this afternoon." Ayuel found it difficult to follow the speech because the interpreter spoke Dinka with an Arabic accent. Mr. Salva seemed to be explaining the objectives of the SPLA. The main goal appeared to be protection of the villages so they would not be burned again. That was good and the boys cheered. Mr. Salva then turned the microphone over to William Nyoun, the deputy. More cheers.

Mr. William spoke in Arabic Juba, the jumble of Sudanese languages that all understood. He talked about how important it is for all Southerners to be united in their efforts to resist the dictates of the government in Khartoum. "They call us rebels, but we are not rebels. We only want to be treated fairly." Every time he mentioned the name *Garang*, the boys shouted, jumped up and down, danced and sang. Mr. William had a great deal of trouble keeping order, and the caretakers didn't want to quiet their enthusiasm. Finally, the guards stepped forward with their guns and the crowd settled down.

Then Mr. William turned to the main speaker and said, "Dr. Garang is a remarkable leader. He will someday be elected president of all of Sudan because he will unite not only the South, but the South with the North as well."

The boys jumped to their feet as the SPLA leader came to the microphone. The guards stepped forward, flanking the platform, but let the crowd express their enthusiasm. Each group shouted a phrase that a teacher had taught them. Ayuel's group shouted, "Welcome, C in C!" over and over.

After several minutes the boys sat down to listen to their commander in chief.

"The SPLA…" His voice boomed over the microphone, deep and rich. The boys clapped their hands and shouted "SPLA." The two other speakers had convinced them that the SPLA was a very good thing, and when Dr. Garang said it, it became even greater. "One thing you need to know is that we came here from Sudan…" The children again went wild at the mention of their home country. "The enemy that burned your villages, murdered your parents and brothers and sisters and killed your cattle, we have chased out." More cheers.

Dr. Garang's voice took on a more serious tone. The boys sat spellbound as a powerful message rolled off his tongue, largely in Arabic Juba, but for the most important parts in Dinka—as he himself was Dinka. "The enemy you fled, that caused you to walk for months with danger and starvation, we have defeated. Your fathers and older brothers have fought with guns against the enemy that wants to destroy us. And we have won the battles. But the war may go on for years. Many of you could go back to your villages now because we have made them safe.

"But—I do not want you to go back with empty hands. Guns alone will not win this war. Your contribution is in a different form—with education, with your minds. The way for you to win back your country is to stay in school and get a good education. Prepare yourselves. Then you can go back armed with knowledge. That way you can change Sudan for the better. We all know how precious are the seeds for new crops. They are cherished and kept in a safe place until the time is right. You are to stay here in this safe place until the fighting is over, learning every day. For you are the *terams*—the seeds—of the new Sudan!"

I need to be well educated… The words of Kiir Chol's song rang in Ayuel's head.

"Knowledge will water the seeds, education will nourish you and you will grow to be leaders of this great country someday. Khartoum is a government of *yierab*—of terror. But you will change that; you will come back with something helpful. You are the seeds!" Dr. Garang held out his hands as if to embrace the thousands of children before him.

And Ayuel believed his life *was* changed.

After the speech he and Gabriel sought out Beny and Aleer.

"I am a *teram*," Beny said, wiping a tear with the heel of his hand.

"We are all *terams* now," Gabriel said. "Until we grow into leaders."

We are the leaders of tomorrow!

Ayuel and Aleer hugged each other as tears ran down their cheeks. "We will get a good education to honor our father and our mother," said Aleer. "We are the seeds of the new Sudan."

TWELVE

A BREWING STORM

Surprised to find Beny and Samuel playing hopscotch with a group of girls, Ayuel stopped to watch. He was looking for something to do after finishing early Saturday morning chores. Making fun of his friends looked promising. A pretty, barefoot girl hopped through the squares, lifting her skirt above her ankle. She lost her balance just at the end.

Beny ran toward her. "Let me try. I know how to jump."

"You can't make it," the girl said. "Boys are too clumsy." Her three friends laughingly agreed.

Beny pitched his pebble and hopped through all the squares drawn in the dirt without a single miss. He threw out his chest and turned to Samuel. "How about that? Guess I'm not so clumsy."

Samuel shrugged his shoulders.

Ayuel watched Beny exchange a few words with the girl before shouting, "So you play girls' games now?"

Samuel waved a greeting and left in the opposite direction, but Beny came over to defend himself. "So? I like girls, especially that one with the short hair. No brothers around. Why not? Besides I think I impressed Samuel."

Ayuel laughed and punched his friend's shoulder. "So what's the pretty one's name?"

"Mary Ajok Malek. She's from Panrieng, like me, but that's all I know. She said they often play here after school. It's near her compound. Think I'll come by after church tomorrow."

★

Several days later, after classes, Ayuel caught up with Beny on their way to their separate minor zones. "Well, did you find your girlfriend playing hopscotch again?" he asked with a snicker.

"She's *not* my girlfriend—just a friend. I like to call her Mary A.," he said looking down, proving she was more than a friend. "She wasn't there on Sunday, but the next day I played the spelling game with her and her friends."

"At least that's not just a girl game."

"I won that too, but the girls are younger—about your age. They had easy words like book, school, pencil. I won easily with 'desk.'"

"Not much to brag about."

"No." Beny grinned and then turned serious. "Afterward, she told me her story."

Without a word, the two boys found the shade of a tree and sat down. In such cases, the children respected another's story, listening closely to every detail and mentally comparing it to their own.

"So what happened?"

"I was getting ready to leave," Beny said, "when I noticed she was looking for something, swishing her toes through the dry grass. I asked her if she'd lost something. She said, 'Yes, my auntie's pen. It must have fallen from my pocket.'"

"So you helped her look for it?"

"Sure, but she found it herself. The others had left, so we sat and talked. I told her my story—the same as I told you. She said, being so young, she didn't remember much about the attack, except how scared she was— and the smell of their *tukul* on fire. Her auntie, whom she lives with, has told her about what happened. When the black Arabs of Darfur came to Panrieng, they would set a *tukul* on fire then wait for the people to come out. Like it was a game, they'd shoot them when they did.

"As soon as their *tukul* was torched, the children started crying. Her father said crying wouldn't do any good. He tore out a place at the back and told her mother to run with the children through the hole. He then stepped out through the front door to distract the Arabs. Of course, they shot him, but she doesn't even remember hearing the guns."

"How horrible." Ayuel shook his head. "So did they all get away?"

"They fled with a large group, but early the next morning, the Arabs ambushed them as they left the shelter of a grove of trees. Her mother was trying to hold on to her and her two sisters and brother, but after she was shot in the arm, she couldn't keep them together. She handed Mary A. to her aunt, and then they got separated."

"Just she and her auntie made it here to Ethiopia?"

"That's right. Like all of us, she worries about what happened to her mother and the others."

"Sure. We all know what that's like."

With heavy sighs, Ayuel and Beny got up and silently went on their way, adding to their sorrow the burden of another story so like their own.

★

The tension of fear lessened during the second year in Panyido. Ayuel felt safe. Occasionally, he heard of a drowning in the river or an attack by wild animals. He'd learned about a gang from the Anuak tribe who lived in Ethiopia and resented the Dinkas at the Panyido camp. The Anuaks had ambushed some of the boys on various occasions and killed about half a dozen, wounding others. These events seemed remote, however, as he didn't know any of those affected.

Ever since Dr. Garang's inspirational speech, he'd thought about learning in a deeper way. There was a purpose now, a focus to his life. Often he lingered after class to chat with Mr. Kiir whom he greatly admired. Life was good except for the food, which was always the same, and there was never enough of it. Sadness and anger still hung over him like a dark cloud, ready to burst into storm. But now he believed, as Dr. Garang had said, that knowledge, too, is a weapon. That made him feel less helpless and gave him a different way to take revenge.

Since the last clothing donation by the Red Cross, he had outgrown all but one shirt and a pair of pants. That required more frequent washing. Two places along the river offered easy access. The most popular was closer and usually crowded with swimmers and other people doing their laundry, but, at age nine, he preferred the more isolated spot down past the river bend where he would have some privacy.

Forgetting the caretakers' advice never to go out of the camp alone, he headed down the dusty path late in the afternoon, balancing on his head a bucket that contained only a bar of soap. No one would see him carrying a burden like a girl. Lots of boys did it when no one was around to ridicule. Since he felt hopeful, he sang one of the Dinka hymns he had learned at the newly-erected Episcopal church:

> *Lord, listen to our call to prayers and see us,*
> *O Creator who created us!*
> *We need the land so we might worship you in peace and freedom.*
> *Lord, listen to the sound of birds eating our flesh;*
> *Lord, see the tall bones lying all over the Land of Dinka.*

Only the sound of his voice and the buzzing locusts broke the stillness until he plunged into the river. He stood naked in the water to scrub his shirt and shorts, then climbed out and spread them on the dry grass. He took his time to cool off in the calm river as no one was anywhere in sight. After splashing and swimming a while, he remembered how he and Aleer used to see how long they could stay under water without coming up. He ducked under, held his breath and counted to twenty before popping up.

He noticed that during his play, the open space by the river had filled with a gang of fighting men—two with guns. *Anuaks!* Their backs were to the river and they faced a larger group of yelling boys who were pelting them with stones. With no place to hide along the barren riverbank, the Anuaks were bound to see him soon. Certainly they would spot his drying clothes.

A gunshot rang out and then another. One boy fell. The others moved around to stand in front of their fallen comrade but continued to throw rocks.

Ayuel got out of the water and pulled on his clothes, thinking frantically. *The Anuaks live to the right. Can't go that way. Got to get to the boys—they'll protect me...*

One of the men with a gun turned and spotted him. The Anuak yelled *Ajual mirec* in his language and fired. Ayuel knew the term meant something like "mean, bad Dinka." The bullet zinged past him into the river. His decision was made. He raced faster than he'd ever done before, right past the men. *If I can only get to the boys. Faster!* Just as he saw out of the corner of his eye someone chasing him, a man threw a large stick at his legs, tripping him. He dropped to the ground and when he tried to get up, a fist clenched around his ankle. It belonged to a fallen man who bled from a gash on his forehead. Several men attacked him, beating him with sticks and clubs. One blow fell across his shoulder at his neck. Everything went black.

★

Ayuel opened his eyes. He stared at the high tin ceiling above him and noticed the wide opening separating it from the top of the walls. When he tried to turn his head, the pain made him nauseous. He closed his eyes again and lay still. A breeze came, stayed a moment, went away and came back again. Over and over the pattern repeated. It was soothing. *Where am I? I don't feel so good.*

"Ayuelo," a familiar voice said. He opened his eyes again.

"Aleer, is that you? I can't see you. Can't turn my head."

"I've been here all night, sitting by your bed." His brother stood and leaned over him. "Thank God, you are coming to."

"Where have I been?"

"You've been unconscious. Some men from the Anuak tribe beat you up."

"They tried to kill me."

"I know."

"Did—did they kill anyone?"

"Rest now. I'm going to bring you some food." Aleer looked around and spoke in a low voice, "This is a dirty place. Very overcrowded. Two people are crammed in some of the narrow beds. Several are outside, but they get the mosquito netting."

"How hurt am I?"

"You're pretty badly beaten up. Lots of blood. Your ribs may be broken."

"My head hurts really bad." Ayuel put his hand to his head and saw that his entire right arm and hand were wrapped in white bandages. "And my side and arm and knee," he said with a groan. "Where's that breeze coming from?"

"It's a mechanical fan that turns back and forth. It works on a generator."

"Oh." He didn't want a lesson on how it works. "Feels nice."

"The police came and sprayed the Anuaks with tear gas to stop the violence. That makes their eyes burn. The Ethiopian police brought you here last night."

"What about the boy who was shot?"

"I don't know," Aleer said with hesitation. "Oh, I almost forgot. You are supposed to take these two red and black capsules. The nurse said to give them to you when you woke up." He placed them in Ayuel's free hand and pressed a cup of water to his lips.

Ayuel took them one at a time, even though it hurt when Aleer raised his head. "What are they for?"

"The nurse said it's to keep the wounds from getting infected. I'll be back in a couple of hours with some food. They won't give you much here."

Before he left, Aleer laid the back of his hand on his brother's forehead to check for fever—just as their mama used to do when they were sick.

★

The next day, as Ayuel became more aware of his surroundings, he noticed a white sheet hung at the foot of the bed, making a sort of wall. Behind it he saw the shadow of a standing woman and heard her talking softly to a patient. Since he couldn't turn to either side of his cot, he guessed there were a lot more patients nearby from the sounds of movement and someone working hard to breathe.

Then he heard muffled voices of Dinkas that gradually became louder. The sheet parted, held open by a nurse who said, "You've got visitors."

Four boys of various sizes whom he'd never seen before stepped into a line beside his bed.

"So you're not dead?"

"We came to see how you are."

"Who are you?" Ayuel said with pleasant surprise.

"We threw rocks at the Anuaks who were beating you with clubs," said the tallest, smiling broadly with his hands on his hips.

"They were kicking you, too."

"You saved my life," Ayuel said in wide-eyed amazement. "Thank you, all of you. That was a brave thing to do. You didn't even know me."

"We could tell you were Dinka."

"Did they kill anyone?"

"Seven. One died after he came here."

"I'd sure hate to be in this place. It stinks. How do you stand it?"

"My brother brings me better food and the nurse is nice when I see her," Ayuel said. "But she's always in a hurry. I even had a mechanical fan for a while, but someone else needed it, I guess."

"You are one of nine boys the police brought in here."

"I'm so sorry about the ones who died. Were they your friends?"

"Sure. We knew all of them," said the tall one. "We weren't doing anything to bother those men. We were just going to swim."

"There were about thirty of us, so we thought it was safe. What were you doing out there alone anyhow?"

"That was foolish of me," Ayuel said with a sigh. "I just felt happy, safe and wanted some privacy."

"Yeah, we saw you get out naked." The boy snickered.

"We're just glad you didn't die."

"Thanks."

★

The third afternoon after the beating, Ayuel pulled himself up and sat on the edge of the bed. Although he was weak and a bit dizzy, it felt good to sit. The taped rib cage gave some pain but his head felt better.

He watched a woman with a tray making her way down the long row of beds. Two boys about five years old lay in the bed next to his, their feet toward each other. They looked very sick. The woman bent over them and said, "I'll be back to feed you two."

"Ah, young man, I see you can sit up," she said turning to Ayuel. "God has smiled on you."

"Yes, Mama, He has."

"Let's see if you can walk outside to pee. There's a door just on the other side of the curtain. I'll be back with your food."

She watched him stand, then walk out past the curtain. When he returned, he lay down exhausted on his bed, his clothing soaked with sweat. In a few minutes, the woman returned with a small plate, which she placed on his chest.

"If you can walk, you can feed yourself," she said.

"What is it?"

"*Papa.* You've never heard of *papa?* It will give you strength. It's made with white flour and sugar."

Ayuel rested several minutes before pinching off a bite with his fingers. It was soft and spongy.

"Hey, Ayuelo, I hear you are well already."

Ayuel recognized his brother's voice. Aleer came and sat at the foot of the bed.

"Who says so? I feel terrible." Ayuel took the last bite and handed the plate to Aleer. "You ever eat this *papa* stuff?"

"No, is it any good?"

"Not bad. Just not enough of it."

"Well, I brought you a bowl of lentils and a spoon. But first let me wash your hands and face. You're sure sweating a lot." Aleer had brought a damp cloth and began wiping him down. "The nurse told me you could go home this evening when it gets cooler. She said if you are well enough to walk, you have to go home so they can have your bed."

★

"Ah-ha! I caught you skipping my class." Ayuel, who now lay in bed in his own *tukul,* turned and saw Mr. Kiir standing in the doorway.

"Good afternoon, Mr. Kiir." Ayuel's broad smile revealed the delight he felt. "How did you know I was here?" He reached out his left hand to shake his teacher's.

"Word gets around." Mr. Kiir sat on the next bed, facing his student.

"You've missed lots of lessons, so I thought I'd bring the lessons to you."

"Are you still teaching about the war, Mr. Kiir?"

"Oh yes, everyone is interested in that. But first, here are some new words for learning the meaning and spelling." He handed him a two-inch pencil and a list of twenty words written on a sheet of spiral-notebook paper. "Write them several times until you can spell them, and keep the pencil hidden under your blanket so no one will steal it while you sleep."

"*Sharia?* That's a bad word, Mr. Kiir. Why do I have to learn that?"

"Bad or not, it's important to know. The government forcing strict Islamic law on us is a chief cause of the conflict. They love to carry out the punishments: cutting off arms and legs, beatings, denial of jobs. All these words on your list have to do with the war: greed, oil, amputation…"

Another visitor stepped through the doorway. "Hello, Mr. Kiir." Beny shook the teacher's hand and sat down on the foot of the bed. "Hey, Ayuelo, that Anuak gang certainly left their marks on you."

"I guess so. I'm getting better though. Walking all the way from the hospital was hard, really painful."

"Yeah, Aleer told me. He said you had to stop every few minutes just to get your breath."

"My friends take better care of me here. They bring me all the food and water I want, change my bandages, tell me when to take my capsules. Yesterday I ate outside with the other sick kids who get to eat first."

"Not much incentive to get well," said Mr. Kiir with a laugh.

"Oh, yes, there is. I need food for my brain, too. I'm a seed," he answered boastfully. In spite of his lighthearted tone, Dr. Garang had really given him a sense of urgency about education.

"With education we can fight, but we also have to defend ourselves against thugs—like those who hurt you." Beny leaned over Ayuel and confided his plan. "Aleer and I, Gutthier, Madau and Gabriel are going to take several with us and look for those Anuaks. We'll lie in wait near their village until we find a few leaving without guns. Then we'll follow and attack them with heavy sticks—maybe spears—for what they did to you. We'll beat them up."

Before Ayuel could agree, the teacher said, "Now, now Beny. Think about it. What are the Anuaks going to do next, after you beat them up?"

"Come after us, I guess."

"Right. And with a lot more Anuaks. That's how wars start."

"But we can't let them get away with these murders. They killed seven Dinka children!" Ayuel said. "You said in class we have to fight back against evil."

"Yes, but pick your fights. Leave these crimes to the police. The South will never win against the northern Muslims if we keep fighting each other—tribe against tribe—those with one idea fighting those who have another. We're all Southerners."

But those Anuaks just hate us. They aren't thinking about the civil war and ideas, thought Ayuel, but he said no more in argument to his teacher.

THIRTEEN

WAR AND PEACE

Ayuel and Gabriel remained in their schoolroom after dismissal of classes to finish some homework. Ayuel's wounds had healed long ago and he was well into his third year at Panyido. He frowned as he struggled with the more difficult lessons. Looking up, he saw Beny and his friend Samuel Kiir enter the doorway.

"We're looking for a dictionary," Beny said, glancing around.

"Over there," Ayuel said, pointing his stubby pencil toward a table at the front of the room. "Gabriel and I are just finishing the math problems Mr. Kiir put on the chalkboard. Say, is he related to you, Samuel *Kiir*?"

"Probably so. I know you think you're related to him with a name like Kiir *Ayuel*. Even you and I could be cousins."

Beny finished writing something on his half notebook and closed the dictionary. "I met a very interesting man in Itang who was related to my mother. I don't think I ever told you about Tiop."

"Isn't he the old man whom you went to visit in the family section?" asked Gabriel. "I think you said he was always joking, but sometimes he had serious things to say. That's all I know."

"You'd said he just had one leg," Ayuel said, still frowning at the math problem.

"Well, I met him back in Itang before I came here. Samuel and I and a bunch of others were invited to his house for a New Year's Eve celebration. We'd never met him before, but our friends said to come anyway. After that, we would fetch water for him or help him in other ways."

"That evening he served us several different foods and plenty of Sudanese *mou* to drink," Samuel said.

"Yeah, I'd never had wine before. That was a great party," Beny said. "The man's name is Tiop-dit. When I came in his house and gave my full name, he said, 'You look like some of my relatives back in Unity with that name.' After we talked a while, we discovered he was related to my mama."

Ayuel and Gabriel, sitting on the dried-mud steps, closed their notebooks and faced their friends who seemed ready to say something interesting. Beny and Samuel sat down on the raised platform where Mr. Kiir usually stood.

"He's disabled, handicapped," Samuel said. "He fought with the SPLA against the National Islamic Front, which is Sudan's main government party. That was back in 1984 before they attacked our towns. They were fighting in the tiny village of Jok-kou just across the border in Sudan. The enemy cut his leg off."

"You remember I told you there were a lot of amputees in Itang. Tiop lived in the family section, so we had to get permission to visit him. I'll never forget that evening and all the things he told us," Beny said, his eyes lighting up. "I didn't really understand what he was saying until I heard Dr. Garang speak to us two years ago. But we understood enough to want to come here. Tiop had a lot of the same ideas that I guess he got from Dr. John—as he called him."

"He lost his wife and daughter in the war. Their village was attacked while he was out fighting. He's not heard anything about them," Samuel said.

"So, what did you talk about on New Year's Eve?" Gabriel asked.

"After we finished eating and the others had left, he poured Beny and me some more *mou* and asked us if we knew why the Arabs were killing us. We said 'no' because at that time we knew hardly anything about the war."

Beny picked up the story: "Tiop said, 'You are small children, and most of you who made it here to Itang are boys. It is good for you to know why you left your homes where you were eyewitnesses to so much death. The Arabs want you to have Islamic names, like Mohammed.' I asked what Mohammed was. He said, 'Mohammed was a great prophet. The Muslims think of him like some of you think of Jesus, our Savior, the Son of the living God. They want to force you to be Muslims—they demand the boys and men dress like them and the girls and women dress like their women. They want you to say you are Arabs, take on a whole new identity and not be Dinkas or Nuers, Christian or Animist. They want to rule over you, despite your qualifications, if you are not Arab Muslim. But *we* have no rights to rule over them.

"'In addition, now that they have found oil under your land, they are forcing you out, not only from Panrieng, Gokrial and Bor, but all over southern Sudan. That is why we took up arms and fought against them. That is why you see people here who have no hands, no legs—like me. We were wounded in the war fighting to free you from radical Arab Muslims who are *yirabian*—evil terrorists. They bomb us and use machine guns and tanks against us. All we have are AK-47s...'

"I interrupted him and asked where they got all that heavy military equipment. He said, 'From their Muslim brothers in other countries.'"

Samuel broke in and said, "I asked Tiop where our *Christian* brothers were. I thought maybe the other Christians in the world didn't have guns or don't know how to make them. But Tiop said, 'Oh, that is not the case. They have guns, tanks, bombs and all of that. Christian brothers in other parts of the world know how to build guns that are more powerful than what the Arab Muslims have.'

"I said, 'What are they waiting for? Why don't they help us? If they see what's happening to their Christian brothers, why don't they give us guns?'

"'Ah, that's where your part comes in,' said Tiop, setting down his cup of *mou*. 'They don't understand us because we speak a different language. They only understand English. You must go to school and learn English so you can tell your Christian brothers that the Arabs are trying to change the whole world to their beliefs whether we want to change or not. Then you can tell them we need guns to fight against this oppression.' I said, 'But they don't teach us English here in Itang.' Tiop then told us we should go to Panyido, where they teach English."

Beny looked around the schoolroom and waved his arm toward the table that held the English dictionary and the world globe. "And here we are in Panyido, in school, learning English. At first we thought Panyido was months away like Panrieng where Samuel and I came from, but I didn't care. I said, 'Good. Then we will walk to Panyido. I don't care how far it is. If I can learn English there, I will go. Then I will be able to speak out about this problem and get guns to fight against the Arabs.'"

Samuel said, "So I agreed. A few months later, we left with about two hundred others. It took us only two nights of walking. We were put in the same Group Eight, but different villages, as you know."

"Of course, that's when I met Aleer," Beny said. "Two months later, Tiop came to visit some friends in the family section here in Panyido."

"And that's when you went to see him?" asked Gabriel.

"Oh, yes," Beny said. "But we had to get permission from a caretaker. When we shook hands, he asked, 'Well, have you learned English or not?' I said, 'Not yet, but I can say, *Good morning, teacher*. And soon I should be able to say, *Good morning, Christians*.' He laughed and said that we must learn to ask about the guns and explain the problem we have in Sudan."

Samuel said, "I told him we would be learning a lot more, but that I could spell *gun*."

"He took Samuel and me out to dinner at a little café here in town. He was hobbling on crutches, but, as usual, remained very cheerful. He misses his wife and daughter very much. He left the next day to go back to Itang. He did his part by fighting and losing his leg. Now, we've got to do our part and get an education."

★

Ayuel took off a white cotton robe and hung it behind the screen near the altar in the Episcopal church. He'd served this Sunday as altar boy, lighting and snuffing the candles. Well into his third year at Panyido and now ten years old, he found comfort at church and enjoyed singing the hymns.

"Thank you for helping, Ayuel. God's blessings and peace," said the priest, gathering his Bible and papers from the pulpit.

"Peace to you, Father."

As the minister exited the side door, Ayuel noticed Aleer, waiting for him, halfway back on one of the many rows of dried-mud pews. When he waved to his brother, he noticed Beny was standing near his new friend Monyjok, who was shorter than most Dinkas. They were entering the back opening of the church, followed by Gabriel and Ayuel's half-brother Gutthier. The congregation had already dispersed.

"Ah, it's cool in here," Gabriel said, breathing deeply.

"That's because of the high ceilings," Ayuel said. "Hey, Gutthier, have you heard yet if you get to transfer to Village One?"

"Just found out. Yes!" Gutthier said. "The caretaker of my group said he'd made an investigation and found nothing really bad about you, so we can be in the same group, even though we are related. Of course, I could have told him about the time... No, really, he found you've never been in a fight that anyone knew of—except when the Anuaks beat you up last year. But that didn't count, since they attacked you."

"That's great news!" Ayuel said. "Can you move in tonight?"

"Sure. He said there was a bed in the *tukul* next to yours."

"So that makes three of us relatives in Village One," Gabriel said. "Of course, they still don't know about Ayuel and me being cousins."

"Good, we'll help you move your stuff," said Aleer to Gutthier.

"Say, Beny, how do you like the new Catholic church?" Ayuel asked. "I miss our singing together, since you changed over."

"Bet all those around you are glad," Gabriel said with a chuckle. "When you two stand together, you try to sing louder than everyone else."

"And we do—or did," Beny said. "I like the service there. Same God, you know. Of course, like the others from the Unity region, I went to a Catholic church as a child, so the liturgy sort of makes me homesick. That's where my parents had me baptized the first time as a baby. And my friend Mary A. goes to this church with her auntie."

Beny still claimed that she was not his girlfriend, but Ayuel knew they spent a lot of time together—going to soccer matches, dances and even to her relatives' compound for games and meals. He wished he knew how to talk to girls like that. Before he could ask Beny how he got along with the auntie, Aleer continued the church topic.

"Ayuel and I were always going to church back in Duk," said Aleer. "Our mother taught us to pray morning and evening, not just in church."

"Don't the Dinkas in Duk, and all of Bor for that matter, go to Episcopal churches?" Beny asked.

"Sure. That's because our grandfather, who ruled over the whole region of Jongli that included Bor, was the first to convert from Animism to Christianity. That was in 1912 while he worked with the British, who were Christians. He had a whole bunch of wives—that's why we have so many cousins—but the British didn't insist he change to their ways."

"So after his conversion everyone followed the chief?" asked Monyjok, showing interest.

"I guess so. Of course, we don't remember that. He was later poisoned at age eighty by Arabs—long before I was born."

"Is that when your father became chief?" asked Beny.

"No, actually it was his brother—one of our uncles—who took his place," Ayuel said.

"I've heard he was among the 142 chiefs who were all slaughtered at the same time," Gabriel said.

"Yes, because of their faith; the government did it," said Aleer. "Then our father became commissioner and judge of Duk. Again, that was before I was born. And we assume the Islamic fundamentalists got him when our village was bombed."

"That's why we have to win this civil war. So much unjust killing," Beny said. "My father was a chief, too. One of the minor chiefs, but I'm sure he was targeted as a leader."

"So much dying for no good reason. My best friend, Malual, was the minister's son. We used to sing…" Ayuel's voice broke with the memory.

"Malual had a really good voice. I remember how, during the journey, he used to sing the songs his father wrote," Gutthier said. "Next Sunday is my turn to check out a Dinka hymnal. Why don't we all get together and sing all the old songs?"

"We can meet right here," agreed Ayuel.

"And sing as loud as we want," added Beny with a laugh. "Right now, let's go for a swim."

Aleer and Gabriel helped Gutthier move his few belongings and get settled in. Beny and Ayuel walked to the river—the safer spot, not the isolated one around the bend where Ayuel had been attacked. After a pleasant swim, they filled their water buckets to take back to their villages. Returning empty-handed from the river was considered poor etiquette, but the heavy load made a more tiresome return trip. Halfway back they stopped under the shade of a tree to renew their energy.

"You know, Beny..." Ayuel said, scooping up some water from the bucket and splashing it on his face before he sat down. "I agree with Dr. Garang that knowledge is a weapon, but it will take years before we know enough to do any good with it. Or fight with it. I'm still angry about all we've lost."

"I know..."

"You and Aleer, you're probably twelve or thirteen now."

"None of us remember our birthdays."

"Back home, you would get initiated into manhood, but here you are still boys."

"They give us more responsibility when they think we are old enough."

"Like what?"

"Well, the priest selected me and a few others for a training course called Peace and Reconciliation. We've already met once."

"What are you supposed to do? Go out and make peace with the Northern Arabs?" Ayuel laughed at the idea.

"Guess we aren't quite ready for that. They teach us a lot about dealing with anger—misplaced anger—and solving conflicts right here in camp. We learn a lot of scripture verses. It's already helped me to understand my anger."

"Seems like there are always arguments. More than we had at first," Ayuel said. "They put people of different tribes and ages together. That causes a lot of the problems."

"Yes, but what if your Group Six were all Dinkas and Group Ten all Equatorians? Wouldn't they gang up on each other? We'd have really big fights—like with the Anuaks."

"Probably."

★

A few weeks later, Ayuel found out more about the training course Beny had talked about. A big argument had broken out in his Village One over chores. Mabior and Alepho, both around fourteen, had been told by the caretaker to pound the grain because the boys assigned couldn't do it. They refused to do what was one of the hardest and most tedious jobs in camp. A fistfight broke out between them and others who thought they should just do the job.

Beny and another boy from the peace training course were asked to meet after the meal with those involved. They brought along a caretaker from a different group who would hear about the situation for the first time. Beny invited Ayuel as he had witnessed the fight. They all gathered in the shade of some trees by the Group Six complex where they sat in a circle.

Beny spoke first. "We're not here to judge who was right or wrong in the fight, who struck first or even to give a solution. That's for the guest caretaker to decide. We are here to provide a place for everyone to express his thoughts and feelings without yelling or making threats. Also we may share some teachings from the Bible. Alepho, you go first and tell us why you think you and Mabior should not pound the sorghum."

"Yeah, we could have had bread tonight, but there was no flour," said one of the boys who had fought against him.

"Wait, let Alepho speak."

"We pound grain like everyone else when it's our turn," said Alepho in a subdued tone. "In fact, we did it just last week. Someone else should do it this time."

"You didn't do a good job last week," said one of the boys on the opposite side. "You left chunks of maize in the flour. I was on the cooking committee and had to beat it some more."

"Who else is on the pounding committee?"

Four young boys raised their hands.

"It takes two of us to hold the large mortar," said one. "Alepho and Mabior are lazy, especially Mabior. Last week, he worked just a few minutes and handed the mortar back to us. It takes hours and hours of work. We are too little to do all of it."

"What would you like to say, Mabior?" asked Beny's partner.

"I say this whole pounding routine is women's work. We are men and should be excused altogether. It's humiliating."

"And is your mama here to pound the grain, Mabior?" asked Beny.

Mabior put his hands over his face and didn't answer.

"Of course, none of our mamas is here," Beny said. "And we don't have cattle to tend or other manly jobs, but in St. Paul's letter to the Thessalonians he says, 'If any would not work, neither should he eat.' That is pretty clear. Ayuel, can you tell us how the fight started?"

"Well," Ayuel said with hesitation. "I heard the caretaker tell Mabior and Alepho that they had to pound the grain this week because the two boys who were supposed to do it were in the hospital—which means they had to be really sick to go to that place. And the others were too young to do it by themselves."

"Did they agree to do it?"

"Alepho said 'All right, Mama,' but as soon as she left, Mabior said he wasn't going to do it, and Alepho said it wasn't fair. That's when one of these boys said, 'You better. You never do your share of the work.' And Mabior said, 'You can't tell me what to do.' Then they all started hitting each other. I don't know who hit first. That's when I left."

"Fighting is the manly way to settle things," said Mabior. "I think we got the best of them."

"Fighting isn't always a good way," Beny said. "Jesus taught us to love even our enemies. Let's hear what the caretaker has to say."

The young man who had been listening intently stood up and said, "All of you have plenty of reason to be angry, after all the people you've lost, including your parents. Sometimes what you are really angry about is something deeper. But, be that as it may, a job wasn't done, and it must be done by the ones asked to do it. If the grain is not turned into fine flour for the cooking tomorrow, Mabior and Alepho will not eat. That's all I have to say."

★

Shortly after the incident with Mabior and Alepho, a group of *khawaja* appeared in camp. No announcement was made at first, but they began talking, through interpreters, to curious children who came by to watch them set up tables with a chair on each side. As the crowd increased, they asked the children to queue up. With an interpreter standing beside each table, the child was asked his or her name, age, background, etc. A man with a small camera then took his picture.

Ayuel and his friends got in line. The rumor had spread that the *khawaja* were choosing people to go to the United States or England where their lives would be better.

With high hope in his heart, Ayuel took his place in the chair, facing the interviewer. After the standard questions, Ayuel said, "I want to go to a better country to get a good education and come back to Sudan to help my people." The man smiled and shook his hand.

Two days after the interviews, the *khawaja* left without a word. Ayuel, like the others, swallowed his disappointment, storing it away inside with all the other heartaches. After two weeks, no one spoke of it again.

FOURTEEN

CROSSING THE GILO RIVER

Near the end of the fourth year in Panyido Camp, Ayuel, Gabriel, Gutthier and others from their village were pulling weeds in their group's small field of tomatoes and okra. Mud squished between their toes as the rainy season had begun, but today the sun drew steam from the soggy earth.

"I can't wait to bite into juicy tomatoes," Gabriel said as he stood up between the rows of plants and took a deep breath. He tired easily, but always tried to keep up with the others. He wheezed and coughed a lot. "The plants are a lot better this year than last. Look at all the blooms."

"It's the ground nuts I like," Ayuel said. "That peanut taste reminds me of home and my mama's cooking. Let's head back. It's nearly time to eat."

"It'll be maize mush again," Madau said, wiping sweat from his forehead with the back of his hand.

"Yeah. Better than tree leaves though. I'll be glad when these vegetables get ripe."

The boys gathered their small piles of wilted weeds and carried them to the edge of the patch. Each group had planted their assigned plot of ground the past two years, which for a season added variety and nourishment to their meager diet. Boys from each of the villages took turns tending their fields.

As they wiped their muddy hands on tall grass beside the field and headed back, Gutthier said, "A lot of people are leaving Panyido. Have you noticed? Doctors, nurses—even some teachers and caretakers."

"They're mostly Ethiopians," Ayuel said. "Mr. Kiir says something's happening in the government. He's going to tell us more about it tomorrow, but I'm on cooking duty and won't hear what's going on—just like the time they told us about Dr. Garang coming."

"Our caretaker left two days ago and didn't even tell us goodbye," Gabriel said, panting as he tried to keep up with the others. "The day before she left, she looked into our *tukul* without checking anything. When I spoke to her, she just stared back like she didn't know who I was."

"Guess we can be messy for a while," Madau said. "No one to check on us." They all laughed and hurried toward their compound.

Beny met them with a worried frown on his face. "What's going on?" Ayuel asked.

"I was looking for you," Beny said out of breath from running. "Just at the end of class today, we asked Mr. Mayen why people were leaving. He said, 'I'll tell you tomorrow, but put on your *mutkukalei*. Be ready.'"

"Be ready for what?" all three said at once.

"Well, put on your *mutkukalei* usually means be ready to *go* someplace, doesn't it? But my teacher didn't say anymore. He said he didn't have much information yet, but he would tell us tomorrow."

"That's what Mr. Kiir said. Something big is about to happen," Ayuel said. "But we don't have any place to go—that's why we're here. We certainly can't go back home to Sudan—still fighting there."

*

Apprehension hung in the air. Since no one knew what was happening, they all talked in hushed voices, passing around outlandish rumors. Ayuel had trouble sleeping that night, tossing about and wondering what was in store. He hated missing out on the announcement at school, but knew he must carry out his assigned duties.

Coming back from the river at noon the next day with a bucket of dried dung and an armload of firewood, he could hear thousands of voices, no longer hushed. Weren't the boys to be in school for the big announcement? In the deserted kitchen, he dropped his load and followed the lines of boys heading toward Group Eight. Adults and children from the family section came also. He thought he saw Mary, Beny's friend, among the girls. A voice over the loud speaker said. "Please, stop where you are. We don't have much time. Listen carefully." Ayuel ran and joined those at the back of the assembly.

"We will leave tonight." *Leave for where?* Had he missed the most important part?

"Don't go out of camp to the river or even to the soccer field. Stay at your compound and wait. Pack a small bundle of possessions: a blanket, not too many clothes, soap, a jug of water, maybe a cooking pot and something small that you treasure. Divide whatever food you have among those in your village."

"Where are we going?" Ayuel whispered to a stranger next to him.

"Shoo! He hasn't said yet."

"War has broken out in Ethiopia. Rebel groups have overthrown President Mengistu who has allowed the refugee camps. Those now in power do not want us here. They think we're part of the SPLA and that you boys will soon be their soldiers. It still is not safe in Sudan, so we are going to Kenya. We will have to cross the Gilo River and then walk south across part of Sudan to get there." Ayuel thought about what the Panyido River had looked like while he was gathering the dung for fire—swollen and churning from the recent rains.

The Panyido became the Gilo that separated Ethiopia from Sudan. Ayuel remembered crossing it four years ago in the rowboats that Officer Chol had forced the owners to provide—and the last one had sunk. *Where will they find enough boats to take us all across? Some might get overloaded and tip.* Fear gripped him as images of the long journey of starvation flashed through his mind. He tried to listen to the words coming over the loud speaker.

"The Ethiopians you have seen leaving recently knew what was about to happen. They knew staying with us was dangerous. You must go back to your group and be ready to leave when you are told. Your Sudanese teachers will go with you. Do not try to contact brothers or cousins. There isn't time."

Back at his *tukul*, Ayuel hurriedly folded the green and black striped blanket from his bed and tied a string around it. He pulled a cardboard box out from under his bed and selected two of his favorite T-shirts and a long pair of trousers. In a near sense of panic, he wondered how long this journey would take. *A week? Two or three months?* He wished he had some schoolbooks, but they were shared and he didn't even have one in his possession.

There was, however, the Dinka hymnal from church. It circulated among twenty people and he had taken it home just the day before. He and Beny, along with several others, had planned to meet at the church to sing this evening as they often did. Ayuel placed the hymnal on top of his school notebook and pencil, then folded some clothes around them. He wrapped everything in the sheet of plastic that he'd used to cover his head in the recent downpours and slipped the package into a small grain sack. Ayuel wriggled his toes into his rubber flip-flops and thought of his real *mutkukalei* from the first journey. When he'd outgrown them, he'd given them to a younger boy.

Now he would see what he could add from the kitchen.

To his surprise he found Mabior, one of the boys who had objected to doing women's work, stirring maize in the big black pot.

"I thought we should eat before we go," said Mabior cheerfully. "We started cooking as soon as you brought in the fuel. Alepho is guarding a bag of grain from the store to divide up afterward."

"You didn't hear the announcement?" asked Ayuel.

"My teacher's Ethiopian, and he told me what was going on before he left. He said the new government plans to kill us all. They are against the SPLA and think we are being trained to be their soldiers. He said his life was in danger for working here. I don't want to die hungry."

Others began filing into the kitchen area with their packs of possessions, equally surprised to find food cooking so early in the afternoon. Ayuel made a second fire for boiling river water. *How long will one jug of water last?*

*

Before they finished eating, the first group was called up to begin the journey. Word spread that they would walk two days along the Panyido River before coming to the selected place at the Gilo. Their teachers had made a difficult choice. They would cross where the river was not so wide but the water would be swifter there.

The sky darkened as Alepho rationed out the grain and the boys filled their plastic jugs with the still-warm water.

"We're in for a big downpour... ," someone said, his voice cut off by a loud clap of thunder. The rains came in big drops, then sheets of water, pounding the earth and the heads and shoulders of those dashing for cover.

Once inside, the boys sat on their beds next to their bundles. "Hope this stops before we leave," Ayuel said. "That first group is getting soaked."

"I'll miss this bed," Gutthier said, sounding wistful. After getting permission to be in Ayuel's Group Six, he'd finally made it into the same *tukul* as well. "I guess they'll burn all our buildings."

"Probably," Gabriel said, "but we won't be in them. I don't think the Ethiopian rebels have planes to bomb us."

Talk continued in this manner until the boredom of waiting turned them to simple games. Some played dominos with pieces of whittled wood, the spots burnt on with a fire-heated wire. Others played the spelling game they had learned the first year.

In late afternoon, Mr. Kiir came to the doorway and told them it was their time to go. "If you have any plastic sheeting, put it over your heads," he said before going to the next *tukul*.

Ayuel reached into his sack and touched the plastic, then withdrew his hand. He'd get wet but the Dinka hymnal would stay dry.

In silence, they hugged their packs or placed them on their heads and filed out of their home to join the thousand or so others from Group Six. Teachers and caretakers hurried them along. The rain fell gently now. In the distance behind them, Ayuel heard a few gunshots. Frightening as it was, this experience didn't compare to the anguish of bombs dropping on Duk, losing his mother, running alone in that dark night of terror.

They sloshed through the mud and tall grass in intermittent rain. Ayuel stayed close to his half-brother Gutthier and his cousin Madau. They'd lost track of Gabriel. Group Eight with Aleer and Beny had already gone ahead of them. He wished he could make this trip with Aleer, but he took comfort in knowing his brother would be with Beny.

On the morning of the second day, Ayuel's group arrived near the crossing point. The rain had stopped but the mud left no place to sit or lie down. Beyond the thousands of swarming people, Ayuel could hear the roar of the angry river. A rope spanned the distance, hanging close to the water, and he could see boys clinging to it as they made their way hand over hand through the frothing waves. A few rowboats struggled to navigate the raging currents. He heard screams and shouts but was too far back to get a clear view of the chaos.

A few cooking fires had sprung up, built on piles of rock with dry wood some of the boys had brought. "Why didn't we think to bring some dry sticks?" Madau asked. "We knew it would be damp. I have a pan to cook our maize."

"Let's go see what firewood we can find," Ayuel said. In the morning sun, steam rose from the drenched ground, intensifying the stench and humidity. They wove their way among the throngs toward a wooded area. Ayuel nearly tripped over the feet of an SPLA soldier leaning against a tree.

"What happened to you?" Gutthier blurted out. Blood oozed through the side of the man's uniform. His right hand and the side of his face were smeared with blood.

"They shot me last night halfway here from Panyido."

"The Ethiopian rebels?" Ayuel asked. "Are they coming after us?"

"Yes." The man moaned. "They are coming with tanks and big guns. You need to cross the river now. Don't wait for boats. Swim if you can. There was a terrible battle at Panyido. They've burned everything. We fought to protect you—so they wouldn't follow you, but we lost badly."

"What will you do when they come?"

"I have a young brother here somewhere. I'm hoping he will find me. Now, go jump in the water and get away. The sun is so hot."

Ayuel and Gutthier carefully took the soldier's shirt off and hung it from the top of his head across his body to shade him from the morning sun. They saw the gaping wound in his side but looked away. What could they do?

Gunfire echoed in the far distance. "Let's forget about cooking," Ayuel said.

Rumors of the approaching enemy spread throughout the crowd. The thousands began to gather their belongings and move toward the river.

Ayuel and Gutthier grabbed their bags and followed. Boys cautiously waded into the water. The rope hung limp from a tree trunk on the bank, apparently broken. The boats were not taking passengers, only bundles.

"We have to swim this!" exclaimed Ayuel, stunned at the realization. Earlier he had feared having to cross the churning river in a small boat or hanging onto the rope. This might be the narrowest place to cross but it was still a wide expanse. He watched bodies frantically thrashing in the water—some making progress, others sinking and screaming when their heads bobbed up.

The two stood in soaking-wet clothes, staring at the yellowish-brown foam.

"I'm not sure I can do it," Gutthier said. This was no comfort to Ayuel as his half-brother had always been the better swimmer.

"Gutthier! Ayuel!" Their eyes followed the voice until they spotted Madau.

"Over here!" They both shouted and waved.

They made their way toward each other. "It's not so bad," Madau said, wading in and backing out several times. "It's cold. We can do it."

Ayuel and Gutthier stood motionless on the bank, clutching their bundles, meanwhile others pushed ahead of them. Ayuel imagined himself swimming in the swirling waters—trying to make the feat seem possible.

"Group Six, bring your belongings… !" one of their teachers shouted. Shaken out of their trance, they rushed to add their bundles to the piles in the small boats.

Back at the bank, Madau tried to encourage them. "I wish I was God. I'd take a stick, like God did for Moses, and part the waters so you guys could walk across."

"Yeah, but you're not God…"

A single boom rang out. Thousands rushed into the raging waters, pushing the three boys in. Poor swimmers jumped on the backs of others trying to hitch a ride. If someone made a few strong strokes above the water, five, six or more rushed to cling to him. Of course, all would go under. Ayuel struggled to rise above the surface but then pretended he couldn't swim to discourage hangers-on.

Above all the screaming and thrashing, as he struggled across the river, he heard heavy gunfire close by. Very close. Bullets zinged into the water. Beside him a boy's head split open and the child went under leaving a wake of blood. The foam churned red all around him. The bullets kept coming, killing on all sides. Hundreds of dead bodies floated past, bumping into him. In a gasp, Ayuel took in a mouthful of water. He spit it out and realized the taste of blood. *Abba, Father, help me!*

Numbness set in. Ayuel moved mechanically, thrashing about in the mass confusion for what seemed like hours. He could see the opposite bank looming closer. When someone grabbed him, he allowed himself to go under until the attacker loosened his grip and let go. His lungs felt as if they would burst but he kept repeating the maneuver. Instead of swimming, he was running in water. *Almost there! Keep going.* At last with his head barely above the surface, he felt his feet touch gooey, slimy mud. Someone underneath grabbed his foot and pulled him down. Ayuel kicked furiously, knowing whoever it was would drown. Otherwise, both would sink.

A bullet hit the bank in front of him, splattering mud across his face.

"Get under!" someone shouted. He watched a boy climb out only to be picked off by rifle fire from the far bank. The body fell back into the water and floated out of sight. Ayuel quickly realized that staying under water with only his head above would make a smaller target. People massed at the bank, standing in the mud among the reeds, water shoulder deep, some bleeding from their wounds. He watched as two boys nearby—having made the crossing—sank exhausted into the water and drowned.

"Crocodiles!"

"They're eating people."

Others pressed against him, trying to escape the new terror lurking in the water but he held his ground. He'd found a sapling to cling to, giving him an anchor. The scent of blood from the wounded roused the voracious hunger of the crocodiles. Would he rather be crushed alive by jaws of crocodiles or riddled with bullets by getting out or drown in the churning water? He decided to take his chances and run for it. Most of the people crawled out in the mud on their stomachs, keeping their heads down to escape the bullets.

Ayuel knew a bullet could strike him in the back at any moment as he ran, but he'd made his choice. Now, missiles fired from the Ethiopian side exploded randomly, leaving the dead and wounded sprawled on the ground. *Madau and Gutthier, where are you?* The small boats with the belongings lay marooned in the mud. Boys were snatching bundles, not checking to see which were their own. Ayuel spotted his green and black blanket, grabbed it and ran on.

FIFTEEN

STARVATION

For the remainder of the day, enemy fire pursued those who had survived the river. Ayuel hugged his soggy blanket, running, then walking, much as he had done four years before. Alone among strangers. They'd been taught to lie flat when guns fired behind them, but now long-range missiles exploded randomly. He reasoned the danger was equally great whether upright or lying down, so he went on. As dusk fell, a hand grabbed his upper arm. "Thank God, you made it!"

"Gutthier! Am I glad to see you! Why are they doing this to us?" Ayuel asked.

"Don't know. We're only children now, but someday we will be strong and have guns."

Too tired to talk, they silently walked side by side. After dark, they stumbled into a small village. Mud and puddles of water covered the ground. Some people climbed trees to find a spot to rest. Thousands milled around aimlessly. Finally the shelling subsided, diminished to distant rumbles. Ayuel and Gutthier sat on exposed tree roots and leaned against the trunk. Exhausted and chilled to the bone, Ayuel held his wet blanket across his chest and fell asleep.

He awoke at the first rays of sunlight. Only now did he realize he had grabbed only the blanket, leaving his clothes and Dinka hymnal—so carefully saved in plastic—to someone else. With a deep sigh, he got up and stretched the blanket across the tree limbs to dry. Gutthier lay curled up, his arms wrapped around himself. His bag of clothing pillowed his cheek against the tree.

"Ayuelo! Over here."

Ayuel turned and saw Beny several yards away, just getting up from his place under another tree. Two boys—about eleven years old, Ayuel's age— were with him. He woke Gutthier with a quick shake to his shoulder and together they eagerly ran over to see their friend.

"Where are we?" asked Gutthier.

"Someone said it's a little town called Pinytit," Beny said, hugging his friends. "I'm glad you're alive."

"Glad for you, too," Ayuel said. "Where's Aleer? Do you know anything? Have you seen Madau or Gabriel?"

"Haven't seen those two, but your brother got across the Gilo before the shooting started. After that, someone saw him go to the left. At that time, an SPLA officer was directing the crowd to different camps. By the time we came along, everyone was running this way."

"So he made it across the river? Thank God for that," Ayuel said.

"Has anyone seen Mary A.?" Beny asked.

"I saw her at the big meeting," Ayuel said. "She was with her friends."

"Hope she and her auntie made it across the river." Beny stared wistfully into the distance.

"Mary's strong. She was always playing some sport. She'll make it." Ayuel tried to encourage his friend. "Does anyone know where we're going?"

"To Pochalla, I think." Beny answered, forcing a smile.

"That's near where we crossed the Gilo in boats the first time," Gutthier said. "And one sank. The river was much calmer then."

"Anuaks live there." Ayuel thought of the men who nearly killed him three years ago.

"But they're Sudanese Anuaks," Beny said. "The Ethiopian Anuaks are the bad ones." Then, turning to the two boys by the tree, he said, "Meet my new friends, Mac and Angou."

"Beny's been taking care of us," said Mac, the smaller of the two.

"You've found a good one to look after you," Ayuel said. "You guys are pretty lucky."

"I found them crawling in the mud, dodging bullets, like me."

"He seemed to know what he was doing so we followed him," said Angou. "Now if we can just find something to eat. I smell maize cooking."

The boys followed the scent and found a man sitting on a bag of grain and stirring maize in a large pot. He waved them over.

"Where did you get the food?" Beny asked.

"The SPLA delivered lots of it just this side of the Gilo," said the man. "It's about ready."

The boys sat and waited. A line of other hungry children began to form behind them. Others had made fires, too, their food drawing disorganized groups of survivors.

As the boys finished eating, teachers came by, telling everyone to find their groups. "We need to check to see who's missing. Then groups will head out at different times as we did before. We should be there by evening. When we cross the Pochalla River, be sure to fill your containers with water. Hopefully there will be food for us when we arrive."

The boys thanked the man who fed them. Beny said goodbye and with his new charges in tow, headed out to find Group Eight.

*

When Ayuel and Gutthier met up with Group Six, they were relieved to find both Gabriel and Madau alive and well. As the boys walked in columns through intermittent rain, teachers checked off the names. The water of the Pochalla River ran dangerously fast, though it was only a few feet deep at the center. Surviving teachers formed lines across to take each boy's hand and pass him on to the next. Ayuel thought of Mr. Kiir and the others as real heroes that day as they stood for hours and did their best to help their charges across.

Slick, moss-covered rocks presented the greatest hazard. If a child's foot slipped in the deepest and swiftest part of the current, he was instantly swept away, pulled from a teacher's grasp. Others would be lost if even one adult left the chain to attempt his rescue.

Late in the afternoon as they trudged along, Ayuel hoped the U.N. or

Red Cross had made food deliveries. Up ahead he saw a boy coming toward them, which of course seemed unusual as everyone else was headed to Pochalla.

"Hey, that looks like Beny," said Madau who walked directly behind Ayuel.

"Hello, Beny!" they both called out.

When Beny noticed them, he came over and briefly walked beside them. Out of breath, he said, "There's no food in Pochalla. The SPLA's there but there's been no delivery for us."

"The SPLA dropped bags of grain on this side of the Gilo."

"I know," Beny said. "I'm going to see if there's any left." He held up an empty cooking pot. "Mac and Angou are both hungry and weak. I told them I would find food. I feel responsible for them. See you guys later." He turned and ran back toward that scene of monstrous tragedy on the banks of the Gilo.

"Be careful," shouted Ayuel.

Shortly afterward, as the sun set, the group was told they'd arrived. The town of Pochalla was a two hour walk away, but the camp would be built here. Once the boys stopped walking, mosquitoes descended in swarms. The rain had ceased, but the thousands who had returned home to Sudan found no place to rest, for puddles of stagnant water and mud covered the ground. As the masses milled about they groaned, wept, argued and complained. As Beny had told them, there was no food beyond small portions a few had brought. The group of four found a small patch of flattened grass. Fortunately they each had a jug of water brought from the Pochalla River. They had gathered a few sticks along the way to make a fire, but instead used them to sit on. A foul odor surrounded them from the damp bodies, mud and human refuse.

"Reminds me of coming into Panyido," Madau said. "Only we were really starving then, not just hungry."

"Donayok was carrying Chuei," Ayuel said. "He was dying…"

"The U.N. and International Red Cross must surely know we're here," Madau said. "No one except the SPLA even knew about us before."

"And we have our teachers with us now. They'll find us food." Gabriel gasped the last word.

"Something wrong, Gabriel?" Ayuel thought his cousin didn't look well.

"I feel a little funny," Gabriel whispered, as he pressed his hand to his chest. "Just when I breathe. I'm okay."

★

The next morning, Ayuel and Madau took their cooking pot and went out to look for leaves, roots or, if lucky, fruit. Anything to fill their stomachs. The other two boys stayed with their packs and small supply of firewood.

Once in camp, the groups mingled as they searched for family and friends as well as something to eat. Crossing an area mostly inhabited by Group Eight, Ayuel and Madau discovered Beny, Mac and Angou in the process of building a small *tukul*.

"Hey, Beny, how did you get back so fast?" Ayuel asked, delighted to see his friend.

"You know I run very fast." Beny grinned and put down the sapling pole he'd been working with. "Please, have a seat." He indicated some large rocks that he'd placed in front of their new home. Turning to his charges, he said, "You remember my friends Ayuel and Madau?"

"Sure," said Angou. "Good morning, Ayuel and Madau. Beny didn't have to go all the way back to the Gilo." The two boys continued to mix grass with mud to build the sides of the *tukul*.

Once they sat down, Beny explained, "I met a man this side of Pinytit who was carrying a large bag of maize over his shoulder. When he saw I had a cooking pot, he filled it from his sack."

"Then you have food?" whispered Madau.

Beny nodded. "Don't let anyone see you." He pulled back a blanket that revealed a pot, full of cooked maize. "Just scoop some into your pot and eat it away from here. I got back early this morning while it was still dark and cooked it," he said in a low voice.

As they followed his instructions, Madau asked, "Did the man tell you anything?"

"He said there were bodies, mostly children, lying on the ground all the way from Pinytit to the Gilo. The missiles caused great destruction. On the bank where the SPLA left the food, it was even worse. The man looked for his missing wife and children among the dead but said he wasn't sure he could've recognized them. He said they probably went to Pakok."

"Where's that?" asked Ayuel.

"That's where Aleer may have gone. We know he made it across the Gilo," Beny said, his voice reassuring. "I met up with Monyjok on the way here, but I haven't seen Samuel... or Mary A."

"Mary would be with a lot of adults from the family section and Samuel's probably here somewhere," Madau said. "Group Eight has about 1,400 in it, doesn't it?"

"Yeah, it was one of the biggest," Beny said. "My teacher, Mr. Ayom, came by just a few minutes ago. He said we are missing two or three hundred from the group, but some may have gone to Pakok. When I asked about Samuel, he said he couldn't remember seeing him, but he didn't have the list with him."

"Thanks for this," whispered Ayuel, pointing to the food gift. "We need to get back to Gutthier and Gabriel." He laid some sticks across the top of the pot to conceal the contents.

*

By the third day, hunger raged throughout the camp. The skeletons of *tukuls*—just skinny poles stuck in the ground without their mud walls— stood eerily across the landscape. Famished children had become too faint to finish the buildings.

"I have a bed sheet in my pack," Madau said. "I bet someone in Pochalla would give us food for it."

"Is it in good condition?" asked Ayuel.

"The best. That's why I brought it." Madau pulled it out, wrinkled and damp. "It smells a little funny."

"We'll freshen it up," Ayuel said, agreeing to the idea. The boys stretched it across tree branches and waited for it to dry in the sun, then folded it neatly. They decided Gabriel should stay with their belongings, as he was the weakest of the four.

The sun bore down at its noontime high when the boys arrived, after a two-hour walk, at the pole fencing on the edge of town. They slipped through an opening and immediately felt the unwelcome glances of the villagers. Some stared, but most looked away and talked rapidly to their companions. Several times Ayuel heard them say *Ajual mirec*, the words the Ethiopian Anuaks had once screamed at him. Since then he'd learned that *Ajual* referred to a small homeless forest animal. They were calling them "bad people without homes."

One old woman was cooking sorghum cakes on a flat piece of metal over an open fire. The boys looked at each other and silently agreed to approach her. Gutthier knew four Anuak words and used all of them. "Good day, Mama. Food?"

Madau held out the folded sheet. Ayuel grabbed his stomach and bent over to indicate he was starving.

The old woman looked mildly interested. She took the sheet and spread it out on the ground. The boys nearly passed out smelling the sorghum cakes, for the woman took a very long time making her inspection. Finally she said "yes" in Dinka and gathered up three cakes. The boys all shook their heads and Ayuel held up four fingers. She frowned and thought a while before finally putting four cakes into their cooking pot. "Tomorrow, more," she said, again in Dinka, as she tugged on Ayuel's shirt sleeve.

The bed sheet would be far more valuable at the *souk* than four small sorghum cakes, but at that moment it seemed a good trade. Quickly the boys slipped away through the fence and headed back, slowly savoring the taste of real food. The largest cake remained in the bottom of the pot for Gabriel.

*

The boys had found a secret source of food. Every few days they returned to trade clothing for small amounts of food, usually a cup of maize or flour. Probably the old woman was trading their good United Nations' clothing for something worth more than food in the town. Since it was impossible to eat without sharing with those around them, they cooked in the middle of the night to avoid detection.

On one side of Pochalla, the townspeople kept their domestic cattle. On the other, the SPLA defended their herd. Well into the second week, still with no delivery of food, the SPLA butchered some cattle and roasted the meat for the ravenous crowds. "Hurry," called Madau, who had discovered what was going on. "There won't be enough for everyone." The others followed him to the edge of the camp where soldiers stood guard with guns over the cooking beef. After waiting in line for a long time, Ayuel and his friends each got a piece.

"Well, that saves my shirt for another day," Ayuel said, licking his fingers. Actually, his last shirt was one Gutthier had given him, as he had lost all his extra clothing as well as the Dinka hymnal. Gutthier still wore a shirt, but the other two were already bare-chested. "Then we will have to barter away our blankets."

Later, they heard that some of the boys who had waited all day for a bite of food only to be turned away hungry, stole into the villagers' herd and bludgeoned a cow. They were caught while roasting it in the middle of the night—and shot to death by the owners. A few others got away with the same desperate attempt to lessen their hunger pains, but the teachers went around pleading with the boys not to steal from the villagers. "They already resent our presence."

At the end of the second week, the teachers circulated through their groups with a new message. Mr. Kiir came by telling the boys, "We are going to build an airstrip. Trucks cannot reach us because of bad weather, the rain and mud. Planes have no place to land."

It was a massive undertaking. More than 10,000 had settled in the camp, some had built *tukuls*, but all were slowly starving to death on a diet of boiled grass and leaves. Each group was assigned a stretch of the airstrip to build. As the teachers directed, the able-bodied cleared away the brush and small trees, brought sand from the riverbank, mixed it with mud and spread it over the surface. Weak as they were, Ayuel and his friends labored with enthusiasm.

Often they passed Beny and his charges on their trips to or from the river. They told him how they traded clothes for food in town, but he said he'd found the villagers even more resentful after the cattle incidents and had little success in trading.

Miraculously, the airstrip lay finished and ready in only two days!

Every day, the thousands of refugees sat by their *tukuls* and scanned the skies. They had worked hard to make a food delivery possible, but, after a few days, disappointment and hopelessness set in. At the end of a week of waiting, the voice of Mr. Pieng, the beloved director of their old camp in Panyido, came over a microphone. "We've spotted a small plane approaching from the east. We believe it contains supplies. You may gather far back on either side of the airstrip, behind the line of teachers, which is now forming. Don't rush to the plane when it lands!"

In the huge expanse of settlement, not everyone could hear the entire announcement, but they all got the central message and began to move toward their airstrip. Ayuel spotted the small white dot that seemed to gradually grow wings and begin its descent. He stood between Gutthier and Madau behind the teachers as the plane circled.

Mr. Pieng's amplified voice was louder and clearer this time: "We have just received word by radio that two very important people are on board this plane: the famous Sudanese Catholic Bishop Paride Taban…" Applause rose from the crowd, especially from the Catholics among them who recognized the name. Ayuel searched the upturned faces for Beny, but couldn't find him. "And all of you have heard about the tallest Dinka ever, Manute Bol, who now lives in the United States of America and plays NBA basketball for the Washington Bullets."

If they didn't know much about Manute Bol, everyone at least knew the song about the tallest man in the world and the shortest man. The boys shouted his name and began singing "Manute and Majok Dengdit stayed in Wau…"

The white plane, with a huge red cross painted on the side, touched down and smoothly glided across the new runway, its roar drowning out the song. When it finally came to a stop and the motor cut off, everyone stood in a hushed silence, waiting for the door to open. Though weak from hunger like everyone else, Ayuel felt a ripple of excitement. They were worth important people coming to see them, and bringing food.

The assembly stood breathlessly as one man came out, walked down the steps and said something to Mr. Pieng. The director nodded and announced over the microphone, "The ICRC workers will be unloading the packages and delivering them to the headmaster of each group. He will then distribute them to his village leaders. Our guests want to talk with you briefly while they are doing this. Please be patient. Everyone will get his share."

The workers began unloading the cargo while *khawaja*, two white men and one woman, stepped out carrying huge cameras over their shoulders. The boys stared in wonder. After a few minutes the revered Bishop Taban appeared. The Catholic boys began singing:

> *Praise Him!*
> *Praise Him in the morning.*
> *Praise Him when the sun goes down!*

Others chimed in as the words were repetitious and easy to follow. Behind the bishop a very, very tall man, wearing a Washington Bullets jersey, emerged in the doorway, bending down his seven-foot seven-inch frame and waving as he followed the Bishop down the steps.

Bishop Taban took the microphone and said, "Good afternoon. I am…" His voice choked and he broke down in sobs. Finally, gaining his composure, he said softly, "You poor children. May God have mercy on us all." Then he made the sign of the cross and began praying, interspersed with sobs. "Almighty God, Our Father, look down on Your creation. Have mercy on these poor, starving, innocent children. Forgive us, forgive the world for turning a blind eye, a deaf ear to their cries in the wilderness."

The Bishop continued, crying and praying for several minutes, then spoke directly to the crowd. "I did not know the horrible conditions you were in. I didn't know there were so many of you. We have brought enough for each of you to have a small amount. Your teachers will see to that, but I will arrange for you to receive more. Peace and God's blessings upon you." He stretched out his hands over the crowd and handed the microphone to the basketball star.

"Hello. My name is Manute Bol. I play basketball on a team in the United States of America."

The boys clapped and cheered.

"I grew up just like you in a small town in Sudan, herding goats. I never had a chance to go to school, and like many of you, my future did not look so good. I started playing basketball and a coach seemed to think I was good at it. Basketball opened a door for me, but I have never forgotten my country, its people and its problems." Ayuel noticed the deep scars that had been slashed across his forehead, marks of a Dinka coming of age.

"I support the cause of the rebels. Many of my relatives are leaders in the SPLA. They are fighting for you so that someday you will have schools, safe churches, homes free from violence, lots of cattle and a place where you will never again go hungry."

The boys quietly applauded as they eyed the bags and boxes being stacked at different locations.

"I am working for you, to convince the United States that they need to do more to help, to intervene in this genocide where nearly two million southern Sudanese have already perished. Many more, like you, are displaced. Such things should not be. I have talked to dozens of American congressmen, warning them of Muslim extremists who may someday come to their own doorstep. I beg them to intervene. But right now they are busy with their own war in the Gulf, against Iraq."

"The Americans are in a war?" Ayuel said, amazed that rich and educated people would have to fight wars.

"I guess they are," said Madau, shrugging and changing the subject. "I'm so hungry."

Manute glanced toward the unloading of the cargo and quickly finished his remarks. The crowd cheered and applauded him loudly. The Bishop ended with a short prayer. Respectful applause followed. All who had come climbed back into the plane, last of all the photojournalists who took one more camera sweep around the crowd and caught the two celebrities waving goodbye.

"Hope they show the pictures to the American congressmen," Gutthier said as they queued up for their food allotment.

"They know about us," Ayuel said. "Remember the American congressman we welcomed four years ago in Panyido?"

"Maybe they don't know what happened in Ethiopia," Gabriel said. "All I care about now is getting something to eat."

"That American congressman spoke English," Madau said, "and Manute Bol probably does too. He's doing what he can."

"Maybe someday they will listen and rescue us," Ayuel said while they watched the small plane disappear among the white clouds.

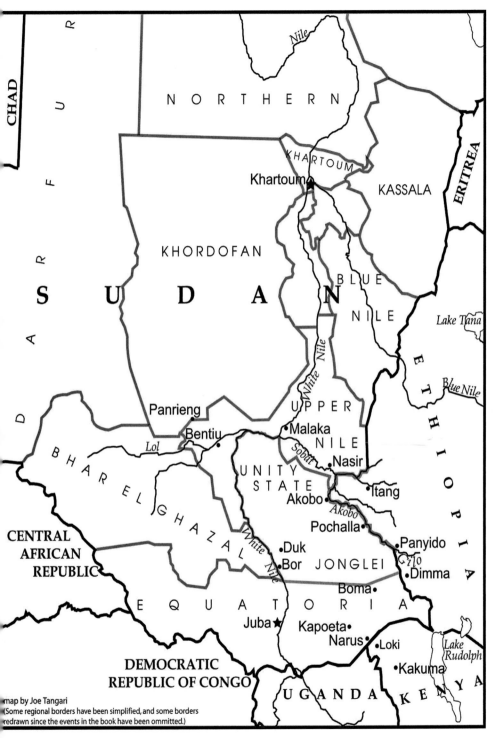

CHAD

DARFUR

ERITREA

NORTHERN

KHARTOUM

Khartoum●

KASSALA

KHORDOFAN

S   U   D   A   N

BLUE
NILE

Lake Tana

ETHIOPIA

Blue Nile

Nile

White Nile

UPPER

Panrieng●

Bentiu●

Lol

Malaka●

NILE

Sobat

Nasir●

UNITY
STATE

Akobo●

Itang●

Akobo

Pochalla●

Panyido●

CENTRAL
AFRICAN
REPUBLIC

●Duk
Bor●

JONGLEI

White Nile

●Dimma

Gilo

Boma●

E   Q   U   A   T   O   R   I   A

Juba ★

Kapoeta●

Narus●

Loki●

Lake
Rudolph

DEMOCRATIC
REPUBLIC OF CONGO

●Kakuma

UGANDA

KENYA

B H A R   E L   G H A Z A L

map by Joe Tangari
(Some regional borders have been simplified, and some borders
redrawn since the events in the book have been ommitted.)

Map of the Sudan, created exclusively for *Courageous Journey* by Joe Tangari.

Salva Kiir, Dr. Garang's Chief of Staff (left) and Dr. John Garang, Leader of the Sudanese People's Liberation Army and virtual Head of State for Southern Sudan, at a reception following his "Seeds of the New Sudan" speech to the refugee children at Panyido Camp in Ethiopia, 1988. Photo courtesy of Ayuel Leek Deng.

Dr. John Garang at the Lost Boys' and Girls' Conference in Phoenix, Arizona, 2004. Photo courtesy of Beny Ngor Chol.

Dr. Francis Deng, Director of the Sudan Peace Support Project, addresses the Lost Boys' and Girls' Conference in Phoenix, Arizona. Photo courtesy of Beny Ngor Chol.

Panel of high Sudanese officials discuss the Comprehensive Peace Accords being negotiated at the time. From left to right: Agnes Lokudu, Sudanese People's Liberation Movement Representative in Great Britian; Pagan Amum, SPLM Secretary General; Deng Alor, Chief Negotiator for the Comprehensive Peace Agreement; Stephen Wundu, SPLM Representative in the United States at the Lost Boys' and Girls' Conference in Phoenix, Arizona. Photo courtesy of Beny Ngor Chol.

An Animist ceremony to celebrate the return of a medical doctor, Manyang Angoth, who has come back after a year's absence to his native Panieng. By stepping over the slain cow, it is believed he will be purified of all his past transgressions. A spiritual healer is in white and holding a staff. This is an important ceremony in Beny's hometown. Photo by Benjamin Majok, Executive Director of the Sudan Relief Rehabilitation Association.

Samuel Kiir, Supervisor of Zone One for the Community-Based Rehabilitation Program (on left) and Beny, Manager of the program. Photo by Ethiopian Community Photo Center.

yuel Leek Deng at eighteen, at Kakuma Camp in enya. Photo courtesy of Ayuel Leek Deng.

Ayuel's uncle, Leek Deng, and his two grown children at home in Kakuma. His teen son, Tiop Leek, is on the left and daughter Mary Leek is on the right. Note the mattress drying on the roof. Photo by unidentified family member.

eny's uncle, Acuil Chol, whom Beny visited in airobi. Photo courtesy of Beny Ngor Chol.

Beny Ngor Chol in front of his *tukul* (on left) in Kakuma Camp in Kenya. Photo courtesy of Beny Ngor Chol.

Stephen Kajirwa Keverenge, Program Manager for International Rescue Committee (far right) and Beny inspecting crutches made in Kakuma Camp. Photo courtesy of Beny Ngor Chol.

Farah Osman in a hand-peddled wheelchair, made in Kakuma Camp by Beny's staff at the Community-Based Rehabilitation Program. Photo courtesy of Beny Ngor Chol.

Some of Beny's Rehabilitation staff at his farewell party. The three girls who called Beny "Mr. Young Single Manager" are in it. Photo courtesy of Beny Ngor Chol.

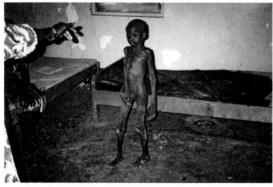

Orphaned child found by Beny's staff, suffering from malnutrition and birth defects. They were able to restore his health, fit him with glasses and teach him to utter meaningful sounds. Photo courtesy of Beny Ngor Chol.

Four-year-old Ahamd Hassan, who is unable to sit alone, now can stay upright in a special chair designed by a technician on Beny's staff. Photo courtesy of Beny Ngor Chol.

Delegates of the Sudanese Youth Conference in Nairobi taste canned soda for the first time (Ayuel is on the far left), 1998. Photo courtesy of Ayuel Leek Deng.

Beny shakes hands with John Chol. Mario from Uganda is center and Anderia Mayom behind him. Kakuma Camp. Photo courtesy of Beny Ngor Chol.

At Beny's farewell party, inside one of the multi-purpose buildings. From left: Frances Kuek, Beny, Dr. Amy and Stephen Kajirwa Keverenge. Photo courtesy of Beny Ngor Chol.

Two Turkanan girls in native dress. The Turkanan tribe lives near the Kakuma Camp and receives services from it. Photo courtesy of Beny Ngor Chol.

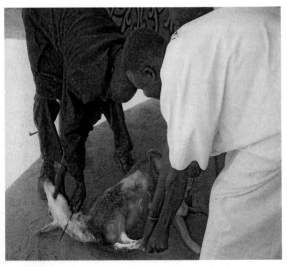

Slaying of lamb for Beny's welcoming party in Nairobi before his wedding with Mary Ajok Malek. This is part of a traditional Dinka ritual for family reunions when a member has been separated for a long time. Photo courtesy of Beny Ngor Chol.

Jacob Gatluak, Rehabilitation Supervisor for Zones Five and Six; Beny, Manager; Abraham Majok, Supervisor for Zone Four, show off their Community-Based Rehabilitation T-shirts, Kakuma. Photo courtesy of Beny Ngor Chol.

Mary Ajok Malek in Kenya. She arrived in Kakuma only weeks after Beny left for the U.S. They reconnected by phone and email. They had not seen each other since he was thirteen and she was eleven. Photo courtesy of Beny Ngor Chol.

Clockwise from right: 1.Anderia Mayom at home in Kansas City, Missouri. Photo by Barbara Youree. 2.Madau Goi in Atlanta, Georgia. Photo by a friend. 3.Beny's younger brother, Abui Ngor Chol, in Sudan. Beny was nine the last time he saw his brother. This photo was sent to him from a family member. Photo courtesy of Beny Ngor Chol. 4. Deng Leek, Ayuel's oldest brother, at his home in Toronto, Ontario. Photo courtesy of Ayuel Leek Deng.

Several of the Lost Boys find their first American home on Olive Street in Kansas City, Missouri.

Manute Bol, the seven-foot-seven former NBA basketball star (center) with Ayuel (far left), Beny (right) and an unidentified individual at Bol's welcoming party. Photo courtesy of Beny Ngor Chol.

Beny learns how to prepare food the American way at his home in Kansas City, Missouri. Photo by Barbara Youree.

Ayuel talks on the phone to his friend Rebecca Kuol in Denver, Colorado at his home in Kansas City, Missouri. Photo by Barbara Youree.

Beny Ngor Chol (left) and Ayuel Leek Deng (right) in front of Beny's apartment in Kansas City, Missouri. Photo by Barbara Youree.

Anderia Mayom enjoys the thrill of driving on the car simulator at a laudromat. Photo by Barbara Youree.

Beny Ngor Chol (left) at his Citizenship Ceremony at the Federal Courthouse in Kansas City, Missouri, December 8, 2006, with the judge and Gina Moreno. Photo courtesy of Beny Ngor Chol.

Ayuel Leek Deng (in ball cap) and Beny Ngor Chol attend a meeting at the Sudanese Grace Church to discuss Sudanese issues in Kansas City, Missouri.

The guys on Olive Street happily receive their GED materials. From left: Dominic Dut Leek, Dominic Leek Leek, Ayuel Leek Deng and Anderia Mayom. Photo by Barbara Youree.

Ayuel Leek Deng graduates from Penn Valley Community College.
Photo courtesy of Ayuel Leek Deng.

SIXTEEN

GOODBYES

No more planes landed. After they'd been in Pochalla three months, United Nations planes dropped packages of clothing, mosquito netting and small amounts of maize, sorghum and beans. Stretched thin, it barely supplied each boy a ration for two weeks. It was not nearly enough. The world apparently was forgetting about them.

When the rainy season ended, even grass, leaves and wild fruit became scarce. The boys were showing signs of malnutrition—emaciation, protruding stomachs, wiry orange hair. They'd been through this before. All anyone seemed to talk about was the lack of food.

Every month or so, as the roads dried, a few trucks brought supplies. With teachers present to enforce discipline, the boys stood for most of a day in long lines waiting for a small portion each. On one such day, Ayuel had just finished eating what he had allotted himself, saving the rest for the next day. He sat on a log, head in hands, and waited for the intense hunger to pass as his food settled. When he became aware of someone in front of him, he looked up and saw Beny with Mary, the girl he'd liked back in Panyido. They stood together, holding hands, both beaming from ear to ear.

"You found her!" Ayuel exclaimed, jumping up. "How? Where?" Though thin and hollow-eyed, Mary's smile and manner were pretty as ever.

"I was standing in line this morning when I saw her walk by, carrying a bucket of water on her head. I called out, 'Mary A., is that you?' She turned, and sure enough it was."

"Always I was looking for Beny and asking everyone," she said, lowering her eyelashes.

"Did your auntie make it too?"

"Yes, Ayuel, she is here with me but she is not well."

"I'm sorry."

"We've found a distant cousin. He wants to go back to Panrieng and look for relatives." Her face brightened when she added, "He thinks that my mother may be in an internal displacement camp in Khartoum, because he's heard many of our clan are there. I'm happy that at least she could be alive."

★

Supply trucks stopped coming, but surplus clothes had a way of finding new owners. Occasionally, a pair of shoes or a shirt was given to Ayuel or one of his friends. They would then make a trip to the village for a food trade. They continued to cook in the dead of night away from camp to avoid detection.

Coming back from the town one afternoon with bartered food, Ayuel and Gutthier ran across Donayok, who was still in charge of Group One. They invited him to come to their midnight meal. Beny, with his two charges, and Monyjok, from Group Eight, came also. And Samuel Kiir, who had been given up as lost in the Gilo, eventually turned up alive as well as the others.

That night, as they sat around the dying embers of their cooking fire away from camp, Ayuel felt less frightened than usual in this isolated spot in the darkness. Donayok had been like a father to him on that first journey of the seventeen. It was comforting to have him here. While consuming their small but equal portions of maize, the boys discussed the news from the outside world. They listened with respect to Donayok, now an impressive young man at eighteen. He had been talking with some of the SPLA soldiers who possessed a radio.

"There's been a split in the SPLA," Donayok said. "One of Garang's commanders, Riek Machar, has turned against him and has gathered forces in Nasir."

"Isn't Nasir where the boys from Itang went from Panyido? That's what I've heard," Beny said, thinking of those he remembered from his first camp, including his handicapped friend, Tiop.

"Right. And some of them have joined what Machar calls the SPLA-United," explained Donayok. "And the strange thing about that is he accuses Garang of using boy soldiers."

"Well," Gabriel said, rubbing his arms to ward off the night chill, "what else can you expect a boy to do who has seen his father and mother killed, has no place to go and is hungry? He wants to grab a gun and go after the enemy. Especially if the soldiers will feed and clothe him."

"I've thought about it myself," Madau said. "They aren't fighting against each other, I hope."

"I'm afraid so," said Donayok. He cradled his head in his hands as if thinking how he might break bad news.

"Come on, tell us," urged Ayuel. "What's happening?"

"It seems the break-away group has attacked the whole region of Bor."

"Where we're from—Gutthier, Gabriel and me," Ayuel said, realizing the tragedy. "And Garang's home. How bad?"

"Very bad. The BBC is calling it the 'Bor Massacre.' Over 2,000 slaughtered. They say it's even worse than what the government by itself has done to the South. In fact, it's the Government of Sudan that is supplying the tanks, planes and AK-47s for Machar's forces. They figure why not let the South defeat itself?"

"That's terrible. Are they out to get all Dinkas?" asked Monyjok. "Riek Machar is Nuer, isn't he?"

"Right. There are a lot of Nuers right here among us who are loyal to Garang and will stay that way, but part of the split is tribal," said Donayok as he shook his head over the horrible turn of events. "Garang's forces have attacked Nasir in retribution."

"Surely Machar's army won't come after us if he accused Garang of using boy soldiers," Samuel said. "Surely there is a solution to a disagreement as simple as that."

"I think that's just an excuse. He doesn't agree with Garang's cause of bringing unity to all of Sudan under a secular government that would protect Southern rights," Donayok said. "He wants the South to split off into a separate country. And I think he hates Dinkas. Garang is Dinka. Also, they are struggling with each other for power."

Distant howls of hyenas prompted a quick departure. They lit a torch, smothered the coals and headed back to camp in the moonless night.

On the way Beny said, "Remember that kid in Panyido who was always going around pretending to speak English?"

"Sure," Ayuel said. "I thought he *was* speaking English. I just met him once, but I remember you talking about him being in Group Eight with you and Aleer. Wasn't his name Emmanuel?"

"Emmanuel Jal. That's him. He did know more words than us, but he would talk fast, stringing a lot of words together. I don't think it was all real English. Anyway, he was from Bentiu, near where I'm from. His father was killed in the same raid. He's Nuer, and he used to brag that he was related to one of Garang's commander's. I believe it was Riek Machar, that rebel that's causing the trouble. I saw Emmanuel here in Pochalla just a few days ago, but he didn't say much."

"Wonder if he knows about the split—and the massacre," Donayok said. "I believe, like I said before, the Nuers in this camp will stay loyal to Garang's SPLA."

Ayuel shivered in the darkness, the comfort he'd felt earlier now turned to a fear, greater than before.

A few weeks later, the word spread that Garang was still in control of the town of Kapoeta that he had captured from the government. This came as good news, but still the SPLA was seriously weakened by the split.

★

The original plan when the refugees left Panyido had been for them to go to Kenya, but that government debated for months over how and where to put so many refugees chased from Ethiopia, as well as the thousands more that streamed out of war-torn Sudan. Remaining in Sudan meant facing constant fear. Government planes occasionally circled overhead. The boys dug foxholes next to their *tukuls* and at the forest edge. Bombs fell on surrounding villages, but so far neither the town of Pochalla nor the camp had taken a direct hit.

As insecurity increased and food supplies diminished, families and older boys began to leave in search of a better place or to return to their villages. Late one afternoon, Beny came to Ayuel's *tukul* with tears in his eyes.

"What's wrong?" Ayuel questioned, putting his arm around his friend's shoulders. "Sit down. I was just making some tea." With a rag over his hand, he lifted a tin can from his wood fire and set it on the ground. "We'll just let the leaves and bark settle. I don't know what they are, but we'll add some imagination."

"Mary A.'s gone." Beny wiped his eyes with his arm and sniffled. "She went with that older cousin she found, back to Panrieng. There's nothing there. They know that, but our village is on the way to Khartoum where she hopes she will find her mother. It's so dangerous to travel in Sudan. I tried to talk her out of it."

"They want to go home, find relatives." Ayuel ached for his friend, but he knew nothing he said could comfort him.

"I'm just thirteen and she's eleven, but we know we love each other."

"Did you talk about that?"

"I told her I loved her and when we grew up, I wanted her to be my girlfriend. And maybe we could possibly get married some day." Beny took a deep breath and let it out. "There, I've said it."

Ayuel handed Beny the tin can of tea. "What did she say?"

"She squeezed my hand and smiled up at me. You know I couldn't tell anyone else this."

"I know."

"Then she said, 'I love you too, Beny.' But she didn't say anything about being my girlfriend or getting married some day."

"She doesn't have to, Beny. No one can be sure of anything. She doesn't know what's going to happen. But, of course, if you see each other again, she will be for it."

"I guess. I'm so worried about her making that terrible trip. About twenty are going." Beny handed the can of hot tea to Ayuel, who sipped and handed it back. "They'll head north and go through Nasir, where Riek

Machar's troops are. They could be captured…"

"They could."

★

After the trucks stopped coming, supplies occasionally fell from the sky, but barely enough to keep life in the children's starving bodies. The delivery would always be dropped a distance from camp to avoid destroying *tukuls* or landing on top of people. One time, the SPLA officers received a message that relief packages would fall just beyond their herds of cattle. Teachers spread the word throughout the camp, giving the time and place.

As always when such news came, excitement spread and hope revived. Ayuel and his friends followed the thousands of others at the appointed time.

"I don't feel hungry; I just feel sick," Madau said, as they walked toward the appointed spot. The drop was to be made in thirty minutes.

"I hate shriveling up and watching myself slowly die," said Gutthier who had always prided himself on his handsome appearance.

"Just think about having something to eat today," Ayuel said and looked skyward. "There come the planes!"

The crowds ran toward the wide, open area, stopping only as the teachers held them back. Several boys rushed on past, hoping to be first to gather packages. The planes flew on beyond the crowd, turned and circled back over the frightened cattle, scattering them in every direction. They let their load loose.

Ayuel's hope turned to fear in a split second as he saw the falling bundles transform into enemy bombs. With his mouth still agape, before any sound could come out, the explosives hit, flinging parts of cattle high in the air. When the planes buzzed off, a dozen boys lay dead and many more critically wounded.

As hunger pangs lingered, they puzzled—and agonized—for weeks over why they had been sent bombs instead of food supplies.

★

For seven months, the children languished. Many died of malnutrition and disease. Then, miraculously, as the Christmas season approached, an abundance of food, clothing, soap and other necessities came from the United Nations High Commission for Refugees and a variety of non-government organizations. Talk of starting up schools again brought hope. Health and hygiene improved. Perhaps they could remain in their homeland.

In Dinka culture, a church building is usually the first structure built in a community. Some of the SPLA officers had been holding services in a grove of trees since the first week, but now preparations for a building had begun in earnest, chopping down and stripping the timbers, marking off the boundaries and carving a pulpit. The soldiers had already worked with the local Episcopal church to order, from Nairobi, a few Bibles and a large number of hymnals for those attending the services.

When the songbooks arrived they were distributed to keepers of books who would each take care of one hymnal for ten people. Ayuel was appointed as one of these book keepers. "This is exactly like the Dinka hymnal I lost at the Gilo, but in better shape!" he exclaimed when the officer handed it to him.

Singing and praying under the trees lifted Ayuel's spirits. Like many of the others, he was hungry to express his faith and sing praises to God. It was food for the soul. Since he was the keeper of a hymnal, he and his friends often sang together in the evenings.

Ayuel's cousin Donayok gave him a nice pair of dark-blue dress pants and a white shirt that had fallen to him. Ayuel treasured wearing them to the prayer services and for special occasions. Now that there was no longer a need for extra food, he had no fear of needing to barter them away. Wearing the new clothes gave him a sense of dignity and worth. He wanted to keep them in good condition.

"Remember how our mamas used to put live coals in their irons to smooth out our best clothes," Ayuel said as he picked up his new pants and shirt from the bushes where they'd dried in the sun, wrinkled from washing. "But we don't have an iron."

"I've seen some guys using quart oil cans," Madau said. "I bet we could get one from the SPLA."

The can was easily obtained. Ayuel washed it out with soap, and that evening after the cooking fire died down to glowing charcoal, Gutthier helped him transfer the hot coals with two spoons into the can. He then wrapped a cloth around the top and tied it tightly so he could hold onto it.

"Now, let's see if it works," Ayuel said. He spread a folded blanket on the hard earth in front of their *tukul*. Other boys gathered around to watch.

He placed a pant leg on the blanket and moved the hot can across it. They all watched the wrinkles disappear. He grinned up at the onlookers.

"Now do mine," Madau said emerging from their *tukul* with his own clothes.

"You can borrow it when I'm done," Ayuel said, as he laid the smooth pants aside and began working on the shirt collar.

He kept them neatly folded in a corner of his *tukul*, waiting for a special ocassion. One day, he and Gutthier returned from the river and found, much to Ayuel's dismay, that the treasured dress clothing had been stolen. Somehow, in spite of all the monstrous tragedies in his life, this still seemed a great blow. He tried to hide his anger, but it surged up greater than the loss deserved. It was as if even his dignity had been snatched from him. When finally alone, he sat in his hut and cried, feeling he had no control over his life, no future, no goals. He reached over and picked up the Dinka hymnal and held it to his chest. *At least they didn't take this.*

SEVENTEEN

BLOOD, SMOKE AND EARTH

Weeks before Christmas, the boys began preparations, prompted by the nostalgic memories of family and community. A large supply of bedding had recently been delivered by the U.N. and the white sheets became robes to wear in the traditional marching. Everyone needed a sash to wear across his chest with a cross attached—red, green, white. It didn't matter, as long as the cross contrasted with the color of the sash. An oversupply of solid-colored skirts were thus put to a good use. Boys were chosen to portray Bible characters and began practicing for the grand Nativity pageant to be performed at the Episcopal church under the trees on Christmas Day. As yet, not even the frame of the building had gone up.

Beny returned from the Christmas Eve Mass at the Catholic church in town. Most Sundays, he made the two-hour trip so he could worship in the way he'd learned as a child. He enjoyed the music and chants, liturgy and banners—the experience of being inside a religious sanctuary. The Anuak priests provided several services, one specifically in Dinka for the refugees.

He stopped at the *tukul* of Ayuel and his friends and found them dressing for the procession that would begin at five o'clock that evening. "I hurried back," Beny said, peeking through the doorway. "You guys ready?"

"Hi, Beny," Ayuel said, stepping outside. He placed a green sash across his chest and tied it to one side. "How do I look?"

"Like you're ready to celebrate."

"How was your service?"

"There were so many of us, they did the Mass outdoors. I wished Mary A. could have been there. Hope she's celebrating Christmas somewhere." Beny slipped on his marching robe with red sash that he'd carried with him.

"She probably is." Ayuel didn't pursue the topic further when Madau joined them.

"It was great," Beny said. "We all lit candles and sang. The Catholic Mass is very solemn and short. Not like the hours and hours that the Episcopalians take to celebrate."

"But you're going with us, I see," Madau said. He tied his blue sash across his chest. "We have a torch for you."

Over the loudspeaker a female voice began singing a Dinka song in English: *Today we pray, because the birth of our Lord Jesus, twenty-fifth day of Akoch...* "It must be time to line up," Gutthier said, as he emerged from the hut. He passed out the torches they'd prepared, ready to be lit when darkness fell.

Thousands of boys marched in long lines, some beating drums, stepping in rhythm. As darkness fell, the participants lighted their torches, passing fire from one torch to the next and the next, making a spectacular sight moving down the slopes and across the vast expanse of the camp. The young voices echoed from column to column in songs of praise. Light shone in the darkness of the refugees' lives—obscuring the misery and squalor, pain and fear of only a few short weeks before when food had been so meager. The Christ Child was born, symbol of peace, joy and hope.

The boys stopped at several stations, or chapels, for prayer and a short reading of scripture. At midnight, they all gathered at the usual place for Sunday services. Gas lanterns hung in the trees, spreading light over the thousands gathered. Following more singing and scripture reading, one of the SPLA officers gave a brief message about God's love for all, while the audience sat on the ground, listening with intense devotion.

The marching then recommenced and continued throughout the night until seven o'clock in the morning. All that exercise in the humid air left the boys eager to plunge into the Pochalla River. Ayuel, Beny and their friends carried clean clothes with them to put on after a quick morning bath. Carefully, they folded the sheets to return them to their intended use.

"Remember how every family would bring some special food to church on Christmas—back in Duk?" Madau said as the boys trekked back for the Christmas Nativity pageant. "And we had meat to eat from the slaughtered cattle."

"My mother brought yams made with something sweet," Ayuel said. "I was always afraid it would all be gone before I got to her dish."

"We did the same in Panrieng," Beny said with a faraway look in his eyes. "My mama made a wonderful pudding with milk and sugar."

"We don't know how to make any of those things, even if we had the ingredients," Gabriel said. "We just have maize or beans like any other day."

"Maybe we'll marry girls someday who know how to cook all those things," Gutthier said. "We'll herd the cattle and do the fishing, build the houses and tell stories to our children."

"About the time we celebrated Christmas in Pochalla," Ayuel said.

They all laughed with happiness because, by any measure, it *was* a good celebration. They raced back to get a good seat under the trees for the Nativity drama, complete with sheep and a donkey for Mary to ride.

*

One evening in *Aduong*, the second month of the year, Beny prepared a large pot of beans and rice. He and his charges invited Ayuel, Gutthier, Madau and Gabriel. Monyjok and Samuel Kiir came as well. Ayuel's group brought a box of biscuits that had fallen to their village. They all sat in a circle enjoying a social evening.

"I've not heard any more about starting schools," said Ayuel. He was eager to resume his studies.

"Mr. Ayom tells me Kenya still hasn't decided on a place for a refugee camp," Beny said, scooping more beans into the common plate.

"Do you think we'll ever move out of here?" asked Gutthier.

Before anyone could answer, a loud—though distant—boom split the air, followed by rapid gunfire.

"That's on the other side of the Pochalla River," Gabriel said, coughing with his arms crossed over his chest. He took a shallow breath, struggling to breathe.

An unusual amount of loud talking rose across the camp as people reacted to the new threat. A half-hour later, Mr. Ayom walked through the camp, as did the rest of the 300 teachers. He stopped at Beny's *tukul* and announced, "Good evening. We are leaving Pochalla for Kenya. Pack your belongings and be ready. Put on your *matkukalei*. We will leave by groups as before. Group Eight probably won't leave until morning." He recognized Ayuel and his friends. "Group Six will most likely leave even earlier in the morning. Just be ready."

"Thank you, Mr. Ayom," they all said.

"May God be with you," the teacher said as he hurried on to the next hut.

*

With plenty now to eat at their village meals, there was no need to trade clothes for food or to hide their cooking. Early in the morning after Mr. Ayom's message, as Ayuel and his three friends prepared to leave, they cooked a large pot of maize to take with them. Around five o'clock, just as stars began to fade, Group Six was called.

"We're going to our new home," Madau said with a sense of high expectation.

"We should be safe in Kenya," Ayuel said. He could hear the shooting in the distance, but it hadn't come closer during the night. "They'll have to find a place for us now. I just want to be safe and go to school."

The boys quickly ate some of the maize, then covered the pot with a shirt. "Ayuel and I will carry the pot between us for the first part of the trip," Madau said. "Is something the matter, Gabriel?"

Gabriel had picked up his pack, then set it down, breathing heavily. "Maybe, I shouldn't take so much," he said.

"You starting to feel weak again? Here, put some stuff in mine," Ayuel said, opening up his grain sack. They all had acquired such bags and fashioned them in a way to be slung over a shoulder or carried on their backs.

Ayuel felt excited about the move. Although the shelling continued, fear hadn't dampened his positive mood. With teachers in charge, he felt more secure about this journey, but he thought about the first terrifying trip when, as young children, they had been left to take care of each other. After nine months in Pochalla, he was probably twelve years old by now and experienced in traveling. He wore his best T-shirt and pants that came just below his knees. White athletic shoes protected his feet. He felt healthy and strong as they followed their instructors toward a new—and hopefully better—life.

All day they walked among the crowds, stopping only to sip water from their plastic jugs and once to eat some more of their maize. "To lighten the load," Madau had said.

"Wonder what the towns will be like," Ayuel said. "I think we go through Pakok where Aleer may have gone. I hope that camp was better than ours—I mean in the beginning when we nearly starved to death."

"Worse," Madau said. "I met some people who came to Pochalla from Pakok, thinking it might be better, but it wasn't."

"You all right, Gabriel?" Ayuel noticed his cousin lagging behind. The boys were taking turns carrying his pack.

"Yeah." After a few minutes he added. "I am just tired. It's a long walk." He was huffing and struggling to keep up.

"Maybe we should tell…"

Suddenly, exploding missiles scattered the crowd. Boys dashed for cover though there was no place to hide. Ayuel turned and saw a large number of tanks pursuing them at the base of the knoll they had just climbed. Planes roared overhead. *Boom!* Bombs exploded on either side leaving gaping holes in the ground and flinging shrapnel in every direction. The pot of maize slipped from his grasp as he ran through the mounting mayhem.

Ayuel felt something hit his lower legs and nearly tripped. Assuming he'd stumbled over a dead branch, he ran on. After a while he became aware that he was sweating profusely. Lightheaded, he staggered and fell. Only then he saw a slice of flesh, nearly the size of his hand, hanging from his left calf. Bright red blood soaked his shoes. Then he noticed a large piece of metal embedded in his right shin. Without thinking, he grabbed it and pulled it out, only to realize it had burned his hand. He heard his own voice cry out in agony. People ran past him. His friends were gone. The stench of gunpowder was mixed with the smell of blood, smoke and earth. Behind him came the grinding of tanks and the crack of guns. Two young boys stopped.

"We'll get a teacher!" said one.

The tanks veered to the left. The boys dashed off to the right.

Ayuel pressed the flesh back in place and held it with his hand. In a few minutes the boys returned. "We couldn't find anyone. There are dead and wounded people—and body parts—everywhere."

"I think I can walk," Ayuel said. "Here, help me up."

The boys pulled him up, one on either side. Releasing the grip on his leg, he left the flesh to dangle, and wiped his bloodied hands on his trousers.

"Here's a sturdy stick to help you walk."

"Thanks. Now, hand me my water jug."

The boys exchanged puzzled looks. The one who appeared older said, "Don't you know you shouldn't drink water when you've been hurt like this? It might cause *tetanus!*"

No, Ayuel had not heard that, but he said no more.

One carried his water, the other picked up his pack. They walked beside him into the evening and throughout the night. His tongue remained so dry he gagged trying to swallow. As his heart pounded rapidly, he gasped for breath and thought about Gabriel doing the same.

The bombardment finally stopped. Around four o'clock in the morning, Ayuel sat down to rest. He hugged his water jug and wondered if there was anything to the tetanus scare. It was such a horrible illness that, in some tribes, the elders pulled the lower six permanent teeth of children. That was to enable feeding in case the child ever got lockjaw. He certainly didn't want to get that.

Just as he pulled himself up with his walking stick, Beny called out to him. "Hey, Ayuelo, are you hurt?" Out of the thousands walking in the pale predawn, it was utterly amazing to run across his friends. Gabriel limped along, his arms over the shoulders of Madau and Gutthier.

"I guess I am," he said as the gang approached. "Shrapnel from the bombs." Leaning on the stick, he stuck out his left leg.

"We'll go on now, your friends are here," said the young boys.

"Hey, thanks for helping me." When they were out of sight, Ayuel asked, "Have you ever heard of drinking water causing tetanus?"

"Never."

"Then hand me my water bottle."

"We're taking Gabriel to a first aid station just up ahead. He's just not at all well," Beny said, handing Ayuel his water. "Looks like you need to go, too." Beny bent and tried to examine his wounds, but it was too dark to tell anything.

"Your group left after we did," Ayuel said, taking a few more gulps of water. "Did they bomb the camp?"

"Yeah. The teachers had us sit on that slope of ground just outside of camp," Beny said, as they all began walking together. "They told us not to get up or run until they told us. We could hear the shelling getting louder, coming toward us. They explained that it would be more dangerous if the masses left all together, forming a huge target. Then planes flew over and dropped a bomb on the group next to us. Mr. Ayom, who was just a few feet in front of me, shouted 'Go!' and the other teachers yelled the same."

"Just as Angou, Beny and I started running, soldiers came up from nowhere and started shooting," Mac said.

"They hit Mr. Ayom and he fell on his stomach," added Angou.

"I went to help him with bullets zinging by my head," Beny said. "He said to go on, the Red Cross would get him. Guess I couldn't do anything."

"Could you see how he was wounded?" Ayuel asked.

"Looked like his arm was bleeding. I saw him take off his shirt and wrap up his wounds. I hope they didn't kill him. He's a good man."

*

Once Ayuel and Gabriel were seated in the long line of wounded at the first aid station, the others decided it was best to go on. Teachers monitored those needing attention. When they saw a person in urgent need, they took him to the front of the line. Such was the case for Gabriel, but Ayuel sat in place.

After an hour or so he spotted Mr. Kiir, his teacher from Panyido. He was checking to see if everyone had water. He also carried a couple of boxes of dried biscuits. Mr. Kiir noticed him at almost the same time. "Ayuel, I'm glad to see you!" He had a few more boys to check before coming to Ayuel. When he arrived, he patted Ayuel's head and said, "But I'm not glad to see you in this line. What happened?"

"I guess they got me, Mr. Kiir." He grinned broadly, comforted by the man's presence and concern. He stuck out his legs.

"Those are nasty wounds, but the medics will fix you up. Here, have a biscuit—or two." He whispered the last words as he slipped a double portion into his hand. "I see you still have some water. I'll be back in a bit."

When he returned, Mr. Kiir said, "The Red Cross took your friend Gabriel away in an ambulance. He's got severe problems. I don't know how he walked so far."

"God was with him," Ayuel said.

"Yes, and with you. I'll see to it that you get on a truck so you won't have to walk."

Mr. Kiir stayed with Ayuel until the medic began cleaning the wounds. That's the last he remembered until he woke up and saw the white bandages covering his legs below the knees.

Mr. Kiir leaned over him. "Now comes the easy part of the journey," he said, scooping him up in his arms and placing him on a blanket in the bed of a waiting truck. He handed him his pack and cleaned shoes. "I washed the blood off them, so they're wet, but they'll be dry when you need them."

"Thank you, so much, Mr. Kiir. Thank you." There were no more words he could think of to express how grateful he felt. "Where am I going?"

"Probably, all the way to Kapoeta. See you there or in Loki, Kenya."

★

Ayuel slept much of the day—even as the truck bounced over rough terrain—his head resting on the spare tire, covered with his blanket and his pack under his arm. Plastic sheeting was spread over the top of the truck held up by poles to keep out the sun and the sides were left open. The few times he sat up, he noticed they were passing columns of walking refugees. He spoke little with the other sick and wounded, too tired to make the effort.

A terrible smell, like death itself, lingered in the truck bed. Several of the wounded, not used to traveling in a vehicle, vomited over the railings from motion sickness—one not quite making it over the side. The boy leaned over Ayuel, reaching for the side of the truck, but erupting on Ayuel's chest. After cleaning that up and changing his shirt to one in his pack, Ayuel felt nauseated too, but somehow kept from throwing up. He lay back down and pulled his clean shirt up over his nose to block the odors.

When darkness fell, the Kenyan driver and a caretaker made their third stop and came back to check on the patients, bringing food and water. That's when they discovered the source of the deadly smell: a boy had died from his wounds and no one had noticed.

The driver and caregiver gently wrapped the body in a blanket and placed it away from the road, under a small tree. They covered it with dry bushes and briefly bowed their heads. Even if they'd had a shovel, the ground was too hard to dig. Ayuel remembered with sorrow that method from their first journey. *Children burying children.*

The caregiver then gave pills to those for whom they'd been prescribed and rewrapped a few bandages, but not his. "We're going to park under that tree up ahead for the night," the driver said. "We don't dare drive with headlights on."

"Will we go through Pakok, sir?" Ayuel asked, thinking of his brother Aleer who might have gone there.

"Oh, we passed that camp some time ago," the driver said. "Now, we're going to get some sleep."

Ayuel sat up the second day as he felt better. He noticed the land had become a vast expanse of desert, the earth cracked into odd-shaped pieces. In the distance behind him, he could see the columns of walkers under the scorching sun. "I feel sorry for them," he said to the boy beside him.

"Yeah, we're lucky to be shot up." The boy laughed, and Ayuel laughed with him. It was hard to know who was lucky. As they came to the town of Boma, the trucks merged with the walkers who were queuing up at ICRC water trucks to fill their jugs. The SPLA brought food, which they distributed to the trucks of wounded as well. But no sooner had their convoy left than Ayuel heard gunfire. He looked back and witnessed black smoke curling up from the town. *Thank God, my friends couldn't have gotten to Boma by now.*

No more deliveries of food or water came on the rest of the journey to Kapoeta. *What will the walkers do? Doesn't the U.N. know thousands of us are out here in this desert?* They crossed only one shallow stream. The truck stopped in the middle of the water and filled everyone's container, but other streams were dry beds of rock. Everyone had to get out and walk or be carried across to lessen the weight. Ayuel walked, clinging to the side of the truck, every step sending pain up his legs.

The afternoon of the second day from Boma, as they approached Kapoeta, they noticed a few dead bodies lying along the way. Not a good sign.

"The SPLA captured Kapoeta some time ago," said one of the wounded. "They wouldn't be doing this. Not now."

"This doesn't look like a battle," Ayuel said. "It looks like assassination. They're all Dinkas." He remembered what Donayok had said about Riek Machar breaking off from Garang's SPLA and going after the Dinkas. A helicopter buzzed over the convoy, hovered, then flew toward Kapoeta. Fear gripped him like the terror at the Gilo. "We'll probably go around the town."

"I'm thirsty and hungry, but I'd rather live," the boy beside him said.

Yet they seemed headed straight toward the town.

An hour later, the convoy pulled up to ICRC trucks where workers were hurriedly making a distribution. Ayuel, though frightened, looked with fascination out over the large town with several brick buildings. Townspeople were spreading black plastic over the tin roofs, apparently to make them less visible to the planes. People were scurrying around, digging foxholes or running out of town with bundles of belongings. The driver and caregiver quickly filled their water jugs, pitched a box of biscuits to the boys and passed around individual containers of cold milk—a curiosity they had never seen before. The two men then jumped into the front seats of the truck and took off.

EIGHTEEN

"HOW ARE WE TO LIVE?"

As their vehicle moved in the middle of the convoy, Ayuel watched the town of Kapoeta shrink in the distance. While it was still visible, Ayuel saw several planes fly over it, then gasped as the bombs fell. "They're Antonovs, built by the Russians," said a companion. "They'll completely destroy…"

Explosions cut off his words. The truck increased its speed. Black rolls of smoke mixed with fire curled skyward over the town. The Antonovs made a second, then a third sweep. Ayuel and his companions watched in horror.

"I hope my friends weren't in Kapoeta yet," Ayuel said. "I don't think anyone could live through this."

"I think my older sister's there," his companion said, rubbing his eyes. "Will this never stop?"

"Not until we are old enough and powerful enough with our education to get guns and kill all the Arabs," Ayuel said between clenched teeth. "In the name of all those who've died, we've got to at least do that."

"We'll be rich and buy Antonovs and bomb the capitol Khartoum and kill all their children."

"But we need some help from Christian countries."

The truck sped through the town of Narus. As night fell, Ayuel was surprised to see the headlights illuminated on all the vehicles. A few minutes later, the driver honked his horn several times along with the other trucks in the convoy as they each passed a marker. When all were across and well beyond the marker, the trucks stopped. "What's going on?" asked the companion.

"We must be in Kenya!" exclaimed Ayuel. Cheers and applause rang out from the passengers in the trucks.

The driver and caretaker got out and came around. "We're safe. We're in Kenya now," the driver said. "We'll stay here awhile, put in some petrol and have a bite to eat. I've got a pot of beans up front. We will be in Lokichoggio tonight."

Ayuel couldn't get the images of Kapoeta out of his mind.

*

Although Lokichoggio—often called Loki—was a large town with a regular hospital, huge canvas tents were set up to house the wounded. Ayuel took a place alongside his riding companions with whom he formed a bond of shared experiences. Since the camp in Kenya still was not ready for the thousands of refugees pouring into the country, they would stay in Loki for now. The boys who were able built *tukuls* and settled in.

Ayuel began walking short distances every day but his legs still felt stiff and sore. Since they hadn't kicked him out of the hospital, he kept his place and let the Red Cross workers bring him the meager portions of gruel. He really wasn't up to standing in long food lines. At the end of the week, he had just returned from a stroll with his walking stick and sat down on his mat when he heard a familiar voice behind him. "Hey, Ayuel, I wondered if I would know anyone here." As Ayuel turned, joy leapt to his throat. There stood his good friend and mentor, his cousin Donayok. "Were you hurt?"

Ayuel extended his hand and blinked back the dampness forming in his eyes.

"Hi, Donayok. Good to see you. I'm not as bad as some of these guys. Sit down. How did you get here so fast?"

Donayok squatted as though he might not stay long. "Well, you know Group One left first. We escaped before the bombing at Pochalla. Then I took my group around Kapoeta and, thanks be to God, the Red Cross trucks caught up with us. Otherwise, we'd be lying dead out in the desert. I hear there was a terrible attack on Kapoeta."

"There was. I saw it from the convoy." Ayuel shifted his position. Being in the hospital tent had given him lots of time to think. "Donayok, how are we going to live in this world?"

"What do you mean?"

"Well, when we were just little kids, our own government bombed our villages and killed our families. In Ethiopia, we got chased out with guns and tanks that pushed us into the river. I think Aleer probably died after the Gilo. We came to Pochalla. Bombed again. Chased out once more after nine months. They killed all the Dinkas in Kapoeta. Now we're somewhere in Kenya. They probably don't want us here either; the government still doesn't know where to put us. Where and how are we supposed to live? We're still children." Ayuel waved his arms around as he spoke. Putting his thoughts into words increased the anger and passion.

Donayok placed his elbows on his knees and nodded his head. "That's a big question." He thought a while. "You know, Ayuel, everything comes to an end. All these bad things become history. After our seventeen got to Ethiopia and we lost Chuei and Malual, things did get better. We had schools and food. There were lots of good people who helped us, like your teacher, Mr. Kiir. In Pochalla, Bishop Taban and Manute Bol came. They cared. We had a fine Christmas. We finally got food. Your wounds are healing. When you move to a new place it's not good at first, but then later it is."

"But people die. They don't come back." Though his anger had subsided, his sorrow had not.

"It does test our faith. Tell you what, why don't you limit your worries to your brother Aleer. Just think about him. Pray for him. You don't know for sure that he died."

Ayuel swallowed hard and blinked his eyes. He didn't want Donayok to see him cry, so he changed the subject. "When you were at the Red Cross trucks, did you see those little containers of cold milk?"

"No, but if I see any, I'll bring you one." Donayok smiled, got up and shook Ayuel's hand. "Got to see if any of my charges are here under the tents."

Ayuel watched this young man of wisdom disappear into the crowds and tried to imagine Aleer sitting in front of a neat *tukul*, chatting with new friends—alive, well and at peace.

Three weeks after their arrival, other groups from Pochalla started trickling in and, several days later, Ayuel was united with his old friends. Though skinny and bruised, Beny, Monyjok, Gutthier and Madau had made it through alive and without serious injuries. Ayuel no longer stayed under the hospital tent as his wounds had sufficiently healed, and he wore only light bandages.

The friends sat in swirls of red dust under one of the few trees and caught up on what had happened while they'd been apart. Mac and Angou were off playing soccer with other friends.

"So all of you were in Kapoeta during the big attack?" Ayuel asked. "That must have been really awful."

"The worst," Beny said. "They are vicious, evil people. You said you saw the first Antonovs. We arrived during a lull in the fighting. We were told to dig foxholes by the river and not to wear white, which would be too easy to see. When the bombing started again, I was in the foxholes with Mac and Angou. Poor kids, they were crying; they were so scared. The bombs fell everywhere. Trees split in two right in front of us. It went on and on. We thought it would never stop."

"I'd hoped none of you were there yet." Ayuel frowned and squeezed his eyes tight.

"You'd hear the roar of the planes, then explosions and then crashing," Monyjok said. "I never heard so much crashing and smashing. Then huge balls of fire and black smoke boiled up. Those brick buildings they'd covered with black plastic just crumbled. Nothing was left—not a tree, not a building. The *tukuls* all burnt to the ground."

"Thousands of people died," Madau said. "It was absolutely the worst attack we'd been through. There were three others on the way, but nothing like this."

"We saw them snatching people, carrying some of them off and stuffing them in their vehicles. Others they chopped up with axes—just like in Unity. People screaming—women and little kids—it was horrible. Sickening. The government didn't just recapture the town from the SPLA, they totally destroyed it."

"From the truck, I couldn't imagine anyone living through it. And we were a long way from the bombing," Ayuel said. "I was praying hard, but why does God let these things happen?"

"I don't know, but God makes the choices," Beny said. "As soon as the planes and tanks left, everyone ran. I grabbed the hands of Mac and Angou and took off. I didn't want to lose those two. We just followed the crowds and made it to Narus where we stayed a day or so and then came on to Loki. Thieves are everywhere, even with a lot of police around. Someone snatched my cooking pot in the market."

"I thought we'd be safe in Kenya. At least they aren't shooting us," Madau said. "Samuel was wounded. He's supposed to be in the tent hospital here but we couldn't find him. The Red Cross made several ambulance trips back and forth, or he may have been brought by plane."

"He's hurt pretty bad," Beny said. "We saw Red Cross workers pick him up before we ran. At the hospital here, they have people lying all over the ground under the tents. There are so many it's hard to find any one person."

"I know. I was there. Donayok came by to see me," Ayuel said. "But I never saw a wounded person I knew."

"I'm glad Donayok made it. We found Gabriel there," Madau said, his voice brightening. "He's better. They gave him some pills and something that smells funny to breathe in."

"But he's getting good care," Beny said. "You'll never guess who else I ran across in the tent. Mr. Ayom!"

"Really! After he got shot in Pochalla?"

"He lost two fingers," Beny said. "The bullet hit his hand and went straight up his arm next to the bone. The Red Cross picked him up, just as he said they would. He's staying with Mr. Mayen now, in his *tukul.*"

*

After three months in Loki, word spread that the "unaccompanied minors," as they were now called, would be leaving soon for Kakuma, site of the new refugee camp. Ayuel stood in line with Beny for water at the tank trucks, brought by the International Red Cross. Deliveries of both food and water were infrequent.

"Do you suppose it will be this hot in Kakuma?" Ayuel leaned on his stick to relieve pressure on first one leg then the other. Walking was easier now, with no need for assistance, but standing still made his legs ache.

"Probably hotter," Beny said. "It's farther south and closer to the equator. Mr. Ayom says the schools will be better and a lot of people speak English there."

"Mr. Kiir told me the teachers who came with us will become the caretakers in Kakuma and we will have Kenyan teachers. I just want to get a good education and learn to talk English better."

"I want to learn to read the books that explain about this stupid war," Beny said, waving about the two empty plastic jugs he carried.

Ayuel's fists clenched. "All I want to do is kill the Arabs for what they've done."

Beny began to rub his chin, which he always did when he was thinking. "In that Peace and Reconciliation class I took in Panyido, they taught us that we should love our enemies, be forgiving. I feel the old hatred and desire for revenge coming back after what I saw in Kapoeta. Okay, the Bible says to love your enemies. So you say to your enemy, 'I love you, Enemy.' And he answers by pointing a gun in your face. What do you do then?"

"I don't know," Ayuel said as they took a few more steps in the long line. A sharp pain shot up his shin. "I don't see any other way than to shoot them all. How can you love monsters like that?"

"I want to find out how. In the class, the priest was always saying, 'Define the problem. Then search for a solution.' We need to find out the *reason* they are killing us."

At fourteen, Beny's thoughts ran deep, but as Ayuel watched his friend's sun-baked lips moving, he wondered if the heat had gotten to his brain. His own mouth was too dry to comment. He nodded as if in agreement and looked up the line ahead of them. It would be another hour to the water tanks.

Thankfully, Beny dropped that subject. A little later, however, he said, "Hey, I found out why we didn't get supplies all that time in Pochalla."

"Why? That makes me so angry. I could understand before we built the airstrip—the weather and bad roads. But Bishop Taban said..." Ayuel's tongue stuck to the roof of his mouth. He would just listen.

"I'm sure the bishop tried to send food like he said, but the government of Sudan would not give them permission!" exclaimed Beny. "They have to *allow* relief workers in. And if they want to drop supplies, the organizations have to tell the government the time and place. That's what happened when they bombed the SPLA cattle and killed some boys. They knew where we would be waiting, so they got there ahead of the relief planes and bombed us."

"That's so evil."

"They did the same thing while we were walking to Kapoeta. They blocked the roads in case anyone tried to help us. Different relief organizations came regularly once a week before we got to Boma, and then they stopped after that. We couldn't understand why. The desert was so dry. We thought they had forgotten us or didn't care. But the government just *wanted* to starve us. The teachers said we would find water at the Koragarap River, but when we got there, we found only puddles of muddy water."

"What did you do?" This was interesting and fueled Ayuel's anger.

"There were two ways and they both took a long time. We filled our cooking pots with the muddy water and added ashes. When it settled, the water on top was clear. Or for those who could find Amoyoak roots, you could do the same thing. Put them in the pot of muddy water and wait for the dirt to settle. The roots purified it. We got tired of waiting and ate the mud."

"I could eat some mud right now," Ayuel said with a sigh. They took a few more steps closer to the tanks.

*

In July, the Dinka month of *Lal*, more than a year after being chased out of Panyido, the teachers announced that all the children, wounded or not, would ride in trucks to the new camp at Kakuma, Kenya. The desert was too brutal to walk across. Again they would leave in an orderly fashion according to their original groups. It would take four to five weeks to transport thousands of boys, as well as the families, with multiple trips by all the trucks the United Nations could muster.

Ayuel's legs had healed, leaving only ugly scars, and he traveled in the same truck as Madau, Gutthier and Gabriel. After the long rest in Loki,

Gabriel's condition seemed better. He carried a package of capsules to take regularly and something called an inhaler to help him breathe. The four sat with their backs against the sides of the truck bed, feet to feet with others from their village. On the way, the boys were in high spirits, singing old school songs and hymns. Recently they learned that Kiir Chol—the boy who had composed the song they'd all sung while waiting for Dr. John Garang—had been found among the dead at the Gilo River. Over and over they sang his song in memory: *I am the hope of my people, I am the leader of tomorrow.*

"Wonder what Kakuma will be like," Gabriel said, gazing out over the barren landscape.

"I'm afraid it will be like this. Hot, windy, a few small trees," Ayuel said. "But we will live in safety. And it will be our home."

"We'll have to learn to speak Swahili," Gutthier said. "That's what most of the tribes in the camp speak. And the government and educated people speak English. Turkana is the tribe living in the village of Kakuma. I don't know what they're like or the language they speak."

"How did you learn all that, 'Funny Ears'?" asked Madau.

"These ears hear a lot. I've been asking around." Gutthier grinned proudly at his knowledge.

Up ahead loomed a wide, flat plateau. A little village huddled to one side. Gray lines of smoke from cooking fires rose against the cloudless blue sky. "Look, I think that's Kakuma," Ayuel said, pointing to the area. Heat waves wiggled the panorama. A lone hawk soared overhead and landed in a twisted barren tree. As they neared their new home, the boys saw thousands of people already at the camp site, erecting poles for *tukuls*, mixing mud and grass, carrying water, cooking maize—the domestic activities of people at peace.

NINETEEN

FORMING NEW TIES

One month after Ayuel's arrival in Kakuma in August of 1992, the Dinka month of *Hor*, Ayuel and Gabriel stood outside their tent and watched a convoy of trucks crawl into the Kakuma Refugee Camp.

"That should be Group Eight," Gabriel said. "They are supposed to move into Zone Four next to us."

"But the directors won't let us go meet the newcomers, not until they're all here and settled in," Ayuel said. "That will probably take days." He felt anxious about the welfare of Beny, Samuel and Monyjok. He hoped that somehow his brother Aleer had made it to Loki and would be among them, but he knew how unlikely that was.

"They can get permission to visit us, I think," Gabriel said.

"Maybe," Ayuel said, shaking his head. "Whatever, we'll have to wait. Let's get out of this wind and heat." The United Nations had set up white canvas tents for the boys until they could build their permanent *tukuls*. The sun beat down in the afternoons, sometimes sending the temperature as high as 135°F. Ayuel and Gabriel used a hand broom to dust off their blankets that lay on plastic sheeting over bare ground. The red gritty dust, whipped up by the ceaseless winds, covered everything.

"Wish they'd start the schools." Ayuel lay down and placed his forearm across his closed eyes. Soon he drifted off to sleep, the custom here to escape the afternoon heat.

Two weeks before his group's arrival, he later learned, the Family Communities had been divided along tribal lines to promote solving their own conflicts, but when new families who had survived the Garang-Machar wars poured into the camp, fighting broke out between the Nuers and the Dinkas.

Ayuel was glad that the unaccompanied minors were left mixed, for the boys of different tribes had bonded by living together in previous camps. Refugees from all over Southern Sudan as well as other African countries swelled the numbers to several times that of Panyido. With so many new arrivals, the unaccompanied children were encouraged to look for family members, even distant relatives, who would take them in.

As back in Duk, children were cherished here, and because many parents had lost their own, they readily took in any young relatives they found. As before, the few girls were easily adopted by strangers who had lost their own children. The boys who could not locate a relative were placed in four Minor Zones of mixed tribes with 400 to 500 each. Ayuel's Group Six merged with Zone Three. Security was tight due to the tension in camp and the threat from the local Turkanan tribe.

Everyone in the camp had to register. In turn, they were each given a Registration Card with their official name, birthplace, birth date, parents' names and if dead or alive and date of arrival. When Ayuel registered, he decided, for no thought-out reason, to give his Christian name James. For his surname, instead of Leek, he wrote Garang, because his family had always said he looked like his Uncle Garang. That name was also thought to bring luck—and of course he was aware that the Sudanese People's Liberation Army leader, Dr. John Garang, carried that name.

"And when were you born?" the registrar asked, noticing he had left that part blank.

"I don't remember, sir, but I believe I am twelve years old by now."

The man wrote something in his book and again on the card. As Ayuel left, he looked at his new card and saw his birth date as January 1, 1980. Later he learned that nearly everyone else in camp had been born the first of January, of some year.

★

"Hey, sleepyhead."

Ayuel felt a foot nudge his side. He moved his arm, which had remained across his face drenched in sweat, and sat up. Feeling a bit dizzy in the heat, he said, "Beny, is that really you? And Monyjok and Samuel? So they let you come over. How'd you find us?" Fully awake now, he jumped up and they all shook hands.

"They let us look at a map of where everyone is staying," Beny said. "They're trying to be strict, but they're still pretty confused as to what rules to follow. How are you guys?"

Beny's grin reflected Ayuel's own happiness at the reunion.

"We're all right," said Gabriel, who had never gone to sleep. He came over and sat on Ayuel's blanket. "Good to see all of you again. I take my pills and Ayuel is all healed up. We don't like the heat. It's much hotter here than Panyido. Gutthier, Madau and eleven others stay here with us. They're off at the Family Community looking for relatives to live with."

"They're really looking for girls," Ayuel said with a grin. They all gave a knowing laugh. Gutthier, especially, was fascinated with girls. "So, Samuel, you're all well now? I heard you were in the hospital in Loki, but no one could find you. I was there too."

"Yeah, I was there. This is what those Arabs did to me." Samuel showed the scars on his right hand and thigh. Then he pulled up his shirt and pointed to a long jagged scar on his side. "This was the worse one. A bullet went in here. They had to sew up the gash."

"Shrapnel," Ayuel said, sticking his legs out straight in front of him.

"But you guys are alive," Monyjok said, squatting down in the dust. Short and slight, he had a keen intellect and was always looking for solutions. "God brought us all through, but this killing has got to stop. Someday we'll figure out a better way."

"That's what I think," Beny said. "If we are doing something wrong, we need to find out what and stop doing it. The Bible says that there is a time for war and a time for peace. We need to forgive our enemies. It's time for this war to be over and this horrible life to turn to peace."

"I say kill all the Arabs," Ayuel said without his usual passion. He didn't want to get into a useless discussion right now with his friend who was always struggling with the idea of loving one's enemies. He changed the subject. "We eat in the mornings now. The wind isn't so strong then, but we still get a lot of this grit in our food."

"Is there a river around here?" asked Samuel. "There wasn't even plastic sheeting for shade over the truck bed. We all need a bath."

Gabriel and Ayuel looked at each other and raised their eyebrows. "Lots of *dry* riverbeds," Ayuel said.

"And one tiny stream," added Gabriel. "In Sudan and even Ethiopia, this would be the rainy season, but we've had only one rain in the month we've been here in Kenya. Some people go sit in that little stream all day to keep cool. We did it once, but it was so crowded. Nasty, really. I'd just as soon sleep in the afternoons until school starts."

"Where do you get water then?" asked Beny. "You can't drink water that people have been sitting in—and doing no telling what else."

"It's piped in from a well," Ayuel said. "You have to go to one of the water taps and stand in line for three or four hours to fill five-gallon plastic jugs. Or if you go at night, usually there is only a thirty-minute wait."

"We all go together then, because it's so dangerous," Gabriel said. "Especially when Nuers and Dinkas are fighting. And then there are the Turkanans. They're the local goat and camel herders who will kill you for a bar of soap or a shirt. We saw some carrying spears and shields like the Dinkas. Since they're herders too, we thought they would be like us, but they're not. They sneak into the camp and steal from the storerooms or any tents that aren't guarded and rape the women gathering firewood outside of camp."

"You asked about bathing," Ayuel said. "It's not like in Panyido where we could just jump in the river. Here you put precious water in a gallon jug and pour it over yourself, rub on soap, and then rinse off. Conditions are a little better in the Family Community."

"Maybe we'll find some relatives. You think Gutthier will find you one?" Samuel asked.

"If not, I'm going with him and doing some serious looking." He paused, then turned to Beny. "Did Aleer ever show up in Loki? Do you know... ?"

"Ayuelo, I wish I knew." Beny shook his head. "Some boys did come to

Loki from Pakok, but they didn't know your brother. I asked. You know how it is when there are thousands of people—and all the confusion. That doesn't mean he didn't go there."

★

A few weeks later, Ayuel and his half-brother Gutthier arrived at the gate of the Family Community, late in the afternoon as people began stirring again. The pole-fence gate wasn't locked, so they unhooked the leather strap and slipped through. Naked toddlers stared at them and a few skinny chickens pecked in the dirt. They approached two women who were sharing a pail of soapy water to wash their clothes.

"Pardon me, Mama," Ayuel said. "We are here looking for relatives we could live with."

"Do you know anyone by the name of Leek?" asked Gutthier. Leek could be either the first or last name to be a relative, according to Dinka naming practice.

"That's a Dinka name all right, and this is the Dinka-Bor section," said one of the women, standing up and wiping her hands on her skirt.

"We escaped from the attack on Kapoeta, stayed in Loki a while and just got here last week," the younger of the women said. She wrung out a shirt, being careful to let all the water drip back into the pail. "We hardly know anyone, but keep asking. You'll find your people."

After thanking the friendly women, they followed the dusty path between the compounds, asking everyone they came across. No luck.

"Where are all the descendants of our grandfather? You'd think with descendants of all his wives, some of our relatives would have made it here," Gutthier said with a sigh.

"I think we're lost," Ayuel said. "We've made so many turns."

"We were facing the sun when we came through the gate. Now it's setting over there," Gutthier said. "No problem. Look, there're some girls playing volleyball." His voice lilted. "It's nicer here; I don't care if we don't go back." They stopped and watched, not daring to approach girls they didn't know.

Two boys who appeared to be about their age were playing pitch with a worn-out baseball at a very large compound of *tukuls* on the other side of the path. "Hello," Gutthier called out to them, loud enough for the girls to hear. "Do you know anyone around here named Leek?"

"Hello. There's Leekmaduk here in this compound," said one of the boys. They stopped their play to come over and shake hands. "I'm Maruon and this is my brother, Majur. Could he be your relative?"

"Leekmaduk was the name of our father's nephew from Duk." Ayuel's heart beat faster. He could barely remember Leekmaduk, but images of home flooded over him as he recalled scenes of family gatherings. "I remember he used to come visit us. Is he married now?"

"Wife and three little kids. Come this way."

Gutthier gave a glance back at the girls who had stopped their play and stood watching. He smiled at them before following Ayuel to their newfound relative.

They came upon Leekmaduk and his wife sitting in front of a *tukul* sipping warm tea.

"I think we've found some of your relatives, Leekmaduk," Majur said. "They say they're the sons of Chief Leek Deng."

"Welcome," said Leekmaduk, who was indeed the nephew. He shook hands with Ayuel and Gutthier and gave them a big hug. "I don't think I would have recognized you. Let's see." He held Gutthier by the shoulders at arm's length. "Aren't you the one they called 'Funny Ears'?"

"That's me, Gutthier," he said with a wide grin, glad to be recognized. "And this is Ayuel."

"Yes, of course. And your father and my father are brothers from the same two parents. My goodness, you boys have grown up! How happy I am to see you alive! This is my beautiful wife, Alual."

"Welcome," his wife Alual said, getting up from tending the pots over the charcoal fire and shaking their hands. "I am baking *daboo*. There will be plenty for you to stay and eat with us."

The smell of *daboo* brought back memories of his mother's cooking. He breathed in deeply.

"There are eighteen of us here in this compound," Leekmaduk said. "Majur, why don't you bring some tea out for our newcomers and mats for them to sit on?"

When they were all seated in a circle, drinking tea, the family shared their stories and were interested to learn what Ayuel and Gutthier had endured: the attack on Duk; their long, terrible journey together; a better life in Panyido with schools; the incredible crossing of the Gilo; Pochalla; Loki; and their arrival in Kakuma.

"My family miraculously survived the strike on Duk," Leekmaduk said, "but we fled the burning village. I don't think a *tukul* was left. We hid in the grass on the edge of town. After the bombing, soldiers came and shot the men. We watched them round up the women and girls and take them off. I've learned they were sold into slavery in the North.

"Most people set out for Ethiopia like you boys, but we stayed in the area around Bor for about three years. That's where Alual and I married and started our family. Then came the Bor Massacre... in 1991..." He paused to get control of his emotions, then continued, "The southern renegade forces, followers of Garang's rebel commander Riek Machar, ruthlessly attacked the civilians of this vast Dinka area, simply because they disagreed with the Dinka SPLA leader. Some say Machar didn't order it, but he surely knew the Khartoum government supplied the arms.

"Then Garang's army attacked the Nuer stronghold at Ayod. By then it wasn't safe to go to Ethiopia. We escaped with a cow and some supplies. We traveled with a smaller group to Kapoeta. We lived there a while until we were again attacked by government Arab forces."

"Some of our friends from Panyido were in that awful attack," Ayuel said. "Did you go to Loki?"

"Yes. We had some help, thanks be to God, from the International Red Cross. Again we lost everything, but escaped with our lives. Then the U.N. finally brought us by truck here to Kakuma. We had little ones with us so that made it especially difficult, but God is good."

Ayuel listened intently while his relatives finished sharing their stories, at the same time savoring every morsel of the bean and maize dish. Leekmaduk explained that with money he earned at odd jobs in the camp, Alual was able to buy herbs, spices and other extras in the town of Kakuma. He also learned that the two boys they'd first spoken to were his cousins on his mother's side. Being among his people from Duk lifted his spirits and filled him with the warmth of well-being.

When the sun dropped below the horizon, taking with it the day's heat, Ayuel realized it was time for him and Gutthier to head back to Zone Three. "Thank you, Leekmaduk and Alual. The meal was wonderful. We haven't eaten like this since our mothers cooked for us." The boys got up and rinsed out their bowls as the other children were doing.

"You don't need to be considered 'unaccompanied minors' anymore," Leekmaduk said. "You may both have a home right here with us and enjoy Alual's cooking every day. Only a woman knows the secret of making ordinary food really delicious."

"We would love to do that," Gutthier said, pressing away a tear with the heel of his hand. "I feel like this is home."

"So do I," Ayuel said. "We'll build a *tukul* here among you, but we want to keep our place with our friends, too."

"We've been with some of them for over five years," Gutthier said. "We've sort of raised each other."

"Of course you have," Leekmaduk's wife said. "You've suffered so much together, but you can have two homes."

After all the hardships of living as orphan children, at last they were part of a family with a mother and father. In the following days, they built a *tukul* with the help of Leekmaduk, Maruon and Majur.

*

Schools opened and classes formed, with Maker Thiang still the Director of Education as in Panyido. Ayuel learned that unlike the volunteers from the refugee population in Panyido, who might be anyone with a minimum of education, these teachers were paid for their services. Most held a teacher's certificate, but some were gifted high school graduates who had demonstrated skills in a particular subject.

With no buildings yet, the children sat under trees by the dry riverbanks. Math and English were the only subjects offered at first, and teachers with those specialties rotated among the classes of about thirty-five students each. Mr. Kiir, like many of the other Panyido teachers, became a caretaker of unaccompanied minors in Kakuma. He now lived in the Family Community.

Director Thiang had somehow managed to bring along the scholastic records of those from Panyido. As a result of Ayuel and Gutthier's good grades, they were moved up, at age twelve, to Class Four. Beny, two years older, was promoted to Class Six. They eagerly pursued their studies with determination, still clinging to the goal of getting a good education.

Ayuel and Gutthier usually stayed in Minor Zone Three during the week so they could study with the other orphan boys and then spent the weekends at Leekmaduk's compound. In the zone, Ayuel had just finished his turn of pounding grain on an afternoon of 130°F heat and decided to go sit in the stream. It was even too hot to nap. Every time the temperature got this high with the wind and dust, people came down with malaria, dysentery or typhoid. On the way to the stream, he came across Beny, walking with a wet T-shirt draped over his head. "Leaving so soon?" he called out to him.

When Beny didn't answer, he ran to him. "Are you all right, Beny?"

"I feel dizzy and weak," Beny mumbled. "I'm so thirsty, but I didn't dare drink from the stream. People are getting cholera and malaria. I don't know what's got me."

"I've heard about the illnesses. Here, put your arm over my shoulders. I'll help you to the Medical Clinic."

With several stops to rest, they finally made it to the clinic in Zone One, only to find a long line of sick people, sitting and moaning. "You stay here," Ayuel said, "I'll bring you some water."

He returned several minutes later with a jug of water from the tap. "Let's wet that T-shirt again," he said, pouring some of the precious water on his head covering. "Drink slowly."

"Thanks," Beny said. "Mr. Ayom is up ahead in line. He's sicker than I am. They may take him out of turn. Someone keeps checking on him."

"I'll go see him," Ayuel said. He moved up the line and easily spotted Beny's former teacher sitting with his head in his hands. "Hello, Mr. Ayom. Beny is behind you in line. He says 'hi.'" He made a gesture to shake hands.

"No, no. Don't touch me or anyone. It's the cholera." When he waved his hand, Ayuel noticed the two fingers missing, shot off by the Arabs in Pochalla.

"May I bring you anything, sir? Water?"

"No thanks, Ayuel. They're coming to get me next, they said." His head dropped back in his hands. "I don't want to be put in that hospital. You can get all kinds of diseases there. Just need some pills. Now, you go wash your hands good with soap, and don't sit in the stream. Say 'hi' to Beny. Sorry he's sick."

*

After another check on Beny, Ayuel went home and followed all the hygiene rules. Two days later, he found his friend in his *tukul*, asleep and sweating profusely. "How's he doing?" he asked Monyjok, who sat beside him, changing the wet cloths on his forehead.

"I think he'll live," he said, looking up with a big welcoming smile. "They gave him pills to take for cholera. He refused to stay at the hospital— it's so smelly there. No place for a sick person. The wind blows down the tents and uproots the poles. It's not even safe to be a patient. Our *tukuls* are sturdier. Not only do they have all the diseases, but there's a lot of mental illness—post-traumatic stress, as they call it, and depression. But Samuel and I are looking after Beny."

"I knew you would. Heard anything about Mr. Ayom?"

"He's in the main hospital in Zone One. That's where they take the worst cases."

"He said he didn't want to be kept in that hospital."

"Not much he could do—unconscious."

Beny opened his eyes. "Hey, Ayuelo, thanks for coming by." He closed his eyes again. "I hate missing school." He picked up a book that was by his side. "When we were passing through Kapoeta, just before the bombing, a captain with the SPLA, Mr. Luol Chol, gave this to me. It's by Majer Gai. It tells about how the Sudanese People's Liberation movement began. I'd just started trying to read it. There are so many words I don't understand, I have to find a teacher to ask what they mean. But I can't read or think like this."

"We'll talk about it later. Tell me what you learn," Ayuel said. "You just get well. Feels like it's no more than a hundred degrees today."

TWENTY

FAMILIES LOST AND FOUND

Ayuel and Gutthier headed to the Leekmaduk compound for the weekend. Ayuel looked forward to Alual's cooking, playing soccer with Majur and Maruon, having small children around and talking about life in Duk with those who shared his memories. Here he found the nurturing warmth of family they'd both yearned for all this time.

On their way, they stopped by Beny's *tukul*. Although he had fully recovered from cholera several weeks before, his housemates still kept a close check on him. His good friend Monyjok greeted them on his way out. "Beny's got some good news. I'll run along and let him tell you."

"Thanks. See you later," they called after him.

Beny was humming a familiar Dinka song and packing a small bag.

"You going somewhere, Beny?" Ayuel asked, peeking through the doorway.

"Hello, guys," he sang out. "I'm going home, home, home!"

"What?" Gutthier questioned. "You found your family?"

Beny stepped outside, grinning from ear to ear. "I couldn't believe it. I was just leaving the UNHCR office where I'd been helping sort papers. Someone tapped me on the shoulder. I turned but didn't recognize the young woman looking at me. 'Do you know you are related to my family?' she said and held her arms out wide. Then I realized she was my mother's niece. Her eyes are so like my mama's. I burst into tears and we hugged each other. She was crying too."

"I know what that feels like," Ayuel said.

"Did she know anything about your parents or brothers and sisters?" Gutthier asked.

"No. She said they got separated from the others in the family compound during the attack on our hometown, Panrieng. Her name is Ayar, and she has a husband and three little ones at home. An older daughter's here in school. I was over there last night. Can she ever make food taste good! They want me to live with them. I'm headed there now."

"We're happy for you," Ayuel said, remembering his first meeting with Leekmaduk and his other new-found relatives. "Nothing's better than going home."

Beny grabbed his bags and the three boys ran to the Family Community, eager to be back with family members.

*

Life gradually improved in Kakuma, much in the way it had at Panyido in Ethiopia—much as Donayok had predicted. Except now, in addition, both Ayuel and Beny had a family to go home to on the weekends or more often if they chose.

As Ayuel continued to struggle with spiritual issues, he was pleased to see Christian leaders come in from Europe and the United States to establish a variety of churches: Episcopal, Presbyterian, Baptist, Lutheran, Pentecostal and Seventh-Day Adventist. The Catholic church provided aid and medical services until the completion of the main hospital building in Zone One. Jesuit Refugee Services and the Lutheran World Federation brought much-needed mental health clinics and counseling.

The Catholic churches built elaborate brick houses of worship with roofs of tin sheeting and bell towers. The African Inland church put up an impressive building also. Ayuel and his friends attended them all, but he liked the Baptist music best. Beny's main allegiance remained Catholic, but he joined in with other religious group activities, too.

For the few Muslims in camp, there was a mosque that regularly called their faithful to prayers. Their worship was peaceful and not considered part of the radical Islamic government of Sudan. The Animists, who followed traditional spirit worship, blended in with the Christians, abandoning their animal sacrifice rituals.

The Episcopalian denomination, adhered to by most Dinkas like Ayuel, made up the largest group. He loved Sundays when they met under a large open-air shelter with a tin roof held up by wooden poles. On Saturday evenings, the young people gathered by the riverbank for singing, dancing and praising God. Ayuel found that the long prayers brought healing for his emotional and spiritual wounds, but dangers still lurked in the camp—tribal fights, looting and attacks by the local Turkanan tribe.

*

"Ayuelo! Come quick! Monyjok's hurt."

Ayuel looked up from the science book he was studying in the shade of his *tukul* in Zone Three. Beny motioned frantically for him to follow. When he caught up with his friend, he questioned as they ran, "What's happened?"

"It's the Turkanans. They attacked him while he was reading under a tree, over by the dry river bed."

A small group of people stood watching when the boys arrived. Some IRC workers were carefully lifting Monyjok's slight, crumpled body onto a blanket. Blood was running out his mouth and ear. Beny knelt beside him and took his hand. "Live, Monyjok. We need your wisdom," he whispered.

Ayuel heard a faint moan. "I think he's alive." He thought of the many times Monyjok had helped them think through problems.

Two men tied the ends of the blanket to a long pole and raised it to their shoulders. Tears slid down Beny's face as they walked along beside the rescuers.

"We saw them," said one of the onlookers. "He was just sitting there reading when four or five Turkanans came up behind him with spears and a club. "They just beat him up. He didn't have a chance. But when we shouted at them, they took off. Someone ran for help."

When they got to the IRC office twenty minutes later, an ambulance was waiting. The men placed Monyjok inside and an aide began cleaning his wounds.

Beny and Ayuel stood around for fifteen minutes or so. "What are they waiting for? Why don't they get him to a hospital?" Beny questioned to no one in particular.

One of the IRC workers who had carried Monyjok said, "We're waiting for a driver."

"Wish I could drive." Beny talked rapidly into the air. He turned to Ayuel. "Monyjok's been my close friend ever since we met in Panyido. He's always looking for solutions. We both want to find a non-violent way of dealing with all the meanness in the world. Now he's a victim of that violence. Maybe there isn't a solution. He never wanted to hurt anyone. He just wanted peace." He paced about nervously, tears shining in his eyes.

"We'll pray for him," Ayuel said. "And you." He hadn't been as close to Monyjok as Beny, but he'd always admired him. He knew what it was like to lose a special friend.

Finally a driver arrived. He sat down behind the steering wheel but left his door open and drank from his canteen. Several minutes later, some men carried a sick woman and placed her in the ambulance. At last the driver closed the door, started the engine, and the vehicle crept out of camp toward the road to Loki.

Beny inquired daily for a report at the main hospital in camp but they had no word. After a week, Ayuel went with him. "They keep fairly good records," Ayuel said. "They're just slow."

"I know. That's how I found out Mr. Ayom had recovered from cholera. Hope we get that kind of news today."

The man behind the desk, who had been shuffling through papers looking for the friend's name, finally stopped and frowned. He looked up at Beny and then turned the paper around for him to read for himself. He pointed to Monyjok's name, after it was scrawled "Dead on ARR."

"He never even made it to the hospital," Beny said and turned away.

No matter how many died, each loss brought its own anguish, adding to the buildup of pain. "Thank you," Ayuel said to the man.

"Sorry, boys," he frowned.

★

The International Committee of the Red Cross set up a mail service at their office. Throughout their African network, an effort was launched to locate family members and to distribute information about those who had died. Large numbers gathered daily at the bulletin board outside their office building to read the posted names of those who had letters.

On their way home from classes, Beny and Ayuel arrived ahead of the crowd to make a routine check. "You know, I love staying with my relatives, but I still miss… Suppose we'll ever know what happened to them?" Beny asked. "So many died or were captured and sold into slavery."

"Or captured and sent to good schools like the survivors picked up at the Gilo River." Ayuel ran his finger down the posted list, looking for any relative's name. Only recently had they learned the fate of the boys captured at the Gilo crossing.

"Yeah, as evil as the Ethiopian army was, chasing and shooting us while we struggled in the water, they treated the ones they caught better than our own government treated us in Pochalla where we nearly starved to death."

"They just wanted to raise up good soldiers for their Ethiopian army. That's what I heard. Wonder if they captured Aleer." Suddenly Ayuel stopped and exclaimed, "Chol! Beny Ngor Chol. That's you. You've got a letter!"

"Let me see!" Once confirmed, the boys rushed into the office. Only three people were ahead of them in line to claim letters.

"It's better to know if they died, isn't it?" Beny asked nervously as he waited his turn.

"I'd want to know," Ayuel said. "I assume my family's all dead, but not really knowing is… I still hope for Aleer. Deng and my parents, I don't think could still be alive."

Finally, the man behind the desk handed Beny a sealed, crumpled envelope from the ICRC in a Ugandan camp.

After he signed for it, the boys went outside and sat on a wooden bench. "I hope and pray there is at least one person still alive."

"I hope so, too."

Beny carefully tore a notch in the corner of the envelope and then ripped the end off. He unfolded the letter and read aloud:

Dear Beny Ngor Chol,

I hope you are well as you receive this. I found your name on a Red Cross list as being in Kakuma. I am a distant cousin, but knew your parents. I have learned that your brother, Lueth Ngor Chol, survived the attack on the cattle camp near Panrieng in 1986, as well as earlier attacks in '82 and '83. He later joined the SPLA. In 1989 he was shot and died instantly, fighting for the cause of the Southern Sudanese liberation. Your sister Acuei is alive and well in the Internally Displaced Persons Camp in Khartoum, Sudan, taking care of your uncle Bol Chol.

"That's the uncle who was the Animist rainmaker and healer, not Acuil Chol, the one that wanted to take me into town to buy a shirt. I chose to go to the cattle camp to take Lueth supplies. Well, it's better he died fighting in a gun battle than being chopped up with axes. My sister Acuei was fourteen at the time of the attack. I've been so worried she was sold into slavery. Thank you, God, for sparing her that! And she's alive and well! There's more." Beny read silently, then folded the paper and pushed it back into the envelope. "My mother, father and stepmother—all confirmed dead. There's no mention of my younger brother Abui."

"What a terrible loss."

The boys sat in silence, shocked by the news. Ayuel's feelings mirrored his friend's. He hoped at least one member of his own family could still be alive—and well. "Do you remember my friend Mary A.?" Beny asked suddenly in a soft, wistful voice.

"Of course, she was the girlfriend you wanted to marry some day."

"Still do. She thought her mother was sent to a displacement camp in Khartoum. I wonder if Mary A. ever made it there, looking for her mother, or if she ever met my sister? That would be nice. I'll write to the cousin and see if he knows any more about Acuei. And if he's heard anything about my younger brother."

"Good. I'm glad your sister is still alive, and you know where she is. I'm happy for that."

★

The schools moved into large mud-brick buildings with tin roofs. Students sat on long rows of mud-dried logs or wooden benches, with about a hundred to a class. They were taught English, Swahili, science, geography, African history, Christian religion and arts & crafts. Agriculture classes and trade schools were set up so students could learn skills for making a living.

Classes ran from seven in the morning until two in the afternoon. All the teachers were certified now. Ayuel, now fifteen, and Beny, seventeen, were both eager students and often discussed what they'd learned with each other and their friends.

Refugees from Uganda, Ethiopia, Somalia, Rwanda, the Congo, Burundi and other countries poured in, escaping war or famine. Kakuma grew to hold 95,000 people, the largest refugee camp in all of Africa, with thatched huts spreading across the parched desert as far as the eye could see. Food rations that had been inadequate from the beginning—maize, beans, sorghum, oil, enough for one meal a day—now strained the facilities beyond capacity. The infertile soil could not be cultivated and the few trees by the dry riverbeds produced no fruit, thus making it impossible to supplement the meager diet. The distribution had been fair, delivered to group leaders in the zones, but providing safe storage for the food and preventing looting had become problems.

As a solution, distribution centers were set up for better control of the supplies. Each person now had to stand in long lines after school for his individual allotment. Often, after two or three hours, those last in line were turned away with nothing. The food rarely lasted the two weeks between deliveries and sometimes the next delivery could be several days overdue. The days without food were dubbed "Black Days."

On one of those Black Days, Ayuel sat in class and tried to concentrate on his teacher's words. He was telling about the Nubian kings of the sixth century who ruled in pre-Islamic times. Ayuel was interested in the great civilizations that once flourished in present-day Sudan, but all he could think about was the hope that food delivery would be today.

From his place in the middle of the room, he noticed Maruon from his family compound lingering outside the doorway. When the dismissal bell finally rang, he rushed out to see why he was there.

"You'll never believe what I have to tell you," his cousin said.

"Has the food delivery arrived?"

"Something better."

Ayuel could see the excitement in his cousin's eyes. *What could be better than the arrival of food?*

"Your brother Aleer is here! He's at home waiting for you. Come on."

Speechless and unbelieving at first, Ayuel slapped his hands over his face. Finally he said, "Aleer has come back from the dead. Thanks be to God!" With renewed energy in spite of his hunger, he hurried home alongside Maruon and found a large gathering of relatives and friends. He could smell rice cooking but his mind had now turned to his lost-and-found brother. He pushed through the crowd and saw a tall, handsome stranger talking rapidly and laughing between sentences. He blinked, his heart pounding, and dared hope he was seeing Aleer. It had been four years, and he would be seventeen now. As soon as their eyes met, the two brothers rushed into each other's arms.

"You've got to say everything all over again," Ayuel said through his tears of happiness. "Where did you go after the Gilo River? I want to know everything."

"You will. And I want to hear all about you." Aleer put his hands on Ayuel's shoulders and held him at arms length. "My, my, you've grown up. And so healthy."

Ayuel beamed with pride and stretched tall.

"Okay, I'll begin again with the Gilo. Like everyone else, I was crawling in the mud after I got across the river. I was so worried about you, Ayuelo. I was afraid you didn't make it. I got separated from Group Eight— Beny and the others. When I stood up, an SPLA soldier shouted at me to go to the left. Along with several hundred others, I made it to Pakok."

"Beny said that's probably where you went." Ayuel sat down with the others from the compound to listen to his big brother, perched on a stump.

"Pakok was a horrid, squalid place at first. I'd lost my possessions and there was no food. Mostly Eastern Equatorians lived there. They were setting up a refugee camp, but after a few days, a family took me in. A while later, I made my way to Maridi where I found our cousin, Agot. I stayed with her and went to school, where I got my primary certificate and started secondary. Their schools were quite good and really helped me improve my English. But since it was not a safe place, six of us decided to go south to Kenya. We followed the Pibor River and, because there'd been lots of rain, we had water to drink and plants to eat. We went through destroyed villages and picked up a cooking pot, calabash gourds and the like.

"We spent a short time in Kapoeta. Not many people lived in that bombed-out town, but the ones we met were generous, giving us food and clothing. When they told us most of the people from Panyido had gone to Kakuma, I knew I had to come look for you. And here you are!"

Ayuel, Aleer and their relatives in the compound talked far into the night, catching up on all that had happened to each other. Leekmaduk and his wife insisted Aleer live with them.

In the days to come, Ayuel wanted to spend as much time as possible with the only other surviving member of his immediate family. He'd lost and found him twice. Ayuel tagged around after him as he had done as a small boy, but they didn't fight or compete as they had done back in those normal times. He admired him now, just as both of them had looked up to their oldest brother Deng.

After that first night together, Aleer spoke little about what had happened to him. He was more serious and thoughtful now. He demonstrated a firm faith in God and seemed sure of himself and the beliefs he held. For the first time, Ayuel realized what a brilliant mind his brother had. Not only did Aleer read during every spare moment, but he was determined to complete high school in three years and then find a university where he could finish his studies.

TWENTY-ONE

OSAMA BIN LADEN

Late one afternoon a few months later, Ayuel and Beny found a spot of shade under a tree by the dry riverbed to study. Ayuel finished his English assignment and slipped his textbook into a plastic bag to protect it from the swirling dust.

Beny held on his knees a thick book by Francis Deng called *War of Visions: Conflicts of Identities in the Sudan.* His lips moved silently.

"You learning anything important about the war?" Ayuel asked Beny as Ayuel leaned back against the tree trunk and stretched. He rubbed the dust from his eyes.

"Some," Beny said not looking up.

"I've read part of Majer Gai's book that you lent me. That one looks even harder."

Beny pulled his concentration away from his book and looked up at Ayuel. "Not really, just longer. I'll be glad when I can read English with more understanding—not have to study each word. But this is really interesting. I'm learning about the attack on Unity that killed my family in 1986. It makes me angry."

"What's it say?"

"Control of oil is part of what this war's about. Guess we knew that, but this gives the background. The American company Chevron discovered

vast oil reserves near my village of Panrieng. That's just below the border
that separates northern and southern Sudan. The Addis Ababa peace
agreement that ended the first civil war in 1972 had given regional
autonomy to the South and hostilities settled down for a while."

"Guess it didn't do much good. We're still at war," Ayuel said. "What
happened?"

"Well, President Nimeiri broke the agreement by making plans to
redraw the border to put the oil fields in the North. That's where I lived,
right on the border. He never carried out his plan, but our people took it to
mean the North was trying to enrich itself at the expense of the South."

"So is that how the war started? Over oil?"

"That was just one factor. It gets very complicated after that. It says
here that to accommodate the northern conservatives, President Nimeiri
aligned himself with the radical Muslim Brotherhood. He began his
program of Islamization, imposing the harsh sharia laws in 1983. Since most
of us in the South are Christian or Animist, this didn't set very well. I
remember some talk about that at church, but nothing had been forced on
us yet. I was a little kid and didn't understand much about it then."

"We're still fighting for freedom of religion now," Ayuel said, leaning
forward with great interest. "Dr. Garang believes that's only right."

"That is when John Garang became involved in the resistance. The
South was being shortchanged on many fronts and a rebel movement had
already begun by soldiers who had gone to Ethiopia. When the North began
to transfer southern military forces to the North to integrate the army,
government soldiers stationed in Bor mutinied. They considered these orders
an attempt to limit their capacity to defend their region. President Nimeiri
then sent his trusted Colonel, John Garang, to stop the uprising."

"Garang was in the government army?"

"He was. But, instead of putting down the rebellion when he got
there, Garang joined them! He and the soldiers fled to Ethiopia where he
organized the Sudanese People's Liberation Army. From other readings, I
know that President Mengistu of Ethiopia led a repressive regime, but since
he held many things against the Sudanese government, he agreed to help
the rebels. In the Cold War—whatever that was—Ethiopia was aligned with

the Soviet Union and Cuba. Sudan's dictatorship received aid from the United States, which encouraged the oil exploration in my region of Unity."

"And we were chased out of Ethiopia when Mengistu was overthrown."

"Exactly. No more aid from the Soviet Union, and the new government didn't support the SPLA."

"What else does it say about oil and the attack on Unity?"

"Not much, but alliances are interesting arrangements. You probably know from history class about the Anglo-Egyptian rule in Sudan and how they'd invaded and incorporated the Darfur region into Sudan in 1916. Though black Africans like us, the Darfurians had been Muslims since the fifteenth century. They were marginalized—it says here—and denied resources from the central government. Conditions got worse after the drought and famine in the 1980s.

"Thousands of people died and rebel groups began to protest. That's when the government came up with their policy of divide, displace and destroy. The Baggara tribe from Darfur in the Northwest started coming down to loot our villages and steal our cattle. The government made no effort to stop them. I remember my parents talking about it but I was too young to worry much.

"The government wanted to clear the land for oil exploration. That's what brought on the violent attacks that killed my family. The government in Khartoum gave automatic weapons to the Baggaras from Darfur and allowed them to destroy our whole area. They weren't paid for killing us off, but with the guns and supplies they were free to do whatever they wanted. It was easy to talk them into it because they, too, were Muslims.

"The radical Islamic government told them it was a shame to be ruled by Christians who are infidels. At the time, as I watched them killing people, I thought it was strange they spoke Arabic, but were black. Just like the government extremists, they captured women and children and sold them as slaves to the North. They had horses, which we didn't. Our spears were useless against their guns."

"What kind of government does that to its own people?" Ayuel asked. He recalled images of the attack on Duk. "Why is oil that important?"

"I don't understand that either," Beny said. "I think they make petrol out of it to run cars and trucks. I know they have to refine it, and all the refineries would be in the North."

★

Later that evening, as they stood in line to fill their five-gallon water jugs, Beny and Ayuel continued their discussion.

"Seems to me," Ayuel said, "that anything would be better than war. Let them have the stupid oil. I don't drive a car, so it doesn't bother me."

"Do you want to be made into a Muslim and follow *sharia?*"

"Well, no, but we don't have to obey those laws here in the camp."

"Do you want to live your whole life here?"

"No, of course not!"

"Look at all the disabled people who come here with their hands or feet chopped off. Some of that was done to them for breaking one of their *sharia* laws, even by accident. It's wrong and it makes me angry, so we have to resist. But also I've done a lot of thinking. If we keep faith in our God, one day peace may come. Maybe God tests our faith by giving us a terrible life."

"Well, I'm tired of this testing."

"I've studied a lot about this. I think we can accept God's plan or we can abandon God. He can bring about miracles. Someday, Sudan may change or maybe there will not even be a Sudan. Maybe it will be a different country. We are on a long journey of hope."

"You've got more knowledge than I do, Beny," Ayuel said. They were almost to the tap to fill their water jugs. "I know Dr. Garang told us that getting a good education was a way of fighting back. I believe in God and all that, but it seems to me that if we could kill off our enemies before they kill us, that would settle it. Then there would be no more wars."

The boys filled their water jugs, said goodbye and went to their separate minor zones. Thoughts swirled in Ayuel's mind as he lugged the heavy jugs. He wasn't sure if killing off all the Arabs would bring permanent peace, but somehow reading and studying wasn't bringing peace either— not personally and not to his country. He admired Beny's wisdom and faith. He seemed so much farther along on his journey of hope than himself. Beny was much like Aleer, both older and much wiser than he.

Ayuel, along with Beny, Gutthier and Samuel, planned to spend their Friday evening watching CNN International in the hospital building near the IRC office that housed the only television set in the whole camp. By pooling the Kenyan shillings they'd earned at odd jobs, they had enough to pay the admission.

"Probably more bad news on the war in Sudan," Ayuel said, as he handed his coins to the man at the door.

Gutthier glanced around for choice seats. "Say, let's take the bench behind that row of girls. I know some of them. Monica lives near the Leekmaduk compound."

"Wonder how they got in," said Samuel. Girls were generally not allowed to watch television, especially when boys were present.

"They probably got special permission. Maybe something important is happening." Just as they sat down, the topic on the screen switched from the British parliament to Sudan. The audience became quiet and leaned forward.

"After several terror attacks around the world," the newscaster said, "Osama bin Laden has turned back to Sudan where he has been living since 1991. He has, indeed, brought his wealth to that country, but now he is using his influence to have *jihad* declared on the South where radical Islam continues to be resisted. Thousands of troops have been strongly armed to clear the southern people from their homes—in essence, genocide. 'The way to heaven is through Southern Sudan,' bin Laden has said. Each troop has been given a key by the government in Khartoum. They are promised that if they die destroying the areas in the South, they will go straight to heaven. The key will open the door to Allah's house where they will be richly rewarded."

"What lies they tell," Beny said under his breath.

"We certainly didn't need Osama bin Laden messing around in our country," Samuel said. "Wish they'd send him back to Saudi Arabia."

"Or Afghanistan."

"Just look at those destroyed villages. Dead people everywhere," Ayuel whispered as he pointed to the screen. "Nothing has changed since we were chased out, it's only worse."

"Shoo! Listen." Monica turned around, her finger to her lips, and grinned. Ayuel had often noticed the vivacious girl with the sweet smile when he came to the Family Community on weekends, but, of course, he had never talked with her directly.

The newsman was saying, "... pressure on the Sudanese government to remove him from Sudan."

"Who's pressuring?" Samuel asked.

"The United States of America," one of the other girls looked back and said. "Pay attention."

As often happened, the generator failed, causing the screen to go black. After they were outside, Gutthier invited the five girls to walk with them along the dry riverbank. The sun had just set, lowering the temperature in the dust-filled air. The conversation turned to less serious topics—gossip about mutual friends, teachers who were too harsh and opportunities to earn money at odd jobs around the camp.

"Samuel and I may get a real job working with the handicapped," Beny said. "We've signed up for a two-week workshop that begins tomorrow. Ever since I met the many disabled people in Itang, I've been impressed by their courage and wanted to help them out."

"Remember Tiop with the one leg?" Samuel added. "He's the man Beny and I spent New Year's Eve with back in Itang. He told us to learn English so when we grew up, we could ask Christian countries for ammunition to fight the Arabs."

"It's more complicated than that, we know now," Beny added. "But that's why we went to Panyido, to learn English. And that was a good thing."

"Tiop's here in Kakuma," Samuel said. "Beny and I talked with him last week. He's learning English himself now."

"I'd like to go see him," Ayuel said. "Sounds like an interesting person."

Ayuel looked back at Gutthier, who had lagged behind with the girls, and noticed how easily he chatted with Monica. He wished he could have the nerve to talk one-on-one like that with a girl instead of just making remarks to everyone in general.

Gutthier began singing a Dinka folk song and the rest all joined in. A full moon rose, lending its light as the young people strolled back to the Family Community where the young men bade goodnight to the ladies. Ayuel waved and mumbled, "Bye, Monica."

★

Ayuel still struggled with anger and revenge. He felt those emotions now as he joined Aleer and Beny in the queue for the bi-monthly rations of food. His history teacher had said some things in class the day before that disturbed him.

"I see you've got your own umbrella, Ayuelo," Beny said. "Where'd you get it?"

"Nice," said Aleer, looking up from the book he was reading. The handle of his own umbrella was snuggly tucked under one arm, freeing both hands to hold his book in its shadow.

"Majur gave it to me. Said he paid 200 Kenyan shillings for it."

"What for?" Aleer asked. "Why would he give it away? I know he's been making some money by bringing water to the construction workers."

Ayuel laughed. "You know Majur. He gets embarrassed about the least little thing. He said only women carry umbrellas."

"I bet someone teased him about it," Beny said. "Doesn't bother me, it keeps the sun off when we have to stand for hours in this heat." Beny held a very large umbrella that he usually shared with Ayuel. Only about half of those lined up carried them.

"We didn't have to stand in line for food or water in Pakok, but there weren't nearly so many people either," Aleer said.

"This only started a few months ago. The new routine takes much longer, but it's supposed to cut down on the looting."

After a few minutes, Ayuel decided to share his frustration over what his teacher had said. "My history teacher thinks he knows why we have wars over religion in Sudan."

"That's what we've all been trying to figure out," Beny said. "So what's his idea?"

"Now I'm getting mad all over again. He insulted us." Ayuel wanted them to agree with him that his teacher was wrong, so he chose his words carefully. "He says it's because we live in such a *primitive* society. The Sudanese, especially the Southerners, aren't educated. He told us that here in Kenya, they have Muslims and Christians that live in the same communities, but don't kill each other. He thinks that if the Sudanese were educated, they would figure out the answers. They would find diplomatic ways to end the wars. What do you guys think of that?"

Aleer closed his book and gave Ayuel his full attention. "I think he is partially right. It's true not many Southerners are educated, but that's largely the government's fault. They've destroyed what schools there were."

"You went to school before the war, didn't you, Aleer?" Beny asked.

"I went for about a year before going to the cattle camp. It was all in Arabic because they wanted to make Muslims out of us. Here's where your teacher may be wrong. The Muslims in Kenya are moderate, like the ones here in camp. They don't bother anyone. We respect them. But in Sudan, the government is run by the Nationalist Islamic Front. They're radical. They want to take over the whole world and make everyone follow their rules, have Arabic names, follow their customs."

"Garang and even Machar are well-educated," Beny said. "They have degrees from American universities. Still they wage war and even fight each other. They're hardly primitive."

"Why did Garang have to rebel against the government?" Ayuel asked. "I partly blame him for all this."

"We do need freedom to practice our own religion. We should have equality with the North and profit from the sale of our own oil. We have to defend ourselves when they attack us," Aleer said. "Garang has courageously led this struggle."

"You're right about that, I guess," Ayuel said. "I wish I was an American so I could bomb all the Arabs in the North."

"Even the women and children?"

"Why not? They killed our mother and father and little sisters—and Deng."

"We have to resist," his brother agreed. "But if we do what you suggest, the killing would go on and on. Somehow we have to break that continuing violence."

"Well, I don't think we're *primitive*."

"In a way we are," Aleer said. "Most Southerners don't value education. Remember what Dr. Garang told us in Panyido: the army fights with guns, but our job is to get a good education so someday we can solve the problems of our country."

"I think when God says to love our enemies, he means it. Certainly not to take revenge," Beny said. "Defending ourselves is different from killing for revenge. I still struggle with this idea, but that's what I believe now."

The line moved up a few steps. Ayuel looked ahead to see how long the queue was and estimated the time. "About one more hour," he said with a sigh. Aleer returned to his book. Beny started talking to a classmate in front of them. Ayuel felt less angry as he contemplated what Aleer and Beny had said about killing just for revenge. Deep down he believed in God and the importance of education, but he was impatient. He longed to see a change in his country. He wondered if ever—in the distant future—he could be part of that change, of making a difference. *I'm just an orphan kid in a refugee camp in a foreign country. What can I possibly do?*

TWENTY-TWO

VYING FOR A
LOST LOVE

A yuel saw little of his brother now, but he was pleased to watch him reach the goals he set for himself. Aleer received his high school diploma—in just three years as planned. Although the school director, Maker Thiang, had been able to provide the students with mostly certified teachers, he recognized Aleer's high academic achievement and asked him to teach GHC (government, history, civics) in the high schools. Aleer agreed to take on the responsibility but told Mr. Thiang that he had applied to attend the Kampala International University in Uganda where he hoped to earn a Bachelor of Arts degree. At nineteen, he would be the youngest of the faculty at the high school. He left the Leekmaduk compound and moved in with other teachers. Taking his new assignment seriously, he spent much time in preparation and in the evaluation of his students.

This left little time for the brothers to be together, but, when possible, Ayuel went with Aleer to the IRC office to check for an acceptance letter from the university. One day, Beny came with them. They searched the postings—with little hope—for a letter about a family member.

"You know," Beny said, as the three scanned the names on the bulletin board, "I've written to my cousin about my sister Acuei and little brother, Abui. I've never gotten an answer."

"That's discouraging," Aleer said. "But it could mean many things. The mail is unreliable. Perhaps your sister is married and was able to leave the camp in Khartoum. Abui could've been adopted by a family…"

"I know. It would just mean so much to find them. Or to know… Say, Aleer, here's your name."

They got in line behind a dozen or so people. Ayuel felt nervous, knowing what he should be hoping, but finding selfish emotions pulling him back. When their turn came, the man behind the desk handed Aleer a large brown envelope.

"That's good news, I think," Aleer said as they all moved outside. "A small letter would mean rejection."

Ayuel could see the excitement in his brother's eyes, but his own feelings remained mixed. While he shared Aleer's joy, the old anguish of his absence swept over him. They stood in the shade of the office building as his brother carefully opened the envelope.

Aleer pulled out a small stack of papers and silently read the letter on top. "I'm in," he announced with a broad smile. "The next semester starts in three months. I'll have to tell Mr. Thiang right away."

"He'll be happy for you," Beny said, slapping his friend on the back. "He knew you might not stay on."

"You don't need to leave right away," Ayuel said. "You can take a bus to Uganda."

That evening, Aleer visited the Leekmaduk compound. The relatives crowded around him, proud of his success. After a delicious—and almost filling—meal, they danced, sang and told stories: a celebration in the Dinka tradition.

Before going to bed, Ayuel and Aleer sat by the still-glowing embers of the charcoal fire. Ayuel told his brother, "Congratulations. I wish you a good life. I'll miss you." An ache deep inside choked the last words. Twice he'd lost this only remaining member of his family, not knowing if his brother died or lived. Now again he must face separation.

"I'll miss you too." The fire reflected in Aleer's eyes as he looked at Ayuel. "Keep studying and searching. You will find your answers. Don't ever give up."

Ayuel recalled those words, *Don't ever give up*, that Deng had said their last time together in Duk. "I won't. Please, write to me."

★

When Beny was nineteen, Ayuel watched him rise to new positions of leadership. Ever since his training in peace and reconciliation back in Panyido, he continued leading small groups in his church, solving disputes in peer groups and organizing youth activities. He also worked with the handicapped and had just finished the second phase of that training. Adults recognized him as a deep and analytic thinker as well as a compassionate counselor.

When an inter-denominational youth conference was planned to take place in Kakuma, Beny's priest and other pastors chose him as a delegate, based on his previous work to promote harmony. Participants came from Uganda, Congo, Burundi, Rwanda, Sudan and Ethiopia as well as Kenya for leadership training. Renowned ministers and Bible teachers led the sessions. Representatives from the United Nations came to speak. Much more comprehensive than the class he'd taken back in Panyido, the conference carried the auspicious title: *Justice, Peace and Reconciliation*. They met in the largest church building, the Saint Bakhita Chapel.

On the Saturday evening following the week-long conference, Beny met Ayuel, Gabriel and Samuel as they arrived early for the weekly praise service at the dry riverbank. The setting sun shed diffused light through the dust-filled air, casting long shadows of gnarled and mostly dead trees. The friends claimed one of the few wooden benches near the front where musicians were setting up their instruments. Latecomers would sit on the rocky bank or stand.

"So how was it?" Samuel asked. "The conference, I mean."

"A fabulous experience," Beny said, his face aglow with exuberance. "If you ever have a chance to do something like this, don't let it pass by. I almost didn't go as a delegate, because I thought I couldn't miss that much school. Believe me, it was worth it!"

"So what was the best part?" Ayuel felt a bit jealous, thinking he'd probably never have such an opportunity.

"I guess it was the music that moved me most. Fantastic! In addition to the drums, they used a stringed instrument called the *donga*. They left us one. We'll be singing some of the songs tonight. Over the next few months we'll be repeating what we learned for the rest of the camp. I'm supposed to give a little talk later tonight."

A short while later, young people started gathering in small groups, talking and laughing as they arrived. Gabriel sat down and remained quiet, because he was short of breath. He perked up, however, when he spotted a boy wearing a white T-shirt with the words *Justice, Peace and Reconciliation* printed on the front. "Hey, Beny, is that kid a delegate from the conference?"

Beny turned and looked. "Well, not exactly. All the delegates got T-shirts like that, but mine was too small. So I gave it to the first bare-chested kid I saw. That's him in *my* shirt."

"I guess that's Biblical," Samuel joked. "He was naked and you clothed him."

"I'm not that saintly," Beny scoffed. "If it had fit, I'd be wearing it now. My talk's about someone saintly though—Saint Bakhita, whom our church is named for, the patron saint of Sudan."

The musicians began tapping their drums. Ayuel noticed the new stringed instrument and was fascinated at how it was played. By this time several hundred people sat on the rocks or portable wooden benches. A song leader, wearing the official conference T-shirt, stepped forward and held up his hands to gain the crowd's attention. He began with a song they all knew: *We all belong to You, O Lord. Come Lamb of God and make us all One.*

Everyone stood and sang loudly, some joining hands and swaying to the music.

"Now, I have a new song from the conference about peace and unity in Christ. I will sing a line. Then you echo my words. Okay?

> *Jesus is Mighty God.*
> *Everyone bows before Him.*
> Maker Thiang…
> *Maker Thiang bows before Him.*
> Kofi Annan…"

The crowd quickly caught on and sang out, *"Kofi Annan bows before*

Him."

After a few more recognizable names, the song leader sang, "President Bashir..."

The crowd obediently followed in form but not so forcefully. *Why would the Sudanese president bow before Jesus?* Ayuel wondered as he turned to Beny. "Why?"

Beny finished singing the line with enthusiasm, then answered Ayuel. "We can hope. You know, 'Love your enemies.'"

No one protested the mention of the Islamic leader. The singing of various praise songs continued for a half hour or more until the leader announced, "Now, we will hear from one of our conference delegates, Beny Ngor Chol, who will say a few words about the patron saint of Sudan. Beny."

Beny bounded to the front, shook the hand of the song leader and turned to the audience. "Good evening. I know not all of you are Sudanese. Most of you are not of the Catholic faith and some not even Christian. That doesn't matter. You can be inspired by the life of one woman who made a difference in the world—Sister Josephine Bakhita. All of us are refugees from our own countries; all of us have suffered and have lost many loved ones by violent means. Sister Bakhita was born in Sudan to a loving and prosperous Muslim family. Then at the age of nine, she was kidnapped and sold into slavery."

Ayuel recalled that Beny had been nine when his life also took a violent turn, and that he often worried about the possibility of his sister being sold into slavery. Ayuel listened closely as Beny told of the girl being tortured, whipped, beaten and left for dead on more than one occasion.

"At age thirteen, she was forced to have tattoos etched with a razor over much of her body. Salt was poured into the wounds, producing excruciating pain. After being sold many times in the market, she was bought by an Italian Consul in Khartoum. Much to her surprise, no one used the lash against her. For the first time since her kidnapping, she experienced peace, warmth and moments of joy. The Consul's family had rescued her and treated her with kindness.

"He took her to Italy, where a wealthy family begged him to let

Josephine stay with them and be a nanny to their little girl. A few years later, this family needed to go on a business trip and left both girls in the care of Catholic Sisters at a convent. When they returned, Josephine asked to stay with the nuns. She had discovered the God who had brought her such good fortune. She said throughout her anguished life, she had experienced Him in her heart without knowing who He was. Later she became a nun and served God for fifty years. She comforted the poor and suffering and encouraged all those who came to her. She became known as the 'woman of faith and forgiveness,' the woman even able to forgive the slave owners who whipped her, the men who cut her with razors, those who had treated her as an object. And she was beatified by Pope John Paul II."

Beny continued to speak about the saint's good deeds, but Ayuel was lost in his own thoughts. *Wish I could be like that. How could she forgive those who treated her so brutally?*

*

Ayuel had stayed relatively healthy in Kakuma on the one meager meal of maize mush a day. When the short rainy season came, leaving puddles of rain, mosquitoes rose in swarms. And with mosquitoes came malaria. Ayuel fell victim. He lay ill at the Leekmaduk compound, feverish and chilled at the same time. Unable to keep down food or even water, he was rapidly dehydrating. On the third day, Leekmaduk's wife brought him some hot tea.

"Drink this and you will get better," she said. "You should be able to keep this tea down." She knelt by his bed and held the cup to his lips, steadying his shaking hands. After only two sips, he waved his arms for her to help him outside. He retched that up and remained on his knees in the hot sun. The air was full of steam, swirling from the puddles. Shivering, he crawled back to his bed and muttered, "Please, Alual, can you bring me another blanket. I'm so cold."

Just as she laid the blanket over him, Gutthier came home from classes. "You look terrible, Ayuelo. Don't you know how hot and humid it is?" He wiped his face with a cloth.

"Get Donayok. He saved my life once before." Ayuel fell asleep as soon as he heard Gutthier leave.

Ayuel lost all sense of time but it seemed like hours later when Donayok pulled back his blankets. "You're soaked in sweat, Ayuel. We must get you to the hospital. We've brought a couple of your friends. They have some poles to make you a stretcher."

"We'll use this one," he heard Gutthier say. "It's not quite as wet as the blanket next to him."

When they had tied the corners of the blanket to the four ends of the poles, Donayok and Gutthier lifted him to the waiting stretcher on the ground. The four men hoisted the poles to their shoulders and carried him to the Zone One hospital.

Donayok stayed with him through the evening, wiping his hands and face with a damp cloth and seeing that he took his medicine at the right times. He sat all night at his bedside, caring for him as his mother would have done. In the morning, he brought Ayuel a bowl of porridge. "Here, try a little of this."

Ayuel sat up and took a small bite. "You're like a father to me, Donayok. You have so many responsibilities as head of Zone One." Exhausted, he lay back down. "But here you are taking care of me."

"You just get well. Can you eat a little more?"

Ayuel sat up again and finished the bowl. "What would I do without friends like you and Gutthier?"

"Gutthier's coming tonight to sit with you. The nurse says you might go home tomorrow." Donayok stood to go. "I'll be back to check on you around noon." Ayuel watched him leave and thought of how much his mentor had meant to him through the years. He rarely saw his friend since coming to Kakuma. Both led busy lives and lived some distance from each other. Yet he knew Donayok would be there for him in any circumstance.

Ayuel recovered and had his full strength back in a few weeks.

★

When Ayuel turned eighteen, Gutthier reminded him it was time he looked for a wife. "You're not even in the first stage of relationships with girls—where you talk to them in secret and hope their brothers don't beat you up," he often said in fun.

"I know, I know," Ayuel admitted one night when Gutthier mentioned the subject again. His half-brother had just returned to the compound late from a weekend party with several young couples. "You and Beny don't have any trouble talking with girls, but, well, I get nervous. The traditional ways are better. When the parents agree that there is a good match, they encourage you."

"Hey, I could introduce you to someone," Gutthier offered. "You just tell me someone you like and leave it to me."

The two sat down on a log by the pole fence. Most people had gone to bed by this late hour and the night was still. Ayuel held his head in his hands. Gutthier knew lots of girls and always claimed several as girlfriends.

"All right. How about Monica Bol? She lives right here near our compound and besides, she's from Duk. I think she's about fifteen." Ayuel paused to gain courage. "I've said 'hi' to her a few times."

"That'll be easy. You won't need an introduction." Gutthier seemed to be forming a plan in his mind. "You see each other in groups all the time. I'll tell Monica you like her and that you have a letter for her. That's the usual way."

Ayuel could feel his face heat up just thinking about it. "I guess I could write a letter. That's better than talking."

"See how easy it is? We'll go by her school after classes."

★

The next school day, Gutthier waited with Ayuel until they spotted Monica alone in the crowd of students. When she moved off by herself as planned, Ayuel walked casually toward her and made eye contact when they passed. The 'hi' he had so carefully prepared stuck in his throat. He took a few more steps and turned to watch Gutthier approach her.

Gutthier easily said his words of greeting mixed with a few gestures. Ayuel saw his friend's lips form the planned words: *Ayuel likes you and he has a letter for you.*

Ayuel's sigh of relief was quickly interrupted by Monica's very audible response: "I don't want to talk to boys. And I don't want to get a letter!"

After politely exchanging a few more words, Gutthier headed toward Ayuel and called out, "Bye, Monica. See you later."

"So I guess we lost that one," Ayuel said, trying to sound as if it didn't matter.

"Not at all," Gutthier assured him. "I know when she goes to the water tap. I'll just drop the letter in her empty bucket as I pass by. I won't even say anything. That should work."

★

"I've got good news for you," Gutthier said as they entered their classroom the next day. "She took the letter out right after I dropped it in her bucket. She didn't even look around to see who did it, so I think she's interested."

Ayuel was skeptical. "I passed her at the Community gate and said 'hi,' but I don't know if she'd read my letter. She just looked at me and then turned her head away, without saying anything. That was rude."

"Girls have funny ways. Just don't speak to her for a while. Ignore her," Gutthier advised.

Ayuel took the advice and started looking around at other girls. He didn't like the way it felt to have a girl reject him, but after a few weeks, he'd quit thinking about her every single minute.

While standing in the water tap line one evening, he felt a pull on his sleeve. He turned to see a small girl who handed him a tightly folded paper. Before he could say anything, the child slipped away.

Ayuel set down his empty water jugs and slowly unfolded the paper. *Meet me at that dead tree outside my schoolhouse tomorrow after classes. Monica.*

A flood of emotions gushed over him. Happiness, of course, because the note was from Monica. Revival of lost hope. And last of all, hurt. He still felt the sting over the way she had treated him. Well, maybe he just wouldn't show up.

But he did.

When she didn't appear after her classmates had all left, Ayuel became agitated and started to leave. And then, there she was, standing in front of him. She smiled up at him but he looked away and said, "What do you want from me?"

"I just don't want my sister to know I talk to boys. She's always around, so I can't speak to you. I got your letter."

"I know."

"You said you liked me and wanted to talk to me."

"I did. I mean I do." Already he was stumbling over words, but he no longer was upset at her. "How was your school day?"

"Good. No, really it was boring." Monica laughed and started talking about a teacher whose lecture put her to sleep. From there, she chattered away non-stop until they got to the Family Community fence.

"I'll just go on back to Zone Three, so your sister won't see us," Ayuel said, feeling confident enough to be gallant. "May I see you tomorrow after school?"

"You can wait by that same tree, but I'll be late. I can't come by until my sister has left." She smiled and rolled her eyes at him.

"I'll be there." Ayuel strode back to his minor zone, head high, confident of his newfound manhood. He wondered if Monica was really avoiding her sister, or, if she even had a sister.

TWENTY-THREE

HEALING EMOTIONAL SCARS

As the weeks passed, Ayuel became comfortable being with Monica. Since she did most of the talking, he could relax and let her bring up any new subject. They went to soccer games and church activities together. He discovered she was really interested in education. Since he had become active in Debate Club, he invited her to join also, which she eagerly did, enjoying it as much as he.

Before long, Ayuel became aware that other young men were competing for her attention. As long as Gutthier was around—always funny, creative and a great storyteller—she enjoyed being next to Ayuel. Together they laughed and cheered Gutthier on. Yet without him, conversation lagged, and she paid more attention to other suitors.

Ayuel discovered his words flowed best when debating before a group. He loved taking sides on ideas like *Should religion play a role in politics?* and *Should abortion be legalized in Africa?* When Monica was in the audience, she seemed to follow his words very closely. That gave him incentive to do his very best. When his peers elected him chairman of the club, he felt that added prestige in her eyes.

★

Resolved: More women should hold governmental positions. The debate topic was not one Ayuel felt strongly about, but he came prepared. He and his female partner drew the negative side of the proposition. As he sat in front of the outdoor gathering, waiting for the debate to begin, he smiled at Monica in the front row and wondered what she thought on the subject, since they hadn't discussed it. She returned the smile, giving him encouragement.

He glanced over at the affirmative team. A second glance drained away his confidence. A comely girl sat upright on her stool, her head held high, ankles crossed. Everything about her, from her carefully arranged hair to her crisp beige blouse and brown, striped skirt shouted self-assurance. Photographs he'd once seen of such women in an American magazine flashed across his mind. How could he have missed seeing her among the hundred or so members of the club? His heart melted.

The moderator was introducing the participants. He heard his own name too late to acknowledge it, but he certainly didn't miss the name of his formidable opponent: Rebecca Kuol. She stood and waved to the crowd.

At the beginning of the debate, Ayuel felt he performed nearly as well as the opposing team in the constructive speeches. All four stuck close to their prepared notes, full of statistics and quotations from knowledgeable sources. Ayuel ended his remarks by arguing that few women had been either elected or appointed to public positions because their natural talents of child raising, cooking, cultivating the crops and creating artistic crafts made a greater contribution to society. He pointed out that a smaller percentage of girls in the camp *chose* to continue their schooling past the elementary grades, thus leaving few women well-educated enough to take jobs in the government.

Rebecca rose for rebuttal, handing her notes to her partner. "I concede that most women do indeed possess the domestic talents mentioned." She paused for dramatic effect. "But many women are equally gifted in leadership and are as capable as their male counterparts of holding high positions that affect the direction of a country." She proceeded to cite women leaders who have made outstanding contributions. "Chandrika Kumaranturge was elected president of Sri Lanka with sixty-two percent of the votes cast. Ruth Perry, just last year, became the first African head of state, leading Liberia to peace after a long civil war. Margaret Thatcher was a formidable prime minister of the United Kingdom, and Madeleine Albright is presently the first woman Secretary of State for the United States."

Ayuel was stunned by the way Rebecca trilled off the foreign names without hesitation. She concluded her argument, passionately stating, "Girls do not continue with their education, because they are discouraged by the adults around them who see only discrimination, lack of opportunity and failure waiting for females in the outside world. But in the attempt to protect young girls, adults are not only condemning them to an unfulfilled life but robbing the world of future leaders toward peace. Women bring a different, and often more humane, perspective to government. By far, these strong women in high positions have tried to turn their countries away from war, through diplomacy and other peaceful means. Yes, the world needs more women in governmental positions."

Afterward, Ayuel, not in the least surprised that the affirmative won the debate, extended his hand to Rebecca. "Congratulations. You were terrific!" *You are terrific and exactly the kind of woman we need in government. Besides, you are incredible and beautiful!*

Out of the corner of his eye he noticed Monica leaving with one of his competitors. At this moment, it didn't bother him in the least. Ayuel found himself totally absorbed by Rebecca, who was easy to talk with, in spite of his fast-beating heart. After an exchange of a few more words about the debate, he asked, "Rebecca, would you like to go watch the cultural dances this evening? I think there's a drum group from the Congo performing."

"Sure. I like that sort of entertainment. Especially the music." They walked down the path toward the performance area. Her eyes twinkled when she looked up at him and remarked, "You are really tall, even for a Dinka. Could you be from the Bor region?

"I am. My father was chief of Duk."

"So you're Chief Leek Deng's son? I'm from Duk too, and my father was one of his sub-chiefs."

Ayuel loved the enthusiasm in her voice. In fact, he loved everything about her. She moved on to talking about woman's place in society. He'd never thought much about the subject and only studied about it in preparation for the debate, but she took it very seriously. No wonder she spoke with such passion.

"You know, women have been struggling for over a hundred years—maybe forever—to be equal with men. I consider myself part of the world-wide women's liberation movement."

"Women's liberation? What does that mean?" He let the back of his hand brush against hers.

Rather than move away, she slipped her hand into his. "For me, it means I want to get the best education possible. Hopefully, I will be able to go to the United States someday and attend a university there. I'd like to study international law and come back to Sudan to help our poor, broken country. Especially, I would like to help women start small businesses to bring their families out of poverty. If this horrid war would only end."

"And you think it's mainly men who want war?" Her nearness thrilled him with excitement. Whatever she said seemed right and true.

"I don't hear women calling for war. Women and their children suffer the most. Often they are raped or sold into slavery."

"That's true, but shouldn't we fight against injustices? Our own government is slaughtering the Southerners. They try to force us to follow their *sharia* laws and convert to Islam. They destroy our villages and our culture, take away our oil-rich lands. That's surely wrong and worth fighting against." He searched her face for reaction, but the setting sun shone in his eyes, making it difficult to see her clearly.

"There are other ways to fight," she finally said, as if debating the point. "We need well-educated men and women to go before the United Nations and present our case. We need the world's help, not just their guns but also their power, to expose our evil government. And we need Sudanese people who can negotiate a settlement and bargain for our rights."

Ayuel thought of Tiop who had said they needed to learn English to ask for guns and of John Garang who said education was as important a weapon as a gun.

Rebecca laughed and squeezed his hand. "You think I'm too serious, don't you?"

"No, no. I agree with everything you say. I too want to get the best education possible so I can help our country. I don't know how you're going to get to the United States of America though." He was awed by her ambition.

"I'll find a way."

They arrived at the area just as dusk was falling. Surprised to find no gathering of spectators, nor sounds of music, Ayuel went over to read a hand-written paper tacked to one of the posts at the entrance. He read aloud the hand-written notice: "Cancelled. No program tonight."

"May I walk you home then?" She agreed—neither cared about missing the performance. The wind had settled to a soft breeze and stars hung close in the moonless night. They no longer spoke of grand ideas or women's liberation, but commented on present happenings at camp or strolled in silence, listening to crickets, night bird calls and the distant sounds of children at play. At the pole fence, Ayuel placed his hands on her shoulders and looked down into her upturned face. "I want to see you more."

"Me too," she whispered.

Ayuel walked back to the minor zone with joy—and maybe love—in his heart. It had been only two months since he'd started seeing Monica. They were certainly good friends, and he felt always would be. But Rebecca was different, well, really extraordinary.

★

Drama Club became another school-related activity that intrigued Ayuel and gave him an idea to help younger refugees. After several weeks of instruction, the teacher-sponsor decided they needed an audience. He arranged for a cast to present a skit before an elementary school. It concerned a court case and the role of judge fell to Ayuel. A man was accused of stealing several cows from a neighbor and attempting to change their markings with paint. Ayuel relished the part, as he had witnessed his father judging such cases, sitting under a large oak tree back in Duk. The skit illustrated the consequences of stealing.

What fascinated Ayuel most was how the children reacted. They had come to Kakuma from diverse countries, speaking only tribal languages. Not only did they carry the emotional scars from horrors witnessed and family members killed, but also they often could only communicate with a few others from their tribes.

However, he noticed they responded emotionally to drama, cheering the victim and yelling at the villain. When the lawyer poured a bucket of water over the cow borrowed for the performance and the paint washed off, the children went wild with laughter. *Why not have children act out their own traumas to express their emotional scars, since they often could not communicate their feelings in a recognized language?*

Within a few weeks, Ayuel had talked to several elementary school teachers who applauded his idea. He and two other Drama Club members met after school one day in an elementary classroom with fifteen children, who ranged in age from nine to twelve. Most remembered Ayuel from the court skit in which he played the judge.

"I wanna be the judge!" Dominic, a boy of about eleven, called out in Swahili. Ayuel, like most of the high school students, had learned some Swahili and Arabic, both of which were common second languages in camp. He hadn't planned to begin with such an elaborate script, but *why not?*

"Okay. And who wants to be the cow thief?" he asked in Dinka, Swahili and Arabic, waving an imaginary stick to herd the cows. Several hands went up. In no time, he had the entire cast, including some willing to portray the stolen cows. The children went through the drama with such enthusiasm—yelling in their own tribal dialects—that Ayuel and his two assistants had to stop the chaos several times. By any measure, the venture was a grand success. The children switched roles and repeated the skit three more times.

Finally, Ayuel had to announce the end of the session. They would meet again on Thursday and twice a week after that.

The following Thursday more than thirty children showed up, ready to perform. Communication became more difficult with a new subject but Ayuel divided the children into four groups and let them plan a scene based on a problem at school. He and the two other Drama Club members went around to each group, helping them prepare their presentations. Ayuel encouraged a great deal of "acting out," so that the spectators could understand the skit.

As the weeks passed, Ayuel chose topics of greater emotional interest, such as unfair distribution of rations or being bombed by the enemy. Anger and real tears became common as the children acted out the traumas in their lives. Ayuel chose some of the best skits to perform in elementary classrooms. One of the most popular carried the title, "No Doctor Around." Dominic, the boy who had acted as the judge in the stolen-cow skit, had suggested the idea. "My brother died on our journey because there was no doctor to help him," the boy said.

He volunteered to play the sick child. A twelve-year-old girl became his mother. Others took the roles of brothers, sisters, aunts, etc. Dominic's class became the first audience for the skit. The Drama Club directors stood by the door to direct the entrances and exits.

Dominic lay across two chairs, moaning and groaning. The mother brought him a gourd of water. He waved her aside. She moaned, placing the back of her hand across her forehead, and left. Other family members came one by one and offered help—such as pulling the blanket up over his shoulders, fanning him with a sheet of paper, giving advice and bringing food. Each time Dominic would wave them away with a groan and plead, "Wanna Doctor."

A healer from the Animist religion came in, dressed in bright clothing, and performed a ritual around him. He held a cup of liquid to Dominic's mouth and insisted he drink all of it. A Christian priest came in a black robe, knelt and prayed over him.

Finally, the stage became bare except for Dominic, who lay still across the two chairs. The rest of the cast then entered solemnly and stood behind him for several seconds. Dominic gave a loud groan, rolled off onto the floor and again lay perfectly still. Some of the students snickered. The other actors sobbed loudly. Two boys came in, rolled Dominic onto his blanket on the floor and tied the ends of the blanket to a pole. They lifted the ends of the pole, laid it over their shoulders and carried him out. The class of students sat in silence. They'd all witnessed something similar when no doctor could come to cure a sick family member.

Suddenly, Dominic burst through the doorway, his arms in the air, followed by the rest of the cast. The students clapped as the actors bowed low. Ayuel hugged Dominic and told him, "Glad you're alive so you can play this again."

Dominic nodded. Ayuel knew the child must be hurting, because it brought back the memory of his brother's death. But at the same time, being able to express the emotion of his hidden grief surely had brought some relief.

★

Drama also helped Ayuel deal with his own emotions, but still he worried about the big issues that plagued him: desire for revenge against the Arabs, dealing with the seeming hopelessness of living in a refugee camp and finding a purpose for his life. He admired Rebecca for her clear, though wildly ambitious, goals and sought to define his own.

In spite of his unsettled issues, he found helping others gave him a deep feeling of satisfaction. On Saturdays, as part of the Episcopal Youth, he visited and prayed with those in critical condition at the hospital.

One young man whom he visited often was Madut, whom he knew well from Panyido. One late afternoon, as he walked toward the hospital building in Zone One, he thought of how happy Madut had always seemed in those days, singing and playing sports. Now he'd spent years in pain, writhing in a hospital ward. There was little the doctors here could do for him with TB of the bone. Ayuel never knew what condition he would find his friend in: bad or worse.

Ayuel walked down the long corridor, trying to ignore the groans and bad odors coming from the patients' rooms. The facility was a great improvement over the canvas tents of earlier years, but still an overworked staff struggled to care for the gravely ill with meager supplies. He stopped at the door of Madut's ward. His friend lay on his side facing the wall, rocking back and forth. Ayuel could hear muffled sobs and saw—as he had seen before—the collapsed bones pushing against the skin of his exposed back. The other five boys in the room napped or stared at the ceiling. An oscillating fan hummed in the corner on a stand. Ayuel winced, took a deep breath and stepped forward. *Abba Father, give me words to say.*

Trying not to touch the bed for fear of adding to his pain, Ayuel slipped sideways, between the wall and the bed. "Madut," he whispered in a soft voice. "It's Ayuel."

Madut opened his eyes. With his face twisted in pain, he said, "Thank you—for coming. You're so faithful. I wish God would take me and relieve me of this horrible pain." He closed his eyes again and lay still. Then he said,

"Several people died yesterday. One in this room."

"It was 135 degrees."

"That was a bad day."

"Yes. What can I do for you, Madut? Do you need water? Food?"

"Just pray the pain will not come tonight. I need some relief. I don't know when I've slept."

"Sure." Ayuel placed his hand gently on Madut's shoulder and started praying aloud. It was a long prayer with much repetition—the words no longer his own as energy seemed to flow through his arm to Madut's shoulder. His friend's tense muscles relaxed under Ayuel's hand. When he finally said, "In the Name of Jesus Christ, Our Savior, So be it," Ayuel became aware of tears running down his own face.

"It's let up some, thanks to our God," Madut said. "And thank you."

"I'll be back in the morning before church." Ayuel had two more stops to make at the hospital, but none tore at his emotions like this one.

The next morning, as promised, Ayuel came by to see how his friend had made it through the night. Cautiously, he peeked into the room.

"Good morning, Ayuel," Madut said with a weak smile. He was sitting up in bed and his face glowed, lacking the contortion of the day before. "Thanks to our God! I slept well last night."

"You look much better. You really got a good night's sleep?"

"I did. The nurse says I may get to go home for a few days if I keep improving." His smile faded to a frown. "Of course, I've done that before. It never lasts very long. Each time it's worse when I have to come back."

"I'll keep praying."

"I think God clearly heard you last night. Thanks."

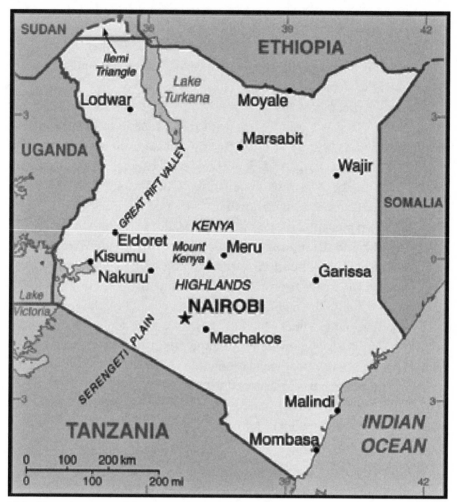

Map of Kenya, courtesy of the CIA World Factbook

TWENTY-FOUR

RAYS OF HOPE

Beny had been working with the handicapped program for two years and had risen to the position of supervisor of the program for Zones One, Five and Six, as well as the Local Zone for the native Turkanans. With these responsibilities and the demands of his last year of high school, little personal time remained for socializing with his friends. Ayuel, too, was busy with his social work and school activities. On this afternoon, as Ayuel was entering the main hospital for visits, he met Beny coming out.

"Hey, what are you doing here?" Ayuel asked. "Don't you usually work at the Multipurpose Center?"

As they shook hands, Beny could not conceal a certain excitement that showed on his face. "I've just had an interview with a terrific man, Mr. Stephen Kajirwa Keverenge, Program Manager for the International Rescue Committee."

"For what? You're already so busy I hardly see you."

"I brought my application in yesterday, and he sent for me today. The job's to be a trainer for the Community-Based Rehabilitation Program."

"So what sort of things did he ask?" Ayuel sat down on the bench by the door, ready to listen.

"It wasn't like that." Beny joined him on the bench. "He didn't just ask me questions and I answered them, trying to make a good impression. We shared experiences about how we felt about the special people we work with. We both enjoy helping them achieve their goals of being independent."

"I know you do, Beny. You have the heart for it."

"Then I said a disabled person is not an unable person. Disability is not inability. Mr. Kajirwa seemed to like that. He offered me the job!"

"Congratulations! You'll be great." In sharing his friend's enthusiasm, Ayuel was getting ahead of himself. "Great at whatever it is. So you'll be doing what exactly?"

"They call the position TOT, for Trainer of Trainees. I will teach the workers in all groups—for the Family Community disabled children, the minors, adults and the aged—both at home and in the schools. Then by next year, Mr. Kajirwa wants me to become the manager of the whole Community-Based Rehabilitation Program."

"That's a lot of responsibility. There are thousands of disabled here."

"I know. It's overwhelming…"

"You can do it." Ayuel felt proud of Beny for finding a meaningful purpose in life.

"I hope. I'll just gradually work up to all the responsibility. Mr. Kajirwa was so encouraging. He promised to work with me."

*

Ayuel and Rebecca continued their relationship, using young girls to pass letters to each other as he and Monica had done. For several months, they shared school and church activities, seeing each other almost daily. They talked endlessly about the war, politics, world affairs, injustice and religion, but avoided speaking of their personal feelings toward each other.

When Ayuel walked her home after attending an event together, they stopped outside the Family Community in the darkness by the gate. There he took her in his arms, and they kissed goodnight. Both the embraces and the kisses gradually became longer and more intense, but no words followed these expressions of affection. Afterward Ayuel squeezed her hand and watched her slip through the pole gate, latching it after her. Increasingly, he wanted the assurance that Rebecca's feelings matched his own. After much careful consideration, he wrote her a long letter in which he declared, "I like you very much."

"What have I done?" he asked Gutthier the next day as they walked home from classes. "What if she rejects me now, because I'm sounding too serious?" He still depended on Gutthier to guide him through his love life.

"Whatever she answers will tell you," Gutthier said with a grin. "She's had enough time to make up her mind."

Before he could respond, one of the little girls who often brought him notes ran up to him. "For you," she said with a giggle, handing him a folded paper and running away.

"Thanks," Ayuel called after her.

"Well, aren't you going to read it?"

"I'll wait until I'm alone. See you later."

Ayuel hurried to his *tukul*, anxious over Rebecca's reaction to his boldness. He sat on his bed and slowly unfolded the letter. He read, "Ayuel, My feelings for you are very much the same—maybe more. Only God knows what lies ahead." Something was marked out that he couldn't read, except for a line at the bottom: "Meet me at the riverbank at dusk. Rebecca."

He fell back on the bed and closed his eyes. *Now, I'm really scared. What can this mean? We've never even talked about love.*

*

That evening, as the huge sun quickly sank into the desert sand beyond the camp, Ayuel made his way toward the dry riverbank. A knot of young men stood on the path, talking excitedly. "What's going on?"

"There's a rumor about other countries…"

"They might take us as refugees," Madau, who was among them, interrupted.

"What countries?" Ayuel asked, not believing his ears.

"Australia, Netherlands. We don't know. It's just a rumor."

"Probably like what happened in Panyido when they took pictures of everyone and said we might go to the United States or England," said Ayuel, remembering the disappointment he'd felt when nothing came of the rumor. "Don't believe it." He turned away and tried to concentrate on seeing Rebecca to suppress the bitterness he felt rising within. *Why do the* khawaja *mock us like this?*

Ayuel found Rebecca standing with her back against a dry gnarled tree, looking especially beautiful. His heart leapt to his throat, blotting out the disturbing news he'd just heard. Her face lit up with a smile and her eyes sparkled when they met his. She reached out her hand and he took it. Together they walked in silence along the riverbank until they came to a broad, flat rock. They sat and faced the dry gully.

Finally Ayuel spoke. "I do like you very much, Rebecca. In your note, you said 'maybe more.' Rebecca, that sounds serious, like we might have a future together." He breathed deeply and waited.

"Have you heard that our future might be in the United States?" Her face glowed with excitement.

"Yes." Mixed emotions swirled inside him. "It's probably only a wild rumor."

"No, Ayuel." She frowned. "This is real. My teacher said there would be an announcement in a few days. Australia, the Netherlands, Canada and the United States have all agreed to take a limited number of refugees from Kakuma. We can be among them!"

"This happened before in Panyido," Ayuel said, shaking his head and feeling deflated. "It's probably a cruel joke or a misunderstanding."

"Ayuel, this could be a golden opportunity for us. Don't you see?"

"What about us?"

"I want to introduce you to my stepmother. I've told her about you and she wants to ask you some questions."

"Of course." The thrill of progressing in their relationship again became Ayuel's emotional focus. "I am pleased she wants to meet me. Could I come to your compound after church on Sunday?"

★

That Sunday afternoon, Ayuel and Rebecca, along with her step-mother, aunt and uncle, sat outside under a young, live tree next to their central *tukul*. Rebecca served tea in porcelain cups. Her stepmother explained, "I found these in the market a few years ago. Of course, for us it was an extravagant purchase, but it gives our home a sense of worth. Sometimes that's more important than food."

Ayuel admired Rebecca's stepmother. She gave him a warm feeling of belonging. Thus with assurance of a positive outcome he brought up the subject of his visit. "As you know, Rebecca and I have been seeing each other a lot the past few months. I care for her and would like to take our relationship to the next level. She agrees." He paused and smiled at Rebecca who nodded agreement. "Of course, we would not continue without your approval." He looked hopefully at the stepmother, then to the aunt and uncle.

"Rebecca speaks highly of you, Ayuel," the stepmother said. "We are impressed by your intelligence, your leadership ability and your deep spiritual faith. But, we have a few questions about your family lineage. My husband, as you know, served as a sub-chief under your father. We very much admired both your parents. I think, however, you and Rebecca may be distant cousins. That is what we need to find out."

Ayuel broke out in a sweat. In Dinka culture, he knew it was forbidden for relatives to marry, regardless of how distant the connection. This idea had not crossed his mind. He swallowed hard. Surely there was some mistake.

For the next hour, he recited his lineage as best he could remember. Aleer had taught him well, back in Panyido. The three older adults pieced together their genealogy, arguing sometimes about who was married to whom. Yet in the end, they had conclusive evidence that indeed he and Rebecca were related.

Rebecca's stepmother sat stone-faced. Gone was the warmth of acceptance. "We all know this relationship cannot continue. It might lead to marriage, which is forbidden. I'm sorry. Good night."

Ayuel rose to go. Rebecca stood as if to say something to him, but her stepmother caught her arm and pulled her back. He could feel the eyes of the woman he loved pleading with him, but he dared not look at her. He dropped his head and said to her stepmother in the strongest voice he could muster, "I will obey your wishes."

★

Over the next few days, Ayuel kept his devastation to himself. His friends talked of nothing else but the possibility of going to a far away country where you could get a really good education, a high-paying job, drive a car and live a fulfilled life. Ayuel refused to believe the news. It was all a rumor, nothing official.

At the end of the week, the *khawaja* from western countries did come, just as before in Panyido. Yet this time there were more of them, and they arrived in several big cars. Their first project was to seek out people in the camp to serve as interpreters. Although English was the official language of Kenya, the teachers had all learned it as a second language. With their heavy native accents, they taught British English to their students who continued to speak their native languages among themselves. This made it especially difficult for the Americans to communicate with them.

One of Ayuel and Beny's friends, Mel Deng, was chosen to interpret. He had risen to be head of all the minor zones in the division of psychosocial concerns. In this position he had the opportunity to speak directly with visiting American officials and journalists. He had practiced his English diligently, not just to be understood, but to speak correctly in either a British or American accent. Often he'd encouraged Ayuel and Beny to speak their best English with him. They decided to seek out Deng for advice on the application process.

In the classes, teachers told all unaccompanied minors and children in foster care, sixteen years of age or older, to gather after school for a big announcement. They were to go to the open area outside the United Nations High Commission on Refugees building. Such assemblies were rare because of the thousands of people who lived in Kakuma.

Ayuel arrived early with Beny, Gutthier, Madau and Gabriel and sat on the ground, not too far from where the speakers' stand had been set up. With two umbrellas among them, they warded off the blistering wind and dust.

"This reminds me of waiting for John Garang to speak," said Beny, as the crowds streamed into the area.

"We thought it was hot in Ethiopia, but we didn't know about real heat, like here in Kenya," said Gutthier, pulling in his umbrella that had just been ripped inside out by the wind. "Where do you guys want to go—if we get chosen?"

"Anywhere I can get some medical care," said Gabriel. His asthma had worsened and his short stays in the hospital did little to help.

"They should take you first," said Ayuel. "But it's the United States of America for me." He hoped for Gabriel's sake this opportunity was real, but he still couldn't imagine himself actually going.

Just as the wind died down, a UNHCR officer came to the microphone. The crowd sat in hushed silence. "Young ladies and gentlemen, a great opportunity is coming to you." Cheers rose. "Representatives are here from several countries that have agreed to take a few thousand of you into an immigration program." More cheers.

"To be considered, you must be a real orphan, both parents dead; have arrived in Kakuma in 1992 or before; and not have taken up arms with the SPLA or any other militia. In addition, they are looking for young people who have shown themselves to be good students by staying in school and making good marks, never been arrested, have shown themselves to be of good character and are willing to work hard when they arrive in their new homes."

Ayuel elbowed Beny. "Guess we qualify," he whispered. An unreal sensation enveloped him, as if in a dream. He would do whatever they asked of him—until he woke up. *But this just might be real.*

"The government representatives will begin interviewing tomorrow. Those eligible will be dismissed from class at different times to keep the lines shorter. This will take several days. Bring with you your life story, written as neatly as possible. You will be asked many questions. Be careful and truthful in your answers for the same questions will be asked of you again before the final selection. Several teachers are standing up front with application forms. Fill out the form and bring it with you along with your life story to the interview. And also your Registration Card that you were issued when you first arrived in Kakuma."

The group of friends sought out Mel to help them prepare for the interview and found him on his way to the UNHCR building. "Hey, wait up, Mel," shouted Gutthier. "We need some expert advice."

"Hello. You guys are going to apply, aren't you?" Tall and handsome with an air of authority about him, Mel turned and shook hands with each of them. "I've got just a minute or two. This is going to be big. I'm working with the Americans and they've given me much to do. How can I help you?"

They all moved to the shade of a tree. "Thanks, Mel," said Ayuel. "We all want to go to the United States. So give us some hints for the interview." Ayuel felt his smile widen across his face as the excitement of possibility filled him.

"The United States is a good place. That's where I want to go, too," Mel said, taking a deep breath as if trying to think of some good advice he could offer quickly. "First of all, do you all still have the Registration Cards that you were issued when you first arrived in Kakuma?"

"They're at home in a safe place, but we all have them, right?" Madau looked at his friends for confirmation. They nodded.

"That's important. They're telling us that they can take only a few thousand people, a fraction of those applying. So they are really looking for names they can quickly reject, starting with those who've lost their cards."

"Doesn't the camp have a record?" Gabriel asked.

"Sure, but officials need to eliminate some people. Also, it's important that when you fill out the application form, everything must match exactly the information you gave for the Registration Card."

"I gave my name as James Garang."

"Who's that?" Beny said. "I thought you were Ayuel Leek."

"I don't know why I told them that. James is my Christian name and…"

"Put that on your application. And all of you were probably born January first, right? Even if you've later found out the correct date from a relative, don't change it."

That evening, until darkness fell, Ayuel worked on writing the story of his life, which was also part of the application process. Since paper was precious, he scribbled his first draft in small script, erasing, marking out and revising. Ayuel wondered if Rebecca was doing the same. He had seen her in the assembly, but she hadn't noticed him. That night after going to bed, the memories of childhood he'd brought to life swirled in his head, mixed with every possible emotion. Restlessly he drifted in and out of sleep. He thought of Aleer. *Is he alive? Did he make it to the university? What if he never knows I've left for a far-away country? What if Rebecca and I both go to the United States? Could we marry there?* He remembered his mother's face and the last time he saw Deng. They would never know what became of him.

At the first light of dawn, he got up and wrote front and back on his best tablet paper the final copy of his autobiography with a borrowed ball-point pen. Writing had brought belief and with belief, hope. He took his composition to his caretaker to look over.

"What do you think?"

After reading the autobiography closely, the caretaker suggested a couple of spelling changes. "You should have no problem based on what you've written here. I wish you luck, but anything can happen. Don't be too optimistic."

Being ready on the first day of interviews proved an advantage. The line outside the Red Cross building was shorter than it would be later, and the interviewers were fresh and interested. Ayuel did feel optimistic. He knew he fit all the requirements. When a grinning boy left the room and tapped him on the shoulder, he entered with confidence, shook hands with the representative and the interpreter. On the other side of the room, he could see Mel standing in the interpreter's spot by a table. Ayuel sat down in the designated chair.

After the standard questions that Ayuel had already written on the application, the representative folded his hands and leaned across the table. "James, why do want to go to the United States?"

To Ayuel that seemed obvious. *Why wouldn't anyone?* He hadn't prepared an impressive answer. "Well, I..." He could feel the heat rising to his face. Laying his hands palm down on the table, he sat up straight and said, "I am a seed, sir. I want to grow and develop, get the best education possible. I believe they have great universities in the United States. They have opportunities. And no war. I could learn a lot from them and someday come back to Sudan and help my country."

Without changing expression, the man put his papers in a folder, wrote James Garang on the tab, and said, "Thank you, James. Tell the next person to come in as you exit."

"I am a seed" must have sounded silly. Of course, the representative wouldn't know about Dr. John Garang's words.

TWENTY-FIVE

THIRSTY FOR KNOWLEDGE

L ife went on day after day at Kakuma Refugee camp. The *khawaja* had left, but they told officials that it would take two or three years to process the names. As people were accepted, they would be notified. For the most part, the unaccompanied minors remained isolated from the outside world, except for what their teachers told them in class. Ayuel, Beny and their closest friends studied hard, thirsty for knowledge. This made them more restless than the children who had given up on education. No one insisted they go to school. Yet all of them fought depression and a feeling of hopelessness from time to time. Beny, now twenty, and Ayuel, two years younger, worried about what their futures held.

From BBC radio and the one television in the hospital building, bits of news leaked out about something terrible that had happened in Nairobi, the capital city in Kenya. Beny and Ayuel had checked out a basketball and were headed toward an outdoor court to shoot a few baskets. They tried to piece together what they had heard.

"Apparently some important building was blown up and lots of Kenyans killed," Ayuel said. "I hope a war isn't starting here."

"We've about run out of countries to flee to. Uganda maybe," said Beny, nervously dribbling the basketball.

"Hey, wait up!" Gutthier was running toward them, waving a newspaper, something they rarely saw in the camp.

"Hi, Gutthier, where'd you find a newspaper? Does it tell about Nairobi?"

"Yeah, right here." Gutthier unfolded the paper to reveal the main headline: *American Embassy Bombed in Nairobi.* "I was hanging around the bus station when I noticed a driver sitting behind the wheel of his bus, reading this newspaper. I just walked up and asked him if I could have it when he'd finished with it."

"Gutthier, you're so bold. So he just gave it to you?" Ayuel said.

"After I waited around a while. Anyhow, have you heard about the bombing?"

"We don't know any details," Beny said. With their three heads close together, they pored over the article, exclaiming the details. Beny kept the basketball tucked at his side.

"... U.S. embassy in Tanzania, too... 257 people dead, 4,000 wounded..."

"... The Kenyan Minister of Education wounded..."

"Osama bin Laden? I thought Sudan expelled him in '96. Didn't he go to Afghanistan?" Ayuel said, surprised to find the terrorist leader operating so close to them.

"But his Al Qaeda is worldwide now," Beny said. "Says here he hates America for the Gulf War and for their bases in Saudi Arabia."

"So he's out to kill all the American infidels," Gutthier added. "That should take a while."

Ayuel released the paper to Gutthier. "Do you realize what this could mean for us here? The Americans supply most of our food. Without them, we would be in real trouble. And if this causes a war, we'll never get to go to the United States."

"Surely, Al Qaeda wouldn't attack the United States of America," Beny said. "Would they?"

"America is too powerful. They have most of the guns in the world," Gutthier said as he folded up the newspaper.

"I hope this doesn't start a war with the Americans," Ayuel said. "We need them."

Trying to get his mind off the news, he changed the subject. "Let's go throw a few hoops."

★

Ayuel admired Beny who, after receiving his high school diploma, had moved up to the position of manager over the entire Community-Based Rehabilitation Program. His position now included the training of CBR employees and teachers in primary and pre-schools. He made referrals for both children and adults in need of corrective surgery and sent them to the hospital in Loki or Nairobi. Classes for the deaf were under his supervision in two primary schools and classes for the blind met in the camp's Multipurpose Center—four wooden buildings with tin roofs. Beny developed thirty-four craft workshops for disabled persons so they could start small businesses and become self-supporting.

After Beny's staff identified a handicapped need, a technician would custom design an apparatus to correct the problem. When they found a four-year-old child in the Family Community who was unable to sit up unaided, the specialist designed a special chair for him that would hold him upright. Crutches were made on site to fit the person who needed them. Due to the difficulty of rolling a regular wheelchair over the rough ground, Beny made a three-wheeled one that could be peddled by hand.

After classes one Friday, Ayuel came by the center to visit with Beny and Samuel, who also worked there. They'd planned to go over to the soccer field to watch a match.

As they walked along to the field, Beny turned to Ayuel and said, "Did I tell you about Samuel's new job?"

"No, what?"

Samuel lowered his head to appear modest. "Beny promoted me to Supervisor of Zone One."

"That's good." Ayuel noticed the pride shining in Samuel's face. "You're skilled at supervising. And, of course, you're always concerned about people. You will..."

Before Ayuel could finish his praise, an unusual greeting interrupted them.

"Hel-lo, Mr. Young Single Man-a-ger!" Four pretty girls in flowered skirts stood several feet away and sang out the words multiple times as they waved and smiled.

"Who are they?" Ayuel asked, surprised that Beny drew such admirers.

"They're girls on my staff," Beny mumbled and gave a weak wave back to them.

Ayuel could see that Beny was blushing. "I think they're flirting with you. They're coming over."

"They just like to tease me by calling me that." When they got close enough, Beny introduced them. "This is Achol, Akoi, Martha and Fatuma. And these are my friends Ayuel and Samuel." After everyone politely shook hands, Beny said, "Fatuma is from Somalia and makes a delicious native dish called *aluo*, from wheat flour and sugar."

"And honey," Fatuma rolled her eyes and grinned.

"They all like to cook for me," Beny shyly admitted.

"Since you have no wife to prepare you good food," Akoi said. "In fact, we have an invitation for you now." She lowered her eyes and pulled out a folded paper from her skirt pocket and handed it to him.

Ayuel glanced over and saw the words printed on the outside of the paper: To Mr. Young Single Manager.

"Thank you, girls, but I really can't come this time. You're very kind, but..."

"You be there, Mr. Young Single Manager," Martha said. "We're all coming and making your favorite *kasira*."

Beny grinned and nodded an okay. The girls skipped away, giggling.

"They're all beautiful, smart girls—and they like you. Why didn't you want to go?" Ayuel asked.

"Oh, I don't know. I'm not sure it would be good to have a girlfriend who's on my staff."

"You're still in love with Mary A. Malek?"

"She was just a childhood sweetheart," Beny said, looking down and scuffing the dust with his foot. "Wonder what she looks like now, all grown up. She'd be seventeen."

"Suppose she made it to Panrieng?"

"Could be, but somehow I imagine her in that camp in Khartoum, looking for her mother. Maybe she found my sister and they are good friends."

"That's a good thought."

★

A short while later, Ayuel, Gutthier, Majur and Maruon headed back to their compound in the Family Community after Sunday morning services. Though all were nineteen now, they danced along the dusty path like children—expressing their recent cause for exuberance.

"It's incredible they selected all four of us as delegates," Gutthier said, jumping into the air.

"We've all been active in the Youth Fellowship, but..." Ayuel said.

"So have lots of others." Majur finished his cousin's sentence.

"Nairobi's a big city ..."

"Where that embassy was bombed last year!"

"Al Qaeda won't be after us, I don't think. Even if we are 'infidels'," Gutthier said, sneering at the unjust term. "Being chosen to go to a conference is the most fabulous thing that's ever happened to me."

"It'll be even more fabulous than the conference Beny was in two years ago," Ayuel said, remembering the twinge of jealousy he'd felt back then. "He said it changed his life."

Pastors from the various churches chose delegates who had proven themselves in leadership, faith and service. Kakuma would send twenty-three boys and two girls—one of whom was Ayuel's and Gutthier's friend Monica—to the Sudanese Youth Conference. Other youth delegates would come from different refugee camps in eastern Africa. Ayuel had no idea what to expect, but the feeling deep inside was like the anticipation he'd felt as a small boy when Dr. John Garang was coming to speak. That had proved to be an important day. It had given Ayuel the will to study and learn in spite of no visible sign that anything good might come of it. Again, he felt hopeful.

★

Two weeks later, the four chosen delegates spent the evening and night at the Leekmaduk compound to prepare for their trip. Leekmaduk's wife, Alual, pressed their best clothes with her charcoal-filled iron. She helped them each pack a small duffle bag that they'd been given along with the official white T-shirt that had *Sudanese Youth Fellowship* printed in black letters across the front. All expenses were being paid by the local churches. She prepared a special evening meal of rice and beans with herbs and spices. They would leave at five the next morning, before the usual mealtime, to meet the public bus at the road by six. Beny, Madau and Gabriel had come for the send-off celebration.

The boys all sat on the ground next to a pole fence Leekmaduk had built to block the harsh winds. They sheltered their plates of food as best they could to keep out the dust. The men and women sat at separate tables. Later, there would be singing and dancing.

"I hear Nairobi is a beautiful city," Gabriel said, "with very tall buildings and wide streets made out of concrete. You're going to have a wonderful time, just seeing all that." He took out his inhaler and breathed in.

"We're staying in a hotel that has three stories," Ayuel said, making an effort to describe what he could only imagine. "They'll have a room for every four people. The four of us will be together. I hope we'll be on the top floor."

"There's a picture on the brochure," Majur said. "I'll go get it." He finished his plate and ran to his *tukul*.

"What will you do all week?" Beny asked. "What's the conference going to be like?"

"Lots of speakers, I think, and discussion groups. It's mostly about peace," Ayuel said.

"About loving your enemies? I wonder if Riek Machar will make a speech. He lives in Nairobi, you know."

"I won't listen to anything he tells us," Ayuel said, feeling his excitement turn to anger.

"We'd probably have finished the war against the Khartoum government by now if he hadn't rebelled against John Garang," Madau said.

"Guess he wouldn't have much to say about peace—at least anything you could believe," Beny scoffed. "You know that kid in Panyido who claimed to be related to Machar?"

"Emmanuel Jal, who pretended to speak English? Machar adopted him, I think."

"Actually, it was his wife who found him in Waat," Madau said. "Some people say she was behind the split with Garang. She's the one who accused Garang of capturing boys to be soldiers. Of course, Machar did the same thing."

"Yeah, she was a British aid worker, a *khawaja*. Strange she would marry a black warlord."

"Emma was her name, and they adopted Emmanuel when he was about eleven," Beny said. "Emma was killed in a car accident only about a year later."

"I didn't know she died," Ayuel said. He tried to put this strange puzzle together—the commander who fought Garang, a white woman who died and the boy they adopted.

"Emmanuel was here in Kakuma for a Christmas celebration a few years ago. I talked with him some. He didn't say anything political but he was with a bunch of Nuers. I think he was still living with Machar."

"Here's the brochure." Majur returned, waving the folded paper. "Look at these buildings. They're called skyscrapers."

Beny took the brochure and studied the picture on the front, a cityscape of Nairobi. "They've got ten stories or more. And palm trees along the wide streets. That will be something to see."

★

The delegates' excitement mounted from the moment the bus arrived on the outskirts of Nairobi. With their faces bunched at the open windows of the bus, they shouted, "Look!" to each other as they pointed to the new sights. Ayuel was most fascinated by the cars. A long caravan of them drove up one side of the road, and another caravan came back the opposite way. Along the edges, cars were parked slanted side by side in a row. "Everyone seems to be in a hurry," he whispered to Gutthier.

"I'm going to have a car some day," Gutthier said, loud enough for Monica and her friend in front of them to hear. The girls turned and looked at him with skepticism. "Like that red one over there," he added.

"But you can ride with me in my large black car with white seats,"

Ayuel whispered and winked at Monica. Gutthier didn't seem to hear the remark as he stretched his neck not to miss a single detail.

"Sure. I'll be ready when you drive up," she said with a laugh.

Only fourteen hours after the boys had boarded the bus, they pulled up to the conference hotel. A huge banner over the entrance said CONFERENCE LODGING. The building belonged to a large Nairobi church and would house about 300 young people. When the bus stopped, the director of the group stood up to face the eager teenagers. "After we get inside, we will go to a counter for our keys. Wait in your rooms, and I will come by and show you how to use water faucets, the flush toilet and electric lights. Don't go anywhere until I meet with you. Then you can visit each other if you like. Follow me."

They talked in low voices with near reverence as they filed down the bus steps and then gawked up at the three-story hotel.

Inside, Ayuel stared at the wicker chairs and large, potted plants. Huge fans cooled the immense space. The two girls found a full-length mirror where they stood, made faces at themselves and giggled. The man behind the counter handed Ayuel a chain with two keys. "Room 307. The lift is to the left. Enjoy your stay," the man said in English.

"Thank you, sir," Ayuel said and turned to Gutthier. "Lift?"

Their director laughed. "You get to ride up to your room. I'll show you. Follow me." At the end of a short hallway he stepped inside a small, windowless box. Six people with their luggage crammed in after him. Ayuel thought he would be smothered. He took a deep breath and held it.

"Everyone going to the third floor?" They all nodded, too awed to speak. "Okay. Someone can punch that button with the three on it."

Ayuel's head felt light and his stomach turned. A second later, the door mysteriously opened to a long hallway. He sighed with relief, stepped out and laughed with the rest of the occupants.

Inside Room 307, Ayuel discovered four beds, two stacked on top of the other two. "I'll sleep on the top one," he said, climbing up to test it. The mattress felt soft and the covers smelled like fresh breezes.

"Come look out the window," Gutthier called. Ayuel joined his roommates to peer down on a huge zoo of roaming animals—giraffes, zebras and elephants.

"Now, this is the way to see wild animals," Majur said. "Up high, behind a window."

During these two weeks, the boys felt like kings. Every day, a housekeeper came to make their beds for them. Like excited children, they turned the electric lights on and off for amusement. No standing in line for hours or carrying heavy jugs of water. Hot and cold water flowed freely, simply by turning a knob. Bathrooms with showers were located at each end of the hallway, one labeled Men and the other Women.

In the mornings, they gathered downstairs for breakfasts of buttered bread with jam and a choice of milk, tea, coffee or chocolate milk. Ayuel didn't care for the strange taste of jam, but the fluffy bread was delicious. The first day they all drank milk, but on the second, Monica discovered chocolate. She convinced the boys to try it and everyone agreed that was the best. Gutthier warned the others not to drink coffee, because it had a drug in it called *caffeine* that was "bad for you."

Other meals were prepared outside the conference building where kitchens had been set up. Sudanese women made traditional dishes, such as rice and beans for lunch and soups for supper. As the delegates made new discoveries, they especially enjoyed these touches from their childhood homes.

TWENTY-SIX

KNOCK AND IT SHALL OPEN

Ayuel, Gutthier, Majur and Maruon stayed close together as they made their way to the assembly hall for the first session of the conference. All wore their new, white T-shirts with Sudanese Youth Fellowship on the front. They found places with the others from Kakuma, about a dozen rows from the stage. The two girls in their delegation sat in front of them. After welcoming speeches and several lively songs of praise, the audience was asked to sit down. Ayuel had never felt so alive, so energized.

Again he thought of the time he'd sat in the sun all day, waiting for Dr. John Garang. That speech had been worth it. Garang's words had inspired Ayuel beyond his expectations. That probably had a lot to do with his presence here today in this big, amazing city, trying to learn all he could because he saw himself as a seed of potential. He expected to hear lots of new ideas, new ways at looking at problems, something to help him conquer his anger and grow up to help his native country of Sudan.

The moderator was saying, "Before our keynote speaker, we have a young man here with a message of hope." This was exactly what Ayuel wanted to hear. He leaned forward, his hands on his knees. "Will you please come up to the stage, Mr. Emmanuel Jal."

"That's Machar's kid!" Ayuel turned and frowned at Gutthier.

"We don't want to hear what he has to say," someone shouted.

Audible groans rose from the Dinkas. The smaller group of Nuers clapped and cheered. Ayuel leaned back and crossed his arms over his new T-shirt. Emmanuel took the microphone and spoke in a clear, passionate voice: "I am here today to encourage you to become part of a new movement that I am organizing for unity and peace—the Sudanese Youth Association. You young men and women are the hope for our country. We need to come together—whether you are Dinka, Nuer, Equatorian or from some other tribe. We are all Sudanese and we all want our country to be at peace..."

"You live with Machar!" someone shouted. "He's the problem."

Emmanuel continued, "Forget the political issues between Garang and Machar; all the youth need to come together. The reason we came here to Kenya is to get an education, to learn, so we can unite all our people."

"We don't want to hear you!"

"Machar put you up to this. You're just trying to trick us!"

"Machar wants only war!" Monica and her friend shouted.

From the other side of the room came opposing words, "Garang makes little kids carry guns!"

The moderator stood and made a motion with his hands for the crowd to quiet down. Emmanuel didn't seem bothered by the outcry. His manner was charismatic and his words powerful. "If we the youth, the hope for tomorrow, do not come together, the discord will go on and on. Our children will grow up as we have, in a war-torn land without hope, without education. We need to carry God's gospel of love to all of Sudan..."

Ayuel and his friends stood with the rest of the Dinkas and shouted insults until Emmanuel left the stage. They were the words Ayuel yearned to hear, but he felt the messenger was false. "His words are too powerful to be his own," Ayuel said to his friends.

"No doubt, Machar wrote the speech," Maruon said. "I don't believe he means a word of it."

"Guess we told him," Monica turned and said as they all sat down.

"We certainly did, and we're right." Ayuel smiled at Monica. He felt comfortable around her now that they were "just friends." He still very much enjoyed her company, for they held many of the same ideas.

The moderator took the microphone and simply said, "There are refreshments in the hallway. Go cool yourselves off and be back in thirty minutes. Remember this is a peace and reconciliation conference."

*

In the hall, the boys found a long table with large, white plastic boxes, filled with green and red cans, sitting in water. Beautiful girls wearing long skirts, leather sandals and the official T-shirt handed out the cans.

"Soda?" One of the girls smiled at Ayuel, holding a can in each hand.

"The red one, please." The can was cold and wet. He watched people pull the little ring on top. He tried, but couldn't get it to work.

"Here, I'll show you," said the lovely girl with the smile. "You just pull it up like this and push back."

"Thank you, miss." He moved back from the table and found Majur, trying to open a green can. "You do it like this," he said.

Ayuel hesitantly tasted his soda, then gulped it down and belched. "What is this stuff?" He felt it fizz up his nostrils.

"Whatever it is, I like it," Majur said. "Ayuelo, how come we've lived in a desert place called Kakuma for years without knowing the world around us is so beautiful?"

"Yeah, and the America we hear about must be even more beautiful," he answered. "But it seems like such a far away dream to think we could ever go there. We've not heard anything since our interviews."

"They said it would be years before we'd know anything."

"Look, there's Emmanuel Jal going through the crowd trying to get people to join his Youth Association. What did you think of that speech?" Ayuel was glad to return to the moment.

"He's just trying to sound important."

Ayuel watched the young man work his way in their direction. He was shaking hands with the willing and seemed unperturbed by those who refused. When he stuck out his hand, Ayuel weakly took it.

"Say, don't I know you from Panyido?" Emmanuel asked, pumping his hand and grinning broadly. Before Ayuel could answer, he said, "Sure I do. I lived with your brother Aleer in Group Eight. How is Aleer?"

"Well, I don't really know. He's not written to me. He was in Kakuma for three years, but left to go to Uganda to continue his studies."

"That's good. Education is good."

Face to face, Emmanuel's personality seemed overpowering. Even though Ayuel still felt resentment toward him, to be polite he said, "That was a fine speech. Unity is a good idea." He felt a small amount of guilt over the protest.

Emmanuel looked deep into Ayuel's eyes and said, "I really meant what I said. Dr. Machar didn't write those words, I did. He's my adoptive father, but I live at a boarding school here in Nairobi. My real father was killed in the attack on Bentiu in Unity."

"That's the area my friend Beny Ngor Chol is from. Do you know him?"

"Of course, he's an age-mate of Aleer and was in Group Eight, too. I came in the same wave of refugees to Ethiopia, but I didn't know Beny until he came to Panyido from Itang."

Ayuel was beginning to like this impressive young man. Somehow, he seemed more sincere and personable up close. "You don't seem bothered that you were shouted off the stage."

Emmanuel took a minute before answering. "I go through the doors that God opens for me. He's given me a message. If people won't listen to my speech, I'll use music. I've already written several songs."

"I wish you well," Ayuel said and meant it.

Emmanuel moved on through the crowd, shaking hands. Ayuel watched him, admiring his confidence and deep faith in God. He was probably no older than nineteen like himself, but far ahead of him in knowledge and understanding.

The crowd began to move back to the assembly room. Ayuel thought of keeping the soda can as a souvenir, but changed his mind and dropped it into the large barrel by the door as others were doing. As he took his seat, someone introduced the keynote speaker, Reverend Ben Otiu, a pastor of the African Interdenominational Church who had written several books.

Ayuel leaned back, took a deep breath and opened his mind and heart in hope of finding some direction to his life.

"If you believe in God, your life will change. Knock and the door will be opened to you. It may take time."

This was the kind of message he'd hoped to hear. Ayuel leaned forward, his chin on his fist. *Tell me how. What do I do?*

Reverend Otiu told his own life story. In Sudan's first civil war, his village was attacked in much the same way Duk had been. His parents, grandparents, siblings—all were killed. Only he and his younger brother were spared. At age eleven, he took his brother by the hand, and together they walked south with other survivors to a refugee camp in Uganda. There was no need to tell of the horrors along the way. Most in the audience of refugees had experienced such a journey.

He planted crops so they could eat. Unlike the government of Ethiopia, the Ugandans didn't protect them. The Sudanese army attacked, killing his new friends. The United Nations then moved the camp to Tanzania in 1972. The conditions and the schools were not good. Few others of his Equatorian tribe lived there, leaving him feeling isolated and abandoned. He decided to take his brother back to Sudan.

"When we arrived in Juba, my life began to change. Until then, taking care of my little brother had been my only reason to live. A Christian missionary befriended us, took us in and found us good schools to attend. A few years later, the missionary brought me here to Nairobi where I finished secondary school and went on to the seminary. God is good. Trust in Him."

Reverend Otiu then invited anyone who wished to come to the front of the room and tell his or her own story. About a dozen young people formed a line. Each told his experience without tears, in a matter-of-fact way. But always at the end, they told of how thankful they were to be at the conference. The anguish of some only came out as they spoke of the grief, trauma and feelings of revenge they still dealt with.

Afterward, Ayuel made his way to the speaker and waited his turn. "Reverend Otiu, those were encouraging words. My name is Ayuel Leek and I would like to ask you a few questions, if you have time, sir."

"Ayuel Leek," the pastor said, looking directly at him as he shook his hand. "I will be happy to talk with you. Wait here a few minutes, please."

When Reverend Otiu had finished shaking hands with those who had come up, he took Ayuel with him out to his car. He reached inside and took out a small, white card from a leather case. "After the first session in the morning, they will play some baseball and other sports. If you don't mind giving that up, we can meet sometime before noon tomorrow. Right now I'm not sure what time I'll be free. Call me after breakfast at the number marked on this card."

"Of course. Thank you, sir." Ayuel had meant only to ask this wise man a few short questions while the line waited behind him. The invitation to actually spend some time with him was more than he'd ever imagined. He found such kindness touching. *Call him? That means on a telephone. How do I do that?*

Ayuel glanced down and noticed the pastor's name printed on the card and several numbers after the word *telephone*. This card he would definitely keep.

*

In high spirits, Ayuel threw himself wholeheartedly into the afternoon activities which included small discussion groups on a variety of topics, an informative lecture on AIDS and its prevention and recreational games on a wide open area of lush, green grass, edged with large shade trees. A panel discussion on anger followed dinner and then a walk with his roommates back to the hotel along the electric fence by the zoo. Every few feet a warning sign said "Danger. Do Not Touch." He imagined warning signs popping up throughout his life: Caution: Bombs Dropping; Danger: Wild Lions; Dangerous Water Ahead; Danger: No Water. *Best not to know what's ahead*, he concluded. *Not much you can do about it.*

That night as he lay on the clean, white sheets of the upper bed, hands behind his head, his mind swirled with all the marvels he'd experienced in one day. *Can my life ever be the same after all this?* He wondered how long he would have to talk with Reverend Otiu. *I'll have to find out how to use a telephone.* He'd seen a phone on the desk downstairs in the hotel.

The next morning, after a cup of chocolate milk, toast and butter, he went to the reception desk and asked the lady behind it, "Please, madam, could you help me make a telephone call?"

"Certainly." She smiled up at him in a way that made him feel helpless and ignorant. He handed her Reverend Otiu's card. She efficiently dialed the number and handed Ayuel the phone.

"What do I do?" he asked weakly.

"When your party answers, just say, 'Hello, this is'—whoever you are." Another condescending smile. "No, turn it this way and talk in here."

Party?

"Hello, this is Reverend Otiu."

The minister's voice was calm and inviting. Ayuel gave his name and said why he had called. The minister agreed to see him. They would meet at a bench under the tree next to the soccer field at eleven o'clock. Throughout the morning, more questions came to him as he listened to speeches and discussions in small groups. *I'll have to select a few of the most important questions.*

★

A few minutes before the appointed time, Ayuel approached the wooden bench under the tree and was surprised to see Reverend Otiu waiting, his Bible open on his knees. The pastor wore shorts, sandals and the official T-shirt. He stood and extended his hand. "Good morning, Ayuel. Are you enjoying the conference?"

"Indeed, I am, Reverend Otiu. I am learning so much."

After they both sat down and chatted about small topics, the pastor closed his Bible, set it aside and said, "Tell me what's on your heart, Ayuel."

"I have many questions, Reverend, but I suppose the most pressing is how to deal with my anger and hatred of the Arabs, the radical Muslims that have ruined my life and my country. I don't seem to get past that."

As Reverend Otiu made no comment, but only nodded his head as though he understood, Ayuel began to pour out his life's tragedies. Then, realizing the minister's time must be limited, asked, "What do I need to do?"

"I can't tell you, Ayuel, why all this happened to you. But I can assure you that you did nothing to deserve this evil. Nor are you being punished for sins of your ancestors. Dealing with it is a matter of attitude. Trust in God."

Ayuel wanted to ask the pastor how he could be sure about not being punished for others' sins. He'd like to believe it, but he'd been taught differently. Instead he said, "It's hard to trust when I have a desire for revenge."

"Of course. You can't just stop hating. You have to put something better in your heart. The more you love and the more you trust God, the more hate will gradually melt away. It's easy to kill. Much harder to forgive." He paused. "What else?"

Ayuel liked what the man said. It was easy to remember, but was that all? *No long lecture on avoiding sin or doing more praying or living a better life?* "Well, yes, I am also concerned about getting an education. I have a brother who went to Uganda. He was supposed to attend the university, but it's been two years and I haven't heard from him. I worry about him, and I also worry that I'm not getting the best education in Kakuma. For the most part, we have good teachers. It's so much better now that we have buildings to meet in. When we were outside, you couldn't hear the teacher half the time because of the wind.

"There're never enough books. If a teacher doesn't know the answer to something, often there is no way to find out. I'm just now learning how big the world is. Being here in Nairobi tells me that. I think about far away places like England and the United States of America. Life must be very different there. Several months ago, many of us applied to be accepted as refugees in a western country, but we've heard nothing yet. I think they have much better schools and we can live in peace in those places. I don't want to spend the rest of my life in Kakuma."

The minister spoke his simple message with feeling. "Build your trust in God."

Reverend Otiu laid his hand on Ayuel's hand and began to pray. He asked God to open the door of success for Ayuel's future, to melt the idea of revenge and show him a better way.

TWENTY-SEVEN

PAINFUL FAREWELLS

Ayuel returned to Kakuma full of hope. The experiences in Nairobi had opened his eyes to a wider world. God seemed to be more real and accessible. His social work became more meaningful. His days lugging jugs of water, standing in long lines and never having enough to eat seemed less tedious. In perspective, the tasks had more meaning, for now he felt that life could be different.

Like others who had progressed as far as high school, he was thought of as highly educated. And, as a returning delegate from the conference, he was assigned by the United Nations High Commission for Refugees to work in his zone, giving counsel to the desperate, the disabled and those who had lost family members. He continued to visit the critically ill through his church.

From time to time, Ayuel received an assignment from the UNHCR office to talk with an individual who was depressed or contemplating suicide. Often he was asked to make a presentation to a small group. As Debate Chairman at school, he had become especially knowledgeable on political issues, religion, war and peace. Other guest speakers came to the Multipurpose Center to talk to interested groups on nutrition, sanitation, job skills and similar topics.

The School for the Handicapped was held in one of the wooden buildings in the Multipurpose Center and supervised by Beny, Manager of the Community-Based Rehabilitation Program. A bus picked up the participants each morning and brought them to the center. One day, Ayuel was leaving the building after giving a talk to a group on the political situation in Kenya when he noticed several men in wheelchairs playing basketball on the outdoor court. As he approached, he realized Beny and Samuel played with them, dodging among the wheelchairs. He watched as a man in his fifties made a free throw, nailing the ball through the basketless rim. The man raised clenched fists in triumph. Everyone cheered and slapped each other's hands, regardless of which team they were on.

"Great shot," said Beny. "That'll do it for today. Some of you have physical therapy sessions coming up."

As the players wheeled off the court, Beny called out to Ayuel. "Hey, there's someone here I want you to meet." Beny grabbed the wheelchair handles of the man who had just made the shot and pushed him toward Ayuel. "This is my friend, Tiop-dit, whom you've heard me talk about since Panyido days."

"Hi, Beny. I'm glad to finally meet you, Tiop." He shook hands with both of them.

"So you're Ayuel Leek. I've been wanting to talk to you," Tiop said with a broad, cheery smile. "If you have a few minutes, why not now?"

"I've got to run," said Beny. "I've got an appointment with Mr. Kajirwa at the IRC office. See you."

Ayuel and Tiop found a spot in the shade of one of the multipurpose buildings. Ayuel sat down on a wooden bench, facing the older man in the wheelchair. Tiop's hair was tufted with white at his temples and his face deeply lined. He wore shorts that exposed the stub of his left leg above the knee, well-healed but scarred.

"They treat us well here," he said as if in answer to a question. "We get better food and rarely have Black Days. Beny makes sure we always have some food. He's a good man."

"He is," Ayuel agreed. "Beny takes his responsibilities seriously."

The two chatted amiably. Then, Tiop wanted to try out his English. *"Today, the air he be hot!"* he exclaimed.

Ayuel couldn't help laughing. "No, no. Say, *'It's hot today.'*"

"Eet's hot today."

"Very good.

"Which is eet you name?"

"My name is Ayuel. What is your name?"

Quickly switching back to Dinka, Tiop said, "That is what I wanted to talk to you about. Do you know what Ayuel means?"

"No, it's a family name. I've always wanted to know its meaning. One of my teachers in Panyido, Mr. Kiir Ayuel, thought we might be related, but he didn't know much about the origin of the name."

"Ah, Mr. Kiir. I knew him as a caretaker here in Kakuma. I told him what I know about the name shortly before he left for Nairobi. Only Dinkas use the name Ayuel and they are all related to each other. You are most definitely kin. So he was your teacher?"

"Yes, and a good friend too. I'm honored to be a relative of Mr. Kiir. Someone told me that somehow he got to the United States and works as a truck driver in a state called Tennessee."

"Glad to hear of his good fortune. Now, about your name—and his too. Ayuel was the great-great-great et cetera grandfather of all Dinkas. He lived about one hundred years before Christ."

"Really? A man named Ayuel started the tribe?"

"One of his descendants was a prophet."

"My mother told me there was a prophet with my name. He could foretell the future."

"Yes. And he could hold a spear in the air, let go and it would stay right there in mid-air. People came to him from far-away places, because he could perform miracles. He was of the Dinka-Ngok, like our friend Beny."

"Does Beny know about the prophet?"

"Sure. We've talked about it. There were many stories about him in that region. In fact, Beny has a Paramount Chief in his ancestry too, his great-grandfather Miakuach de Beny Kur. In 1799, this chief refused to allow the Arabs to build a mosque in Panrieng and in two other towns. Their leaders also wanted to move the border to put these towns in the North, just as President Nimeiri tried to do more recently. Miakuach said 'no.' As a result, they condemned to death all the chiefs of the region, but Miakuach said that since he was the one who answered 'no,' he alone should die. As they led him away, he turned to his sub-chiefs and said, 'When you bury me, leave my right hand sticking out so that you will know I am always with you and my people.'"

"And they did as he said?"

Tiop's eyes twinkled. "Of course."

"I never knew about that. Certainly he was a hero to his people. So what about the prophet Ayuel?"

"Well, one of the prophet's descendents, also named Ayuel, came to the region of Jongli and settled there in the southern part of Sudan, where most of the Dinkas live today, in the region of Bor. He became chief over all Jongli."

"Then my grandfather must have been a descendant of this Ayuel. He was chief over Jongli also. I would have learned all this history if...Well, you know, I was only seven when I lost my family. But even as a small child, I knew genealogy was important."

"That's why I am telling you all this. Was your grandfather Deng Malual? With twenty-nine wives?"

"That's him."

"He was given the name Paramount Chief, because he was so highly thought of by everyone."

"Except those who murdered him."

"Yes, of course. A book was even written about him in Arabic called *Paramount Chief.* He was quite famous."

"So what does my name, *Ayuel,* actually mean?"

"I think it means all the history that goes with it. Not just one word. You have greatness in your past, my son."

★

A short time later Ayuel, Beny and Samuel were leaving the hospital after visiting their friend Gabriel. He'd been having more frequent asthma episodes. With the last attack, he collapsed and was rushed to the hospital. His condition had become life threatening.

"I thought he looked better today," Samuel said. The three walked down a dirt path, discussing their friend's situation.

"The doctors can do little for him here," Ayuel said. "I hope, Beny, you can send him to Nairobi for surgery."

"Of course, I'll do what I can," Beny said, "but he really doesn't fall under my program. So many people have health problems and there are huge numbers of disabled."

★

Eventually, the IRC was able to arrange for Gabriel to be examined in Nairobi. The day after coming back by ambulance, he lay on his bed in the *tukul* he shared with friends. Ayuel sat beside him.

"They couldn't do anything for me. It's too expensive, and they say I really need to be evaluated by a specialist," Gabriel said. The back of his hand lay across his forehead as he stared up at the pointed thatch above him. "I'm getting weaker, and without the oxygen treatment or whatever I need, I'm never going to get well."

"Maybe help isn't too far away." Ayuel didn't want to hold out empty hope, but there was a glimmer he could share. After a pause, he said, "Some American representatives were here last week while you were gone. The rumor is they are choosing the first ones to go to the United States. Maybe they'll pick you. You were called back for the second interview. God must have kept you alive for a purpose."

Ayuel hated seeing his cousin, who used to be such a good athlete, lying there in poor health. He'd watched him get worse over the years. Only the miracle of treatment in the Western world could save him now, but he remembered what Mel had said about the representatives looking for reasons to reject someone. An expensive illness could be a good excuse.

Gabriel didn't answer, but Ayuel saw a tear roll from his eye.

"I'll bring you some tea."

★

At age twenty, Ayuel was in his senior year in high school. He dated several girls now and still enjoyed Monica's company, but he'd found it impossible to lose his love for Rebecca. They talked occasionally about world affairs and the possibility of going to the United States, but he made sure they were never alone together—to honor her stepmother's wishes. They both had been called back for the second interview—a rigorous process in which the applicant must answer all the questions exactly as before. A mistake could mean disqualification.

Only a few days after Ayuel had talked with Gabriel, an announcement that the names of the first applicants to be selected would be posted. As excitement mounted, all talk turned to "The List." *Who would be chosen first?* Ayuel got up early to check the bulletin board. Nothing. As soon as classes were dismissed, the news had spread. Too excited to form a line, the hopefuls bunched up in front of The List and quickly left, most with disappointed expressions on their faces.

One departing young man, Majok Bol, turned to Ayuel and, through clenched teeth, muttered, "It's hopeless. I don't know why I even came to look."

Ayuel could see more than disappointment in his face, something like anguished grief over a death. Putting his hand on Majok's shoulder, he walked with him a few steps. "There will be more postings. You're as qualified as many others…"

Majok pulled away. Ayuel watched him walk down the path with a bowed head. He knew Majok as a fine athlete and good student. He would probably be chosen ahead of himself. Ayuel thought no more about the man's comment.

As more eager, hopeful people were arriving, Ayuel decided to sit on a bench some distance away and wait for the crowd to disperse. He had picked up a booklet the day before called "Welcome to America." He pulled it from his back pocket and sat down to read. A few minutes later he looked up to see Gutthier on a bicycle rushing toward him.

"Ayuelo, good news!" he shouted. A broad smile lit up his face as he dropped the rusty bicycle on its side. Puffs of dust swirled upward.

Maybe my name's on the list. Ayuel swallowed hard and stood up, shoving the booklet back in his pocket. Gutthier had not even been called for the second interview. His teachers assured him it was just a matter of locating his original folder. They wouldn't pass over a young man of such talent.

"It's—Rebecca, the girl you liked, Rebecca Kuol!" Gutthier panted from his brisk ride. "I was just coming from Peace Training and stopped at the edge of the bulletin board. I stuck my head around the corner of it. Of course, I couldn't see the whole list for all the people, but at the bottom a little piece of paper had been nailed on. She's scheduled for a flight on Sunday."

Stunned, Ayuel found himself speechless for several moments. "Don't joke with me, Gutthier." Just hearing him say her name tore at his emotions, but the thought that she would leave without him left him anxious.

"Come see. Yours might be there too. As for me, I can't be hopeful until after my second interview."

"I'm sure they'll find your folder. Someone probably set it aside to review because you're so outstanding." Ayuel felt more concerned about it than his half-brother did, but he wanted to encourage him. Gutthier could be happy no matter the circumstances.

Gutthier picked up his bicycle, and Ayuel followed him to the bulletin board. "This seems so unreal. I can't believe it," Ayuel said more to himself than to Gutthier.

When they got close enough to see, Ayuel's eyes darted first to the attached paper at the bottom, with only the names of the three Kuol children on it: Rebecca and her two younger brothers. Ayuel's heart leapt to his throat. Now he searched the rest of the list. *Maybe we'll both go together. Maybe.*

"No one we know." Gutthier sighed. "There'll be more lists all year. This is just the first fifty." Ayuel slowly read through the list one more time and was starting over when someone pushed him aside. The realization that he might never see Rebecca again overwhelmed him. *If chosen, I might go to Australia or somewhere far from the United States.*

"Gutthier, please help me find a way for us to meet with her. You're so good at that sort of thing. You know I can't contact her."

*

That evening around six o'clock, Gutthier and Ayuel headed to Rebecca's family compound. As they approached, Ayuel could hear a large number of people talking and laughing. He could see Rebecca standing in the center as her friends and family competed to ask her questions and give advice. Never before had she appeared so radiant. He stood back as Gutthier elbowed his way to her. He watched them talk while the others politely waited. She seemed to be nodding her head in agreement. They shook hands when Gutthier left.

"Is she coming to talk to us?"

"Says she's too busy. Too many things to do to get ready," Gutthier said as they retreated. "But she said she would send you a letter tomorrow."

That wasn't enough. He longed to hold her in his arms one last time, to tell her how much he loved her…

★

Saturday morning Ayuel and Gutthier stood talking behind their *tukul* when they heard a polite young girl's voice ask at the front entrance, "Please, sir, where would I find Ayuel Leek?" He could hear Madau telling the girl where to look.

"I'm Ayuel," he said as the girl—about twelve years old—appeared.

"Here is a letter for you from Rebecca," she said in a tone of respect. She held out a folded sheet of paper, not even concealed in an envelope.

"Thank you and tell Rebecca 'thank you' too." He smiled at the messenger and waited until she left before unfolding the paper.

He read silently:

Ayuelo, I will remember you always. I hope you will come to America, and we can get married over there when we are older. But I want you to stop dating other girls. I love you and will see you at the airstrip tomorrow. Rebecca.

He handed the letter to Gutthier and waited until he'd read it. "I won't mess around with other girls, I swear it. That's very little to ask of me. Rebecca is always so optimistic. She really believes I will go to the United States, we will see each other again—and someday we will marry."

"I'm happy for you. That's a good letter and she's a good woman. Believe her."

"I'll wait and see."

On Saturday night, Ayuel could not sleep. Of all the emotions that engulfed him, the pain of Rebecca's leaving was the most overpowering. He tried to concentrate on the love she'd expressed to him and her hope for their future together. That seemed an impossible dream, but the pain of separation was real. Tomorrow she would be gone.

At five in the morning he finally fell asleep. At seven, Gutthier was shaking his shoulder, "Wake up, Ayuelo. It's Sunday morning, time to go see Rebecca get on the plane."

When he sat up, nausea flooded over him. "I can't go, Gutthier. I'll just feel worse if I see her get on that plane and leave me here in Kakuma. You go ahead."

"No big deal, brother. I'll represent you and say goodbye to Rebecca for you." Gutthier picked up his bike, jumped on it and took off.

Ayuel drifted in and out of sleep all morning. He could hear people passing by on their way to the various churches. The bells of the Catholic church chimed at eleven. Rebecca's plane was scheduled to leave at eleven thirty. Dizzy and sick to the core of his being, he got up and went outside. He walked out of the compound and leaned against the trunk of a skinny scrub tree. The hot wind flapped his shirt as he looked out over the vast refugee camp, *tukuls* as far as the eye could see—his home for the past ten years. *This is a forgotten and desolate place. I must get out of here some way, somehow. How can I live with my heart gone?*

The roar of a plane drew his gaze to the hazy sky. He watched the outstretched wings, soaring ever upward, until they became a dot—and melted into the gray.

★

Postings went up every few weeks. Ayuel always went to look, and his disappointment seemed especially painful as he recalled Rebecca's leaving. Gutthier had told him when he came back from seeing her off that her destination was a place called Denver, in the state of Colorado. Sometimes he wished he'd gone to the airstrip to tell her goodbye—sometimes not. When he saw names of friends on The List, he sincerely congratulated them, but always he felt a loss.

His cousin Akon—the only girl among the seventeen children who had walked together to Ethiopia—had found a way, with relatives, to make it to Canada before the first list had gone up. Samuel was sent to a town in Tennessee, the same state where Mr. Kiir had gone. Others were leaving one by one.

Months went by. It was now June, 2001. Anxiety was increasing throughout the camp. Ayuel, like the other applicants, found it difficult to let hope build, only to be dashed over and over again. Some were unable to answer the questions in the second interview exactly as they had the first time. People were rejected for insignificant details, such as a misspelled name or a wrong date. For others, their file folders were just lost. Many had become deeply depressed. Suicide was not uncommon.

Ayuel often talked with his friend Mel about the process. Directors of the Family Community had pushed to have foster children and their adoptive families go first in the resettlement program. In his position as one of the leaders over the minor zones, Mel had been involved in discussions about whether foster children or the unaccompanied minors should have priority. With limited places, Mel fought and won to have the minors go first. As he explained to Ayuel, all the children were orphans but the foster boys and girls already had the advantage of family life. Now it was time for the orphan boys to have their chance.

Today a new posting had gone up. Ayuel felt the excitement rise as he inched toward the front of the gathering at the bulletin board. Mel Deng was the first name he recognized. On second reading, his own name was still missing, but there was his cousin's name: Gabriel Manyang. *Good. He needs to go.* Ayuel rushed to the IRC office and picked up the letter for Gabriel.

Back at their *tukul* he found Gabriel sitting outside reading a schoolbook. "Hi Ayuelo. I'm so far behind in my school work, everyone's passing me by." When he noticed the excitement on Ayuel's face, he added, "But you look like something good's happened to you."

"No. To *you*." He sat down on the ground beside his cousin, glad to see he must be feeling better. "You may not need to catch up. Your name was on The List!" Grinning broadly, he handed Gabriel his letter.

"Praise be to God. He's not forgotten me." He tore open the envelope and read silently. "They are sending me directly to a hospital in Harrisburg in the state of Pennsylvania. Says they have specialists for asthma. What a miracle!"

"That's the miracle I've been praying for." Ayuel squeezed Gabriel's shoulder. "You deserve it. Looks like they're going to treat you immediately. That's wonderful."

"Anyone else going that you know of?"

"Mel Deng. I hope he will be on your flight to see you're well taken care of. But he's going to the state of Missouri."

"Doesn't matter. It's in the U.S.A. and they have a good hospital." Gabriel looked back at his letter. "It says the orientation is on Friday. I may just feel like going."

★

Ayuel carried Gabriel's bag to the gate at the U.N. office where the bus waited to take the people leaving to the airstrip. Though skinny, short of breath and hollow-eyed, Gabriel was well enough to board without assistance. Mel and his younger brother, destined for Kansas City, walked by his side and would be with him most of the journey. "God will be with you, Gabriel. It's your time for healing," Ayuel said. Sad as he was at this parting, he felt optimistic for his cousin.

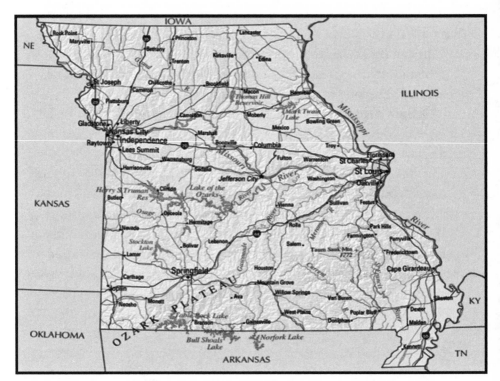

Map of Missouri, courtesy of the National Atlas of the United States of America

TWENTY-EIGHT

U.S.A.: DREAMING AND REALITY

In July, both Ayuel and Beny found their names on The List. Beny would leave that month and Ayuel in August, but it was a somber day. On their way to the bulletin board, they had noticed a crowd gathering at the dry riverbank. A young man's body hung from a high limb of a tree. Moments later they learned that it was someone they both knew—Majok Bol.

In a cruel twist of fate, Majok's name clearly appeared near the top of The List—less than an hour after he had finally given up hope.

*

No news had come back to Kakuma about the ones who had gone, but both Ayuel and Beny were destined for Kansas City, Missouri. Wherever that was, they hoped it wasn't far from Harrisburg, Pennsylvania, so they could check on Gabriel.

The next morning, Ayuel, Beny and Madau sat in a large room with about fifty others at the Multipurpose Center waiting for the day of orientation to begin. Everyone clutched his "Welcome to America" booklet and other papers they had been handed upon entering. The noise level was low, but the excitement ran high as friends grinned and made jokes about how they would become rich and famous in America.

Finally, an officer of the IRC came to the front and introduced a young American man with yellow hair. "Congratulations," he began. "You have been chosen to come to the United States because we believe you will adapt well and contribute to our society. After five years, if you are living a successful life, have a job and are self-supporting, you may apply for citizenship. Or at some point, Sudan may have settled its differences and you may wish to come back to your native country."

After this brief introduction and more advice about working hard and following the laws of the land, he showed a video about how Americans live. The young people were awed by the scenes from cities with their towering skyscrapers and streams of vehicles on the many lanes of highways.

"Wow, this is much grander than what I saw in Nairobi," Ayuel gasped. "How do all those cars keep from running into each other?"

"Bet we'll all be driving one before long," whispered Beny. "Everyone has a car of his or her own there."

The scene changed to the rolling countryside of mid-America. "What funny cows they have! No long horns," Madau mumbled behind his hand. "Look how green it all is—all that grass and forests of trees. That's where I want to live."

The next segment showed a family eating at a large table in their home, passing around bowls of different foods. The camera swept through several restaurants and ended with a fat man driving up to the window of a building where someone handed him a big round sandwich—right through the window. He drove away, munching as he wove his way through traffic. The audience went wild with laughter.

"How can they do that?" Ayuel said in amazement. "Now he's taking a drink from that large cup through a straw." The driver screeched to a halt at a stop light, set down the drink and put a small object to his ear.

"What's he doing?"

The narrator on the film answered. "Americans often talk on their cell phones while driving, but it's generally considered an unsafe thing to do." The driver sped away when the traffic light changed, swerved around another car, honked and slammed on his brakes to avoid hitting a truck. "This is not a good way to drive." The man folded up his cell phone, finished off his food and pitched the wrapping paper out the window. "Throwing trash out the window is against the law. Just because some people do it, you must not." Everyone howled.

"This is unbelievable!" said Beny. "Driving and eating and talking on a tiny telephone. I didn't even see a telephone cord, did you?"

"No. Strange habits these Americans have. But I like their cars."

The *khawaja* turned off the video and said, "The United States is much farther north than we are here. Unless you go to Atlanta, Georgia, or Phoenix, Arizona, you are going to find snow and ice in the winter."

Madau elbowed Ayuel and pointed to his destination on the acceptance paper: Atlanta, Georgia. "No snow for me," he whispered.

The presenter held up a poster that showed a street with houses and cars covered in white, several inches thick. "This is what happens when it snows. These children are building something called a snowman. I'm sure you will make one of these or participate in a snowball fight. That's when you clump snow together and throw it at each other. Since it's soft, it doesn't hurt and it's lots of fun." Ayuel and his friends snickered. It seemed like a strange way to have fun.

"Now here is something you can really get your hands on." He laughed as two of his assistants brought out a large rectangular chest, like the ones Ayuel had seen in Nairobi that held red and green cans of drinks. The presenter reached in and took out a huge clear rock a bit smaller than a soccer ball. "This is a chunk of ice." When he held it up, water dripped from it and ran down the man's arm. "I'll pass this around, and you can see what lakes are like when they freeze over. Also, you may see freezing rain that covers everything just like the snow does. Snow is soft, but ice is... well you can see for yourself." His assistants passed around several chunks of the stuff. Nervous laughter and an occasional shriek rose throughout the room as the Africans made their first acquaintance with ice.

Beny handed his chunk to Ayuel and watched him react. Ayuel's arms began to ache as he tried to see how long he could hold on to it. "This is strange stuff," he said, passing it off to Madau. Water dripped onto his bare legs. He winced and laughed at himself.

"Winter in America," the man said.

"I wonder if Missouri is in the north or the south. I hope it's in a warm place." Ayuel shuffled through his papers and found a U.S. map. Only the states were labeled, no cities. "Here's Colorado where Rebecca went. It begins with C-O, but I don't see an M-O."

"Here it is," said Beny. "Montana—M-O."

"That's far to the north!" *And very far from Colorado.* With his hands still cold and wet, he wiped them on his shorts. "We're doomed to snow and ice."

"Just make a snowman or throw snowballs at everyone," Madau said with a chuckle. "It'll be *fun.*"

★

A large number of Beny's relatives, friends and staff came to see him off, making it a joyous occasion. The girls who worked for him had made a banner, saying "Goodbye, Mr. Young Single Manager. We love you!" They held the banner and chanted the words as Beny approached the gate at the U.N. office to get on the bus. Everyone else had said their good wishes, leaving Ayuel to walk beside him the last few steps. The two friends shook hands. "Beny, have a good trip and I will see you in Montana when I get there."

"Thanks, Ayuelo. I wish you a good flight, too. Just one more month and you will be out there."

The two men had experienced so much together since their days as children in Panyido. Ayuel looked into his best friend's eyes and then threw his arms around him. A lump in his throat blocked any more words. Beny turned, walked through the gate and out to the waiting bus, carrying the one duffel bag he had been issued. Along with twenty-some other passengers he ascended the steps, turned, waved and disappeared inside. Applause rose from the crowd. *A whole new life awaits Beny. May God go with him and bless him.*

★

In August, Ayuel waited in the U.N. office, his duffel bag in his lap. Inside he had placed the Dinka hymnal from Pochalla, the one that replaced his copy lost in the Gilo River crossing—a precious memory of difficult days. Madau had left that morning on the flight to Atlanta. Donayok, their mentor from the days of the long hazardous walk to Ethiopia, sat across from him, next to Gutthier. Donayok had chosen to stay in Kakuma and get married. Gutthier's folder from the first interview had never been found. "Too bad," the social worker had said. Monica's records had met the same fate. With tears in her eyes, she had told Ayuel goodbye the day before. *I know how she feels.*

With all the joy of facing his new life, knowing that in four days he would see Beny and other friends who had gone to Kansas City—and some-day he might find Rebecca—Ayuel still felt the same sadness he'd known so many times watching others leave. Now he was parting from Gutthier, who had been with him since childhood and helped him in so many ways. They'd shared all the experiences of their lives up to this point. His age-mate. And with Deng and Aleer gone, Gutthier was his only remaining brother.

Donayok carried him through the deserts of Sudan after Ayuel had nearly died. At that time, he thought of the leader of their group of seventeen as an adult, but Donayok had been only fourteen. Through the years, Donayok had been his advisor, counselor and friend. The time Ayuel had been sick with malaria, Donayok and Gutthier took turns sitting with him in the hospital.

When it came time to board the bus for the airstrip, Ayuel walked between Donayok and Gutthier. As he stood in line, he asked, "What are you going to do? You can't live the rest of your lives in Kakuma."

"I'm thinking of saving my money and going to Australia," Gutthier answered. "It's not such a fast-paced life there. Monica thinks she will do the same. I might raise some sheep."

"I'm not going to stay forever in Kakuma, but life isn't too bad when you have a job in the camp. After we're married, I'll apply for a permit to work in Kenya," Donayok said, shrugging his shoulders. "See what happens."

Ayuel knew how valuable Donayok was as head of Zone One. He admired them both for their optimism and the way they always looked for solutions when situations turned bad.

"Write us a letter when you get to Kansas City and tell us what it's like in Montana. We'll let you know what we do," said Gutthier.

As they stood in line, Donayok slapped his hand on Ayuel's back. "You be good and follow all their laws. I've never been there, of course, but I've heard some people drink a lot of alcohol and go to places called nightclubs and get into trouble. Don't do that. I also hear there is much violence over there. You could get hurt. So take care of yourself in the Western world."

"I will."

"Get a job as soon as you can so you won't be homeless. Don't do anything wrong and get put in jail," Gutthier added with a restrained laugh.

Ayuel remained silent. He appreciated their words of advice, but there was nothing he wanted more than to have a successful life. He would try very hard.

As his turn came to pass through the gate, Ayuel kept his head down and avoided eye contact. He shook hands with them both and accepted their embraces. Turning toward the bus, he didn't look back, not wanting them to see the tears running down his face.

*

Through the smudged glass window of the small plane, Ayuel watched his past slowly sink away. He could make out the tin roofs of the Multipurpose Center's buildings, the bell tower of the Catholic church, the winding dry riverbed and thousands of round, pointed thatched huts stretching far and wide, but ending where the bare earth began. How amazing to see its entirety! Just as he had watched planes disappear into the sky, Kakuma faded away.

When he walked into the airport in Nairobi, Madau had been waiting and ran toward him saying, "Just like you described it, Nairobi is a fabulous place. We'll be here for two days, and…"

"I know, they told us. We get shots and more orientations." Madau's enthusiasm had swept away Ayuel's sadness about leaving, and Nairobi brought to mind happy memories. International Organization of Migration workers surrounded them and the others from Kakuma. "We'll take you to your hotel in about an hour. Meet back here in this area," said one young man. Ayuel noticed the I.O.M. workers all wore T-shirts with the words, "Lost Boys of Sudan."

"What does that mean, Lost Boys?" Ayuel asked.

The worker looked down at his shirt, "I've no idea." He shrugged his shoulders. "That's what the Americans are calling you guys."

★

Since Ayuel had experienced electric lights and running water at the Nairobi conference, he felt comfortable using them in the much nicer hotel. That evening, he and Madau sat near the front in a hotel meeting room. A man from Somalia, who now lived in Texas, was leading an orientation session. When he asked if anyone had a question, Ayuel raised his hand. On his lap lay his U.S. map of the states. "I don't understand why Kansas City is in Montana rather than in Kansas. New York City is in the state of New York, so…"

"Well, that is puzzling, isn't it?" the man said, scratching his head. "You see, Kansas City isn't in either state. It's in Missouri, right in the middle of the United States. You'll like it there. Next question."

Ayuel had wanted to ask if it snowed there, but at least he was happy it wasn't Montana.

"Still farther north than Atlanta," Madau whispered.

★

Later that evening, a couple of men Ayuel and Madau had known in Kakuma came to their room. "We brought you a few things you will need in America," one of them said when Madau opened the door. They handed each of them a plastic bag.

Ayuel dumped his out on the bed.

"This is a toothbrush for brushing your teeth. Americans don't use split twigs, you know. To make it taste good, you put a bit of this toothpaste on it."

"Soap and towel. Thanks," said Madau.

"What a beautiful blanket!" exclaimed Ayuel.

"Actually, it's called a bedspread. You put it on top of your sheets and blanket. This nice embroidery was made by women here in Nairobi."

"Thank you," said Ayuel, lightly running his hands over the colorful stitches. "Something to remind me of Africa."

★

The next flight took them to Brussels, followed by a long one crossing the ocean. A woman from the I.O.M. met their flight and directed them to the area where they would catch their next plane late that afternoon. Ayuel and Madau spent most of that day in the JFK airport. Afraid to wander far, they gawked in the shops and admired the huge airport. While they were standing in front of a sports shop that displayed shirts with New York Yankees printed across the front, a man stopped to chat. "Where youse guys from?"

Madau and Ayuel looked at each other, unsure of the question. When the man repeated it, Ayuel said, "Kenya—I mean Sudan."

"S'll the same. Africa, right? Youse guys play sports?"

"Not today, thanks," said Madau. The man shook his head and walked on.

"What did he say?"

"I've no idea. The English that people are talking here doesn't sound like what we learned."

English wasn't the only language they heard. People from many different countries in their native dress, some with small children, scurried about trying to read signs, as wide-eyed as they. But it was easy to pick out the Americans.

"I didn't know they were all so big," observed Madau. "Wonder if Americans are like that normally, or if they think it's handsome to be fat."

"I know I don't want to look like that," said Ayuel. "I think it's because they have so much food. In five years, I'm afraid we'll be like that."

"We won't be able to wear these clothes."

"No one is wearing shirts like ours. Or shoes." Ayuel looked down at his flip-flop sandals. They'd both worn their best African shirts, collarless and free flowing with embroidery framing the v-neck. "We do look different from most people."

*

As the plane dropped lower over St. Louis, Ayuel pressed his face to the glass, fascinated by the spectacle of lights just coming on—some in straight lines, some randomly placed—something like the stars over Kenya. Madau had left earlier on his flight to Atlanta. Ayuel's seatmate, dressed in suit and tie, made no effort to speak to him. A few remaining "Lost Boys" at the back of the plane would all get off here, and he would continue to

Kansas City, Missouri alone. He looked at the watch he'd been given at one of the orientations in Nairobi, along with a lesson on telling time. Seven p.m. He'd slept most of the time since New York, but now he felt alert and excited at the thought of seeing his friends in Kansas City.

The plane bumped a bit as it touched the airstrip. Ayuel remembered the I.O.M. lady in New York had told him to remain on the plane in St. Louis. The next stop would be his. When the plane finally crawled to a halt, the passengers jumped into the aisles and opened the cargo bins above for their luggage. After standing a very long time, the line of people began to move up the aisle. As each Sudanese young man passed, he leaned over and shook Ayuel's hand, whether they knew each other or not. "Have a good life." "God Bless." "Good luck."

Two girls he'd talked with at various stops along the way were the last of the group. One leaned across the businessman. "Aren't you getting off?"

"No, I go on to Kansas City."

"Oh," she laughed. "I thought maybe you were a *lost* boy."

★

When the plane finally took off, Ayuel watched the bright lights of the city grow dim and fade under clouds. When the plane descended, again the lights brightened and spread out over all the earth. Apparently, the whole United States was one huge city, or the cities all ran into each other. The lighted buildings and highways with moving car lights stretched as far as he could see, but fear gripped him as the plane slowed and stopped. The tunnel to his new life stretched out from the airport to the door of the plane. He must cross it. Now. *Where will I stay? What do I do when I get off? Will there be an I.O.M. person to help me? When will I see Beny, Mel and the others who went to Kansas City? And Gabriel—did he make it to the hospital?*

Of course, he had these thoughts many times on the journey, but they seemed overpowering in the *now*. The businessman sat unmoving, his briefcase upright on his lap, adding to Ayuel's anxiety. When the passengers slowly moved up the aisle, the man got up and pushed into the line. Ayuel quickly did the same, pulling his duffle bag and plastic sack from the overhead bin. He took a deep breath. *Well, Future, here I come. God will be with me—as always.*

TWENTY-NINE

A ROMANTIC CALL

Ayuel scanned the crowd as he emerged from the tunnel, his bag over one shoulder and the sack clutched in his hand. Only a few steps in front of him stood Gabriel and Mel. He walked briskly toward them. "Gabriel, is that you? I thought you were in Harrisburg."

"I was, but moved here. Welcome to America!" Gabriel looked amazingly healthy and bright-eyed.

"Mel, you've taken good care of him. Glad to see you. What's life like here? Where am I supposed to go?"

"Just calm down," said Mel, taking his baggage. "There's a van and driver from the Don Bosco Immigration Office outside. We're taking you to your new home. You will be living with eight other guys: your friend Beny, Dominic Leek Leek, Dominic Dut Leek, Anderia Mayom, Abraham Deng, David Wuor, Samuel Atak and Samuel Malual. I think you know them all."

"All but the last one." Ayuel had hoped he wouldn't be too far from Beny. Now he'd be living in the same house—and with others he knew. *This is good!* He got in the big car, called a van. Mel crawled into the back seat and Ayuel sat in the middle seat with Gabriel. The driver took off, merging into heavy traffic with barely a glance at the swift-moving vehicles around him. "How do Americans drive like this?"

"That driver is a Dinka from Sudan. He's been here a few years and works for Don Bosco Center. He'll pick you up in the morning to take you there to fill out some papers and get more clothes. I can tell you now that they will pay for your needs the first three months. After that, you're on your own. And you'll have to pay back the air fare of $800."

"That's fine with me. I want to get a job right away." Ayuel remained engrossed in the buildings, the lights, the cars. As they drove through an area called the Plaza, it seemed a magical and fanciful world of fountains, flowers and statues.

"Me and my brother live just down there," Mel said, pointing.

"I go to a good doctor whose office is right up the street," Gabriel said, indicating the opposite side.

"So you're not short of breath and tired any more?"

"Not at all. Good as new—that's an American expression," Gabriel smiled. "They've found just the right treatments for me and are teaching me how to take better care of myself. Now I'm ready to find a job."

"Is that hard? How do you do it?"

"We're waiting for our Social Security numbers—you have to have that number to work—and some other legal papers," said Mel. "The Center is trying to find mentors for us from various churches and organizations. They'll help us find jobs. Soon we'll have to pay the rent, buy food, pay the electric and phone bills."

Ayuel couldn't believe how much they'd learned in just two months. The van now drove down streets that were not so well lit. The houses were smaller and not as nice. Papers blew across the streets and old bicycles lay in the yards with tall grass. "Why is no one walking? Does everyone drive? Even the poor people?"

"Or ride the bus," said Gabriel. "They do walk some, but it's past ten o'clock at night. We're in your neighborhood." The van turned slowly onto Olive Street and stopped in front of a shabby two-story house with a porch. "This is it!"

★

Inside, his friends all rushed to welcome him. Beny got up from watching their very own private television set. Everyone talked at once:

"Would you like a soda to drink?" "We're making you a big dinner." "Did you eat on the plane?" "Did Madau get to Atlanta?" "Let me show you how this works."

Strange as it all seemed, Ayuel felt he had come home to a loving family. Anderia, whom he'd known since Panyido, took him by the arm and led him upstairs. He switched on the overhead light. "This is our room. And that's your bed with a whole outfit of clothes and some shoes. The Center brought these by today." To Ayuel, it seemed like a palace. Someone had already brought his bags up and set them by his bed.

"It's beautiful. I have a bedspread that a friend brought me in Nairobi." He pulled it from the plastic bag and Anderia helped him lay it across his bed. "I'm so tired. Maybe I'll sleep some before we eat."

"Sure. Anything you want. We want you to be happy here," Anderia said. "Let me show you the bathroom."

Ayuel followed him. Anderia, at six feet four inches, was the tallest in his new family. Like Beny, he'd fled from his home in Panrieng at an early age. His six lower teeth were missing, due to his family's fear that he might get tetanus and not be able to eat if his jaws locked.

"Do you know how a shower works?"

"I think so. I used one in Nairobi."

Beny stuck his head in. "We're cooking chicken and rice for you. You hungry?"

"No, but I should be. I've only eaten what they gave us on the plane—which wasn't very good. I had a soda before St. Louis. I'd like to lie down awhile first."

"Sure. We'll come get you when it's ready."

Ayuel lay down on his new bedspread, closed his eyes and heard his friends quietly close the door.

When he woke later from a deep sleep, he thought it must have been early morning. *The driver from the Bosco Center is coming by for me.* He hurriedly showered, put on the new clothes and rushed down the stairs. "Is the driver here for me yet?" he asked, fearful he was too late.

"He doesn't come until morning," said Gabriel, who had not gone back to his apartment. "Hey, you look like an American already."

"You've just been asleep an hour," said Beny. "I was on my way to wake you for dinner." All his friends laughed at Ayuel's mistake, but he didn't mind. He was hungry now and ready for their welcoming party.

★

The next two weeks seemed a blur. There was so much to learn and Ayuel enjoyed every minute of discovering his new world. The nine young men on Olive Street talked endlessly about their adventures and the funny things that happened.

"When I was in the airport in New York," Beny said one evening while he and Ayuel were washing dishes, "I kept seeing these signs that said 'restroom.' I wondered why they had so many dead people and why they would keep them at the airport."

Ayuel burst out laughing. "Sure, that's the word we use for the place to put bodies before they're buried. So how did you find out?"

"One of the other guys told me. So we went in." Beny was laughing now. "I don't remember what they called these rooms in Nairobi, but I remember you had to do something to make the water run. In New York, you just put your hands under the thing and water came out."

"I know. And hot air would blow from a machine and dry your hands for you. This is a strange world."

Anderia finished sweeping the kitchen floor and pulled up a chair. "Remember, Beny, that first week when someone had brought us food? We didn't know what to do with it."

"I can't believe how nice the Americans are, helping us get settled here," Ayuel said, placing a stack of dishes on a shelf.

"A lady from the Episcopal church came by a few days after we moved in," Anderia said. "She brought us this can opener, which solved the mystery of the cans. We didn't know how to get the food out. And these dish towels. Paper towels for cleaning up spills and some cooking pans."

"We had just put the food in different places," Beny continued the story. "She opened the refrigerator and saw the cans of beans and corn. 'No, no,' she said. 'These go up here in the cabinet.' When she opened that door, something that looked like milk started dripping out. 'Oh, my goodness,' she said. 'Ice cream goes in the freezer.' We'd never heard of ice cream, so it was no big loss when she poured it down the sink."

"So what is ice cream?"

"I still don't know, but I know it was in a hard, cold box when I put it up there. It felt like that ice they passed around at the first orientation. She made a list for us of the things that go in the freezer, what goes in the rest of the refrigerator—like milk and vegetables. Sugar and flour should be on a high shelf, not under the sink. She's been back a few times and is helping us understand money. Four quarters to a dollar, and things like that. Her name's Jean."

★

With his friends, Ayuel cautiously explored downtown Kansas City, learned to ride a public bus, eat at McDonalds's, shop at supermarkets with automatic doors, drink from a drinking fountain, go up escalators and down elevators—all with the excitement of a child in an amusement park. For recreation, they had access to an outdoor basketball court next to a closed-for-the-summer school. Their time was full with activities.

Some of Ayuel's housemates had received their Social Security cards and were applying for jobs. Mel had already begun working at a lumber company. Different organizations, schools and churches learned of the Lost Boys. Few seemed to have heard of Sudan or their civil war, but some people were curious and wanted to help them in some way or at least hear their stories.

One day, as several of the young men sat in their living room reading the Sunday newspaper, the one telephone—located in a downstairs bedroom—rang. Always an exciting event, they all stopped, put down their papers and looked at one another. Who would be brave enough to answer this time? Often it would be a person who talked too rapidly or had difficulty understanding one of them.

Anderia volunteered. When he came back in, he announced, "It's for you, Beny. He's talking in Dinka, so no problem."

The others listened attentively to Beny in the next room as he replied with expressions of surprise in the Dinka language. Then in English he said, "Send her my mailing address since you have e-mail and I don't. Thank you, Madau, that's fantastic news!" Not forgetting his manners, he added, "And how is your life in Atlanta, Georgia?"

After a few moments, Beny came back and sat down on the couch, covering his face in his hands, choked with emotion. Ayuel and the others waited in silence, knowing he would share his news.

"Well," Beny finally said, "Mary A. is in Kakuma."

"You just missed her," said Ayuel. He added, "Then she knows you're here?"

"Yes." Beny took a deep breath in an effort to appear calm. "You can e-mail a message now on the computer in the IRC office—for a few shillings. Anyhow, Gutthier sent an e-mail to Madau and said she'd come to Kakuma from Ethiopia. You know Gutthier, he's going to meet any new girl who shows up in camp. Gutthier said she has grown up quite tall and is very pretty. She would be a twenty-year-old woman now. She was only eleven the last time I saw her."

"So is she going to write to you?" Anderia asked, leaning forward to learn the details.

"I hope so. I gave Madau my address here on Olive Street. Gutthier didn't say how she got to Kakuma or if she ever found her mother."

"She will tell you all that, I'm sure," Ayuel said. "Did Madau give any other news from camp or about himself?"

"He said there are a lot of us in Atlanta. They've had their pictures in the newspaper with stories about them. A man from the Catholic church is his assigned mentor. He takes him to church and for job interviews. From Kakuma, Gutthier is still planning to go to Australia and Donayok is already married. He says it's really depressing in camp with so many of the leaders and best students gone."

Ayuel thought of Rebecca. Maybe he could get her address or telephone number from the Don Bosco Center. He'd already learned how to take the public bus there and back.

★

The next day, Ayuel did take the bus to the Center, the first time alone. Immigrants from many different countries had found jobs there. They understood the problems of new arrivals. A man from Mexico helped him find a registry of all the Lost Boys in the United States, listed by state. Under Kuol, he found Rebecca and her two younger brothers listed with a foster family. He wrote the number on a slip of paper the Mexican gave him and stuffed it in his jeans pocket.

Back at home on Olive Street, he punched in the number, the words already formed in his mouth. Instead of Rebecca's voice, a man said, "We cannot come to the phone right now. Please leave your name and number after the beep." By the time it beeped, he remembered about answering machines, one of the orientation lessons. He quickly blurted out the prepared words: "Hi, Rebecca, this is Ayuel Leek. I just wanted to let you know I had arrived in the U.S. safely. I will call you again." For two days, he tried every hour or so. Ayuel began to lose heart, thinking Rebecca did not wish to hear from him.

The following day he got a call from Mel Deng. "Hey, Ayuelo. I just got a call from your friend Rebecca in Colorado. You know, when you leave a message on a machine, you need to give your telephone number as well as your name."

"So she wants to talk to me?"

"Of course. She said her foster parents didn't answer the phone, because they took her two little brothers to Washington D.C. Rebecca is in Florida at a foster children's conference. When her foster mom got home, she telephoned her to say she had received a call from some man—Leek something. Rebecca knew it was you, so she called me."

"Did you give her my number?"

"Yes. She said she'd call. She doesn't want you to call her very much, because the foster mom is so good to them, Rebecca doesn't want to bother her. So just wait for her to call."

Ayuel's happiness soared—for about half a day. Then anxiety set in. He couldn't call Rebecca. Waiting and disappointment were not new for him, but it was still very hard to wait. One evening while Ayuel watched TV news, the phone rang. He could hear Anderia say, "Calling from Colorado?"

He ran to the phone. "Hello?"

"Is that you, Ayuel? This is Rebecca Kuol."

"Of course. I can't believe I'm hearing your sweet voice again."

"I thought you went to New York," she said. "It's good to be a city boy."

"No. I don't like New York. Too big and too many people."

He felt his heart pounding, but he was over his nervousness. They chatted easily about their living conditions. She would be moving in with some other girls and her brothers would stay with the foster family that treated them all so well. Rebecca asked him what his goals were, now that he was in America.

"I want to live the American dream," Ayuel said with a big smile and gestured with his hands for emphasis. "I want a good job, get a degree, nice house and drive a BMW!"

"Good luck," she said, and he could hear her laughing. "I'll talk to you soon."

After the goodbyes, Ayuel sat quietly, savoring the sweetness of her voice.

*

Mail appeared in the box attached to the front of the house every day except Sunday. They took it in only when the box was full and waited for Jean to come by and tell them what was important and what wasn't. She would take the bills to the Don Bosco Center for payment. "The three months will soon be up for most of you," she explained. "Then you will need bank accounts and checks to pay the bills."

Beny started checking the mail every day now, hoping for a letter from Mary A. When no letter came after a week, he made a long distance call to the IRC office and left a message for Mary Ajok Malek, giving the date and time he would call her. Jean had helped them all purchase phone cards so they would each be responsible for their own calls.

Ayuel was the only other person home the Saturday morning that Beny placed the important call. When the connection was finally made and Mary had been called to the phone, he said, "Mary A., this is your old friend from Panyido and Pochalla, Beny Ngor Chol."

"Yes. I've been waiting here in the office. Gutthier told me where you were and I've sent you a letter. So much has happened. How are you? What is America like?"

"It's a nice place. I miss you. I wish I could have seen you before I left."

"Me too. Everyone knows you here. They say you were a big manager."

"Did you ever find your mother?"

"She's in Khartoum. It's all in the letter."

After a few more minutes, Beny said, "I can't talk any more now. I still like you."

"I like you too. Goodbye."

★

Beny was in the living room when the letter came—but not in the mail. A new group of Lost Boys had arrived in Kansas City the day before. A friend from Kakuma, Zacharia, hand-delivered the message. Beny was pleasantly surprised to see him when the doorbell rang. Ayuel heard it as well and was on his way downstairs just as Zacharia came in. After exchanging hugs and sharing experiences of their journeys, Zacharia pulled a folded envelope from his shirt pocket.

"I have something here for you—brought all the way from Kenya from a girl you used to know."

"Mary A.?"

"That's right. I've got to go. Someone is waiting for me in the car to take me to a place called the Don Bosco Center to fill out some papers."

After Zacharia had left, Beny sat down, holding the envelope. Ayuel started to go back upstairs to give him some privacy. "No, stay. You know I'll share it with you after I read it." Carefully he peeled open the envelope and withdrew the folded papers. Three pages. He read and re-read for a long time while Ayuel sat patiently waiting.

Beny leaned back and sighed heavily. "You remember she left our temporary camp in Pochalla with an older cousin to return to our home in Panrieng? That's where our village was burned years ago and her father shot. Mary was separated from her mother and the other children, and she came with her auntie to the camp in Panyido where we met."

"Sure, I remember you telling me all that. You found her again in Pochalla after we crossed the Gilo back into Sudan. She thought her mother might be in a displacement camp in Khartoum."

"Right. Well, Mary A. and her cousin—and the group they were traveling with—got no farther than Nasir after leaving Pochalla."

"Hadn't Riek Machar broken away from the SPLA at that time and made Nasir his headquarters?"

"Yes. Machar was capturing all the children. Mary A. was among them. She was only about eleven then. I'm sure she was terribly frightened, but she didn't tell me her feelings about any of it. Her cousin fought alongside the SPLA and had some fingers blown off. He was captured too and sent along with the children to the Internal Displacement Camp in Khartoum. It didn't take her long to find her mother, who was not in good health. They stayed together in that camp for several years. It must have been a very bad place, though she doesn't say much about it—just that it was unsafe, little food and no school.

"When she heard there was a refugee camp again in Ethiopia, her mother said she should leave with a group planning to go there. Mary A. wanted to stay and care for her mother. Her mother said—let's see, here it is in the letter: *Go with this group. You are old enough, Mary Ajok. You must go to school. There is no school here. I am too old to travel. Let education be your mother and father.*

"Mary walked all the way back to Itang in Ethiopia, but there was no school. She knew her mother, being a widow, would never be able to pay for her to go to school in Khartoum. When she heard about the schools in Kakuma, she went on to Kenya with some others. She got there only a short time after I left."

"But now you've found each other."

"That's good—very good. In five years, I should have my U.S. citizenship. I could go back and marry her."

THIRTY

STRIVING FORWARD

That Tuesday morning, exactly one month after Ayuel's arrival, he and Beny were at the Don Bosco Center talking to a counselor about job opportunities. The man had just told them that Simon Deng, a Lost Boy and friend of theirs, would be arriving at the airport that afternoon. The counselor asked if Simon could stay with them that first night until they could make arrangements for his permanent lodging. They enthusiastically agreed.

In the corner of the large meeting room, a few women were watching the television set turned low. Suddenly a woman began beating her head and screaming, "Oh no, oh no!"

The three of them went over to see what was going on.

"It's the end of the world!" moaned another woman.

"What—what's happening?"

"We don't know yet. Look!" The three stood transfixed behind the women as they watched on the screen an airplane crash directly into a skyscraper.

"See! There goes another one!" a woman shrieked.

"Is this really happening or a horror movie?" the counselor asked. Although from Ethiopia, he had lived in America several years and knew how real fantasy could be.

A woman changed the channel. On the screen another plane was crashing into a building. She flipped through all the channels. Everywhere planes were flying into skyscrapers.

"That's New York City," Beny said. "There's the Statue of Liberty and isn't that the United Nations?"

"Here comes another airplane! I can't believe they keep flying into the skyscrapers!"

"Why can't they stop them?"

"Is this real?"

"That's the same building—and the same airplane. We're seeing it happen over and over."

"No, it's not. Look! That's a different building. The one behind it has already been hit."

A broadcaster was saying, "… no accident. This is an attack on the United States."

"Look at all the smoke… the people running, screaming… they're jumping out windows."

"This is real. Who would do this to the greatest country on Earth?"

"Listen."

Again a newscaster's voice: "No one can locate President Bush. He was reading a story to schoolchildren." The image of the baffled President came on with a man whispering something in his ear. He continued reading. "They've whisked him away—to a safe place, I'm sure. Vice President Cheney is in an undisclosed location. The CIA believes Al Qaeda is responsible for this. Osama bin Laden…"

"Bin Laden? How could Al Qaeda get here?" Ayuel clasped his hands to his face in disbelief. "We came to a safe country and terror has followed us here!"

★

The next morning Jean and her friend, Barbara, from Christ Episcopal Church, came by. "We had a service last night at church about the attacks, to pray for those who lost their lives," Jean said, giving each of the guys a hug. "The whole nation is in mourning. It must be especially difficult for you who have endured so much horror yourselves, and now to see this. We thought it might help to share some of our pastor's thoughts and some scriptures that he read."

They all gathered around the large dining room table while the two women went through the program in the church bulletin. Ayuel found the service comforting but it left him with many questions. Though much older now, trusting in God and understanding the cruelty in the world seemed as difficult now as when he crossed the hostile desert as a child. He excused himself a moment. When he returned, he was carrying a black book.

"Oh, your Dinka hymnal," Beny said, his voice lilting.

"I thought you ladies might like to hear us sing a Dinka hymn. It's meant a lot to us to sing together during bad times."

"Yes, of course," Barbara said. "You brought the hymnal with you from Sudan?"

"Sure. It's really my second one," Ayuel explained. "I lost the first one at the Gilo River crossing. I've had this since I was eleven or twelve years old. Some of the songs have been translated from English to Dinka, but I like this Dinka one about the Children of Israel who endured so much persecution. God promised them blessings if they remained faithful. He would always be with them. When the Jews scattered around the world, they took that faith with them. God has scattered the Dinkas. Good will come from it."

The young men gathered around Ayuel to look at the words and sang in their native language:

> God promised to stay with me forever.
> My government cannot protect me.
> You will protect me from those who want to kill me—
> And I will follow Your will.

"That's beautiful," Jean said. "You guys have great voices and you sing with feeling. Thank you."

"It's certainly fitting for this sad day," Barbara added. "I enjoyed your singing."

"Most people have been very kind to us," said Anderia. "Everyone can tell we're from a foreign country. Late last night someone was banging on the door. Then they seemed to be throwing something against the house. Our American friends wouldn't have come that late."

"And a Sudanese would have called out our names," Beny added. "We think they were trying to break into our house."

"That could be." Jean thought a minute. "You know, this isn't the best part of town. Not everyone will be your friend in America. You have to be careful. You were right not to open the door."

★

The following evening Beny and Samuel Atak were cooking a meal while the others huddled around the television set listening to the news—still all about the attacks. When they learned that no planes could land on American soil, they worried about what had happened to the plane Simon Deng was supposed to be on. He should have stayed with them last night.

"Hey, guys," Beny called from the kitchen. "Salt would make this chicken taste a lot better." After the meager, bland food of the past fourteen years in refugee camps, they enjoyed their flavorful cooking. But they still couldn't get used to eating more than once a day. Food Stamps and the small allotment of money for their first months were quite adequate.

"We'll go get some at that little food store down the street," Anderia offered. Four others, including Ayuel, decided to go along, as it was getting dark. After a couple of blocks, Ayuel noticed a sign in a yard. "No Trespassing."

"Maybe we aren't supposed to be in this area," Dominic suggested. "It could be dangerous here." The five young men stopped to decide what to do.

"There are people on the other side of the street. Maybe we should walk over there," David said, gesturing in that direction. When they all turned to look, they noticed that the people—about six men and women, plus some children—were all staring at them. One man seemed to be making a cell phone call.

"I say we keep walking on to the store and not look back at them," Ayuel said, leading the way.

A few minutes later, a police car with lights flashing, screeched to a stop right beside them. The young men froze in place.

Two officers jumped out. "Put your hands behind your heads! No dummy, like they do on cop shows."

They finally got it right. One officer placed his hand on the handle of his gun and watched them closely while his partner searched them. "Now put your hands behind you. No, put them together. Ain't you guys ever been arrested before?"

After clicking handcuffs around their wrists, the senior officer asked, "Where do you live?"

"Back there on Olive Street, sir," Anderia said.

"What's the number?"

None of them could remember. Ayuel knew it had only three digits, and he should know, but being so frightened he couldn't think.

"Where you from? You don't look like African-Americans. You Muslims?" Ayuel and Dominic were proudly wearing their African shirts and flip-flop sandals. They knew their English sounded funny, but hadn't realized they'd be mistaken for Muslims.

Ayuel hesitated a moment before answering. They'd been persecuted as Christians by radical Muslims. He answered simply, "We're from Sudan."

"Where's that?" The officers seemed more relaxed now, like they were enjoying this.

"Just north of Uganda and Kenya, sir."

The officers stared back at them.

"Below Egypt," Beny offered.

"Oh, in Africa. Why didn't you say so? What are you doing here? Somebody called, said there was a suspicious looking gang of foreigners out here. Could be terrorists."

"We're going to the store, sir."

"To buy salt."

"Stah? Sahl? What's that?" The officer looked confused.

"For food," explained David. "We're cooking chicken. We need salt for our food."

"Humph! Got any I.D.?" When Ayuel and his friends seemed puzzled, the officer said more kindly, "You know, like a driver's license, green card, something with your name on it."

"Not with us," Ayuel said, feeling his brain click back on. "I can give you the number of the Don Bosco Immigration Office." When he gave the number, the officer dialed it on his cell phone.

"Guess they've all gone home, but it's the right number. There's a recording." He and his partner unlocked the cuffs. "You guys take care of yourselves, now."

The officers got back it their car, turned off the spinning light and slowly drove off.

★

After someone tried to break into their house and the near arrest by the police, Ayuel realized America wasn't all paradise. Now, the excitement of new discoveries and incidents of cultural shocks were covered by a cloud of anxiety. Everywhere they went, people talked of last Tuesday's attacks. How could this have happened in the United States of America?

All air traffic had come to a halt. Ayuel, Beny and the other refugees from Kakuma were especially concerned by rumors they'd heard at the Don Bosco Center that foreigners would no longer be allowed in the country. Another rumor suggested the plane carrying Lost Boys—including their friend Simon Deng—had been sent back to Frankfurt, Germany. Ayuel could imagine the pain he must be feeling, to have his dreams dashed.

The tension brought back the old discussions about the plight of their war-torn country, the role of war, understanding God's purpose, forgiving your enemies and their purpose in life. Big questions.

Saturday morning, September 15, Mel and Gabriel came over. With Ayuel and Beny, they sat around the living room of the old house on Olive Street struggling with these ideas.

"You remember the air show that second week I was here?" Ayuel asked. "We watched from the basketball court as the planes flew over in formation. I thought about how I would love to fly over Khartoum in one of those planes and drop bombs on the city. If every Lost Boy could do the same, we'd win the war, but of course…"

"I know you used to say the solution to Sudan's problems was to kill all the Islamic Arabs," Beny said, sipping his soda from a can. "And I thought we should just forgive our enemies."

"So what's the answer?" Gabriel asked. He dipped tortilla chips into melted cheese and unbuckled his belt to make room for more.

"Both force and forgiveness are necessary," Beny said. "But we are all Sudanese. We should learn to live together,"

"But how?" Mel asked. He took a swallow from a bottle of water he'd brought along. Ayuel couldn't understand why someone would pay a dollar for water when it was free from fountains wherever you went and clean water ran from the pipes in the house.

"Well, this is what I think now," Beny said. "We can't forgive our enemies when they will not talk to you. They come to kill you in the night. In 1992, Garang tried twice to set up negotiations in Nigeria between the Sudanese government and the SPLA. It failed. Why? Because the SPLA was in a weakened condition.

"I still believe we must forgive. We must find out what we are doing wrong—and apologize if we need to—but we can't do that until they sit down and talk with us. So what I believe now is that the South must become more powerful and the National Islamic Front weak. Then we can negotiate from a position of strength."

"I agree," Ayuel said. "Of course, I gave up the idea of killing all the Arabs long ago, especially after my talk with Reverend Otiu in Nairobi. I also remember Dr. Garang said education for us was a weapon. The Lost Boys are scattered all over the world now—cities in the U.S., Australia, Canada, Europe. Wherever we are, we can get our story out. Educate people. We've already found some who are curious and ask about Sudan. Let's tell them the horrible things going on in our country. Other countries must help us."

"Right," Gabriel agreed. "The Lost Boys can go out, not in airplanes to bomb, but armed to educate the world."

"But at the same time," Beny said, "we must weaken the enemy. Only then can we sit down and negotiate a settlement between the North and the South. We are not rejecting them, but they are rejecting us."

"You're right," Mel added. "Without fighting, there will be no peace. And, Ayuelo, you are right too. The Lost Boys are the future of Sudan. When we all have our education and become American citizens, we can go back with power and bring unity to our country. Democracy cannot break down the door. It must slowly come in stages. When we visit our homeland, we can bring a vision of the democracy we've seen here. I love this country, because they respect the lives of each person."

"In spite of the attacks," Ayuel said, "this is mostly a peaceful country. I'm so concerned about all the people we've left behind. I want to transfer the peaceful life we've known here in this country to Sudan. Everyday life goes on here just as it did before the attacks by Al Qaeda. I think..."

A ring of the telephone interrupted his thought. As usual they all looked at each other. "Okay, I'll answer it." Beny went to the bedroom phone.

The others heard him exclaim, "What! He's at the Center?... Sure, we'll be here."

Beny came back with a broad smile. "Simon Deng is at Don Bosco Center. They just picked him up."

"His plane didn't go back?"

"It went to Canada. He's been there since Tuesday. Someone from the Center is bringing him over right now," Beny said with excitement. "He can tell us the rest. That's great news!"

"Gabriel, you and Mel stay for dinner," suggested Ayuel, brimming over with joyful anticipation. "We'll make a big meal for him like they did for me."

★

That evening after dinner and cleaning up, the twelve young men sat around the dining table, still in apt attention as Simon told of his adventurous trip. His plane had landed in Toronto, Canada, rather than returning to Frankfurt. He spent three nights in a hotel there. On Friday, he rode an Amtrak train to Boston with other Lost Boys destined for that city, and just this morning was able to take a flight to Kansas City. He wore a brightly colored African shirt he'd bought in Nairobi.

"There's quite a large group of Sudanese people living in Toronto. Some are Lost Boys—as they call us—but also families and others who have lived elsewhere before moving to Canada."

"Did you get to see any of them?" Beny asked.

"I did. The word got out that we were stuck there because we couldn't fly into the United States. There were four of us from Kakuma sharing a room that had an extra sitting space, so a group of them came to visit. Of course, everyone was asking if anyone knew certain people, friends and relatives, you know…" Suddenly Simon stopped.

"What's wrong? Go on."

"Nothing's wrong. I just remembered something very important," Simon said, grinning from ear to ear. "Ayuelo, do you have a brother?"

"Only one who could still be alive. I haven't heard from him in several years, but he's supposed to be in Uganda." Ayuel was puzzled, but didn't expect any news about Aleer.

"There was a man in the group who said he was from Duk. I know you are from there, so I told him your name. He said he knows a Deng Leek who lives in Toronto and he is from Duk. Could you be related?"

"There must be some mistake," Ayuel said, afraid to even consider that this could be his oldest brother. "Both names are quite common among the Dinkas, but it's a pleasant thought anyway."

"Wouldn't hurt to call him." Simon handed him a phone number. "He said there aren't many Ayuels. I gave him the Don Bosco number, which was all I had."

The others seemed more excited about the connection than Ayuel. He sat stunned, seeing in his mind his twelve-year-old brother coming toward him and Aleer while they played soccer. And that last time they walked a path together, the Maradona T-shirt he'd bought for him in Bor.

"It couldn't be Deng," he whispered. "He died long ago."

*

Sunday afternoon, Ayuel called the number. No luck. Finally an operator told him how to dial a Canadian number. Someone answered on the fifth ring, but the connection was bad, full of humming and crackling sounds. He hung up. It was not to be.

Later that evening, the phone rang. A few of his housemates were upstairs, but he was the only one downstairs, near the phone. Not feeling comfortable answering, he waited. It kept ringing. Finally, he went in and sat on the bed. He picked up the receiver.

"Hello?"

"Ayuelo?"

"Who is this?"

"Ayuel, this is Deng, your brother."

"I don't believe you." He stood up as a feeling of irritation, almost anger, came over him. "How can you prove it?"

"Calm down, Little Brother," the voice said. "Our mother's name is Nyayul."

Now he knew. His chest tightened and his throat choked. After a few seconds he was able to ask, "What—what brought you to Canada?"

"Sit down. It's a long story."

"How did you know I wasn't sitting?"

"I just know. Thank God, I've found you! Someone told me they knew you and Aleer made it to Panyido, but I learned that camp was chased out." He heard Deng clear his throat. "I'll try to be brief and write you a letter later. Well, I made it to Itang and joined the SPLA. John Garang was upset there were so many children in his army. When he went to Cuba to ask Castro for arms, he said he was a Communist—which of course he wasn't. But he also asked him to take the boy soldiers, those under fourteen, into his country where they could go to school and avoid the war. Castro, being a good friend, agreed. One hundred seventy of us were shipped over and placed in a boarding school. It wasn't bad, but I had to learn Spanish. Now I'm speaking English and French.

"We had food and a place to stay. In 1998, Pope John Paul II came to Cuba for a visit. I was at the University of Havana and part of a group of students who didn't want to live in a Communist country. We chose a committee to appeal to the Pope. He granted our request and arranged for us to come here to get a better education. I'm studying to be a veterinarian, you know, an animal doctor."

"I know. For cats and dogs."

"I'm more interested in cattle."

"Of course, you're Dinka."

Ayuel tried to tell his brother a few facts about his life over the fourteen years they'd been separated, but his emotion at finding his brother made it difficult to talk. They agreed to write each other.

"Deng, Aleer went to Uganda, to Kampala International University, in 1997. I've not heard anything since."

"We'll find him. Don't ever give up."

THIRTY-ONE

AMERICAN LIFE, SUDANESE DREAMS

Two weeks after Ayuel's arrival in Kansas City, I went with Jean Schmitt for my first encounter with the nine young men who lived on Olive Street. Jean had already been mentoring them and calmed my apprehensions. I was worried about how I would be received. I need not have been concerned, as they welcomed me with handshakes and hugs.

They were all very tall and thin. Ayuel Leek Deng, fine featured and reserved, impressed me with his gentle and polite manner. Beny Ngor Chol seemed to be the one in charge and showed me around the old, two-story house. We were going to take them on a picnic. As we all left, I was surprised to see that the guys rushed out the front door ahead of us. Later, I learned that in Dinka culture the man goes out first in case there is danger, such as wild animals.

Officially, the Don Bosco Immigration Center assigned Beny and Samuel Atak to Jean and Ayuel to me for their mentoring program, but until other mentors were found, we were also involved in the lives of the other young men living with them. At that time, Ayuel went by the name James Garang. I knew him only as James until we began working together in earnest. Now I address him by his African name, as he has requested.

That day we stopped at a fast food place to get our lunch. The guys giggled over their difficulty in filling their cups with ice and soft drinks at the self-serve soda machine. That was the first of the many adjustments I witnessed them struggling through. After we purchased food and drinks they piled back into our two cars, folding up their long legs, and we headed out to a quiet public park for the picnic.

At first, as I watched and listened to them, they seemed to me like children emerging into a bright new world, eager to absorb it all. Yet, they were very serious about their ambitions. They all assured us they wished to work hard, earn their way, hold jobs, get a good education and that they appreciated all that the Americans were doing for them.

I sat across from Ayuel at the picnic table as we munched chicken and French fries. After a short while he laid down his food and faced me directly, though his eyes seemed to be gazing far away. In a matter-of-fact tone he told me some of the experiences of the thousands of boys and girls who swam the Gilo River chased by tanks and guns. He was a child of eleven at that time. As I listened to the facts of the mass murder, I sat stunned, trying to wrap my mind around this incredible event.

Almost as if making a confession, Ayuel told how one boy had clung to his foot in the water, but he'd kicked him away. Otherwise, they would have both drowned. Then he picked up his drumstick and continued eating. Never before had I come so close, face-to-face, with such sheer horror. Whatever I said must have sounded shallow, as there were no words to express how deeply his experiences affected me.

A few weeks later, I invited Samuel, Beny, Ayuel and Jean to my house for lunch. During the afternoon, Beny told me his childhood story. At age nine, he'd stood in stagnant water for hours not daring to move, covered with mosquitoes, and watched enemy soldiers chop up people with axes and even kill a child by beating her against her mother.

Again shocked, I mumbled something inane. From the time I first met these guys, I've loved to talk about them at every opportunity. But I could never bring myself to mention Beny's story. When I finally wrote it down for this book, I let others read it, but I don't believe I have ever spoken it aloud.

Those were the only accounts I got with emotional details for four years. During that time, my encounters with the boys mostly produced bare facts. When they finally began to open up, letting me know more, Ayuel explained that at first, even though they wanted me to write the story, it was too painful to talk about.

I asked myself, *How did they come through all these experiences and be the bright, energetic, personable, entertaining and philosophical young men they are today?* I'm sure there were many people in Africa—teachers, ministers, relatives and fellow travelers like Donayok and Tiop—who guided and shaped their thoughts. But one fact is evident to me: they know God up close in a way I never will on this earth. Often I heard one of them say, "God is good."

*

Once the guys had obtained their Social Security cards, they began searching for jobs. Though intelligent and adaptable, learning the culture and appearing all-American presented the biggest hurdles. When one of the nine, Dominic Dut Leek, landed a job counting and packing money for a casino, he asked me for a quick course on the face value of our coins. The nickel being twice as large but only worth half as much as the dime puzzled him.

Jean and I drove the boys to multiple job interviews and helped them fill out the applications, but we were not the only ones assisting them. Gina Moreno, an employment counselor who worked with refugees from the Don Bosco Center, tells of the day twelve young men walked into her office. They immediately won her over by their sincerity and respectful manners. She has remained a close friend and mentor to them, continuing to help through her own agency: Integrity Staffing. She found jobs for approximately thirty of them and placed seven or eight, including Beny, at Fixtures Furniture. He operated woodworking machinery, assembled parts, packed, shipped, put finishing touches on products and even served as a translator for other Sudanese with limited English.

Ayuel, soft-spoken and reluctant to speak well of himself, was among the last to find employment. We agonized with him. Finally, he called me with the good news. He said he had prayed and cried all night. In the morning, he received two phone calls close together with job offers. After talking it over with us, he chose to work at the luxury Crown Center Hotel downtown. He had already learned how to manage the bus routes. He was given a free lunch, but as he chose the items he felt surprised that so many people chose to eat leaves (from the salad bar) when perfectly good meats and vegetables were available. Later, he also worked at Fixtures Furniture; then Cardinal Health, filling orders and shipping prescriptions, and stocking at Wal-Mart.

Jean and I enthusiastically threw ourselves into mentoring. Jean took on the job of helping the guys pay their bills. At first they pooled their money, handed it over to her and she wrote the checks for rent, telephone, gas, electricity and other expenses. One time, attempting to strike out on their own, they mailed cash for the phone bill in the company-supplied envelope with no identification. Fortunately, Jean was able to track down the right office, identify the sender and have the money credited to their account. Eventually, they had their own checking accounts and individual phone cards for long-distance calls. Cell phones were not far behind.

Jean and her husband, Ed Schmitt, a lawyer, helped several of the guys apply for Pell Grants. By September of that first year, they were enrolled in courses at Penn Valley Community College. The Schmitts also arranged for the nine to get out of their lease on the Olive Street house. The area was dangerous, infiltrated by drug gangs and random violence. They were able to move into two newly-decorated apartments on Knickerbocker Street in downtown Kansas City only a few blocks from the college.

Being a former schoolteacher, I helped them with their English and tutored them for their classes. One day in October while working with one of the guys, a group burst in, brimming over with excitement and waving books in the air. Since they were all talking at once, it took a few minutes to learn the cause of the fuss. Richard Berry, mentor to Anderia Mayom and Dominic Leek Leek, explained that he had just taken the group to purchase books to prepare them for the GED exam. Like kids on Christmas morning, they stretched out on the floor and couch, thumbed through their treasures and shouted out new nuggets of knowledge. Their eagerness for learning was a joy to behold.

That fall, I witnessed their enthusiasm in many other ways as we helped them acclimate to a new culture. I took Ayuel to the public library where he got his first library card. There, I began our initial interviews for this book. My head spun as I tried to envision *his* culture of cattle camps, spears and family compounds of grass and mud huts—culture shock in reverse.

The five or six guys that Jean and I took to a Laundromat one afternoon adjusted easily to the process of wash, dry, fold. Their main focus, however, turned to a simulated driving apparatus set up for children to watch a screen and make the moves behind a steering wheel. As I watched six-foot-four Anderia scrunched down in the seat with the others crowded around, cheering him on as they waited their turns, I realized how eager they all were to begin driving. Afterwards we treated them to ice cream. They said there were too many choices and that the cold hurt their teeth. Well, not everything turned out to be as much fun as we'd expected.

We took them for doctor and dental checkups. Anderia got his six lower teeth replaced that had been pulled when he was a child, so he could receive nourishment in case he got tetanus. Having never eaten sweets, most of them still possessed a reasonably good set of straight white teeth. As small children, before the attacks when cows were plentiful, they drank lots of milk. However, Ayuel and Beny both developed stomach ulcers—due to stress and diet change—that needed treatment. Ayuel's was serious enough to land him in the hospital. At one point, Ayuel showed Jean and me the deep scars on his legs and the back of his neck where he'd been hit by shrapnel from helicopter fire.

Fall and winter were busy times. Jean and I took turns picking up the guys at the Knickerbocker apartments for services at Christ Episcopal Church on the Kansas side of the state line. There were barbecues at Jean's, a Renaissance Festival and making a jigsaw puzzle of the states among the many activities. On Thanksgiving Day, Beny, Ayuel and Samuel Atak came to my house as well as both my children, their spouses, six grandchildren and others, including a homeless man. My daughter Renée and her husband are both jugglers as are their children. They all had a fun time giving the guys lessons juggling balls and clubs outside. In the afternoon, my son,

Gary, gave them their first driving lesson in a school parking lot. They loved it and actually did quite well.

They had all feared snow ever since touching a chunk of ice at their orientation in Kenya. They discovered it really wasn't so bad. Jean outfitted them with boots. Coats and knit caps came from somewhere, and they threw snowballs and made a snowman in my front yard.

When the guys were first processed at the camp, the U. S. Government agents had guessed their ages and assigned them all the birth date of January 1 for their legal documents. The older Sudanese in the area threw a grand birthday party for all of them on that date. Several of their friends were able to travel to attend also.

★

The people of Kansas City slowly became aware of the "Lost Boys" who had been assigned to their city. Schools and churches invited them to share their stories. Articles appeared in the *Kansas City Star*. A rally for support of Southern Sudan was held at the Lenexa Christian Center. It was sponsored by Christ Episcopal Church, Kansas Senator Sam Brownback and the Sudan Support Network. They called it "You Are Not Forgotten— Sudan: the Hidden Holocaust."

Before the program, Beny, Ayuel and Jean were interviewed by local TV Channel 41 and appeared on the ten o'clock news.

Several hundred Sudanese families who had settled in the area packed more than half of the center's auditorium and local people filled the rest. Senator Brownback, who has worked tirelessly for the Sudanese cause, gave an encouraging speech.

But the most emotional presentation was by Bishop Bullen Dolli from Southern Sudan, who was in the United States to receive the prestigious Religious Freedom Award. Having felt personally the devastation of Sudan's war and persecution, he told of being led to the edge of his freshly dug grave by members of the National Islamic Front. When they started to blindfold him for his execution, he refused the courtesy, saying he'd like to pray first. The men sneered but allowed it. He ended his prayer with the words, "Father, forgive them for they do not know what they are doing." The men loaded their guns, but not a shot was fired. They stood silently until the leader of the group fell to his knees and muttered, "Your God is alive." They released him, and he walked back to the church where his people welcomed him with palm branches.

Senator Brownback later graciously invited Beny and some of the others to his home for dinner with his family where they continued discussing the Sudan situation and what the United States could do to help. Shortly before 9/11 President Bush had appointed former Senator John Danforth from Missouri as American envoy for Peace in Sudan.

CBS began filming "The Lost Boys of Sudan" for *60 Minutes* with correspondent Bob Simon. This would be the first time a large segment of the American public would hear about the Sudanese tragedy and the willingness of the U.S. Government to take in these orphaned young people as refugees. The guys eagerly watched their story unfold on TV. The program opened with applications at the Kakuma Camp in Kenya and quickly moved to their American experiences. It included many of the guys in Kansas City. One of them, Joseph Taban, was featured with a memorable scene of his first attempt at driving a car on a sunny day in which he skidded off the road.

A Hollywood producer, Bobby Newmyer, was so impressed by the *60 Minutes* show that he called CBS. The producer of "Lost Boys" knew Gina Moreno, the employment agent who also had been captivated by them, and told Newmyer to call her. Newmyer had often said, "I have done well in my life. When I turn fifty, I want to stop doing well and start doing something good." He was still a few years short of that age goal, but here was his opportunity. "I want to make a movie about these Lost Boys," he told Gina in the phone call.

Newmyer came to Kansas City and met many of the guys there as well as other Lost Boys from around the country who gathered to share their experiences. Later he invited Beny and these other Sudanese advisors to come out to his home in Los Angeles. Trips were made back and forth.

Not only was the movie idea put in place, but also Newmyer realized how much the refugees—scattered throughout the United States—longed to see each other again. Newmyer and others then made and funded plans for a grand reunion to be held in Phoenix, Arizona, in 2004.

Since Newmyer soon became aware that Beny was the recognized leader of the sixty-five Lost Boys in Kansas City, he called him Beny George Washington, after America's first great leader. Actually, the word *beny* in Dinka means leader, as Beny explained to me. The day he was born a beloved Dinka leader, whom everyone called Beny, died. His parents named him in honor of this leader. It is certainly a fitting name for him.

In April 2002, I moved to Arkansas. Jean threw a going away party for me at her home with the guys from Knickerbocker. With much sadness I bid them goodbye. They were off to a good start in America, and I knew they would continue to flourish. Beny and Ayuel eventually moved to separate apartments in North Kansas City, each with multiple roommates. We continued to work on the book by phone and email. I made the four-hour trip every month or so to meet them in one of their apartments. They were always gracious hosts, taking time from their busy lives to tell me their stories. It was intensely emotional for the three of us.

★

In August 2004, the big reunion in Phoenix materialized at the Lost Boys Conference. It drew over 2,000 attendees, including Sudanese families. Gina was there and told me she'd watched the busloads arrive at the downtown hotel. In an emotional frenzy, the young people sought out their friends from Kakuma whom they had not seen since their days at the camp. Their happiness spread with hugs, tears and laughter.

Most exciting of all, Beny and Newmyer had arranged for Dr. John Garang, the SPLA leader of Southern Sudan, to come and give the keynote address. The fact that Garang's niece, Rebecca, is married to a Lost Boy, John Akui, and they live in Kansas City, helped in making the contact. At the Phoenix hotel Beny enthusiastically shook the great leader's hand and welcomed him to the conference. With him were other high officials, including Deng Alor, chief negotiator for the Comprehensive Peace Agreement, which at that time was still in progress. Since Beny had helped arrange his hero's appearance, he had an opportunity to speak personally with him. Garang told him, "You are getting a good education. Bring your skills and knowledge back to your country, and especially the American dream for human freedom, to help build a new Sudan."

In his speech at the Convention Center, Garang repeated the importance of education, just as he had done back at Panyido in Ethiopia so many years before. He told the young people he was happy to see their progress. The great leader reported that the peace negotiations were going well. He said the United States was with them in their struggle for freedom. He urged them to come home to the new Sudan and change it to a peaceful nation.

Beny gave an inspiring speech. The National Lost Boys Foundation was established. Filming had begun on the movie and everyone felt excited that Bobby Newmyer was supporting their cause in such a visual and far-reaching medium.

A few months later, on January 9, 2005, after nearly three years of negotiations, Sudan's government in Khartoum and the SPLA, led by Dr. Garang, signed the Comprehensive Peace Accords to end more than twenty-one years of civil war. Part of the agreement was that Garang would be elevated to the post of vice president, thus becoming the first southerner and first Christian to hold such a high position in the Islamic government. He and President Bashir, former enemies, would work out a power-sharing democratic government. Hope, at last, had come to Sudan. Celebration spread across the South and in the Sudanese community of Kansas City.

But only three weeks after being sworn in, Garang was killed in a helicopter crash on his way back from a trip to Uganda. Rejoicing turned to mourning. When his supporters feared foul play, riots broke out in Khartoum and in Southern Sudan. In Kansas City, the Sudanese community mourned for a week and marched in the streets, calling for an investigation. Beny and Ayuel were devastated. When they first heard the news, they couldn't believe their hero was dead until Beny made a call to General Maker Deng in Nairobi who confirmed the nightmare. Beny was feeling so much grief that his employer offered him some time off.

In May 2005, I attended Ayuel's graduation from Penn Valley Community College, where he earned an associate's degree in applied science and a paralegal technology certificate. Like proud parents, Jean and I applauded as he came forward in his cap and gown. The next fall, he enrolled at Avila College.

In December 2005, I got an email from Beny telling me that their beloved movie producer Bobby Newmyer had died suddenly of a heart attack. He was only forty-nine years old. The movie was placed on hold, but he had already made a huge difference in the lives of many young people by making the conference possible. He will not be forgotten.

*

In January 2006, Ayuel took a trip to Denver, Colorado, to visit Rebecca Kuol, his girlfriend from Kakuma. I had talked twice to Rebecca by phone. She was charming and warm, spoke beautiful English and told me she was enrolled in University of Colorado Denver, pursuing a degree in International Studies.

Rebecca and Ayuel were forced to end their romantic relationship back in Kakuma when they'd discovered they were distant blood relatives. Dinka culture forbids such marriages. After renewing their relationship in America, Rebecca's stepmother, still in Kakuma, continued to phone and write, reminding them of the Dinka tradition. Out of respect, they finally gave in to her wishes. Today they remain best friends, calling each other often with encouragement and advice.

Ayuel and his oldest brother Deng, whom he discovered was still alive and living in Toronto, Canada, finally were reunited by meeting in Michigan, where some of their relatives now lived. They met at a gathering of cousins late one night. When Ayuel walked in and the two brothers faced each other, they both were confused and speechless for some time. Ayuel said he could feel the warm tears crawling down his face. Finally, Deng spoke: "You were just a toddler. Now you are a grown man." Ayuel said he could hear his own voice, soft but bitter for all the time lost. "So many years without hearing or seeing you." After a warm embrace they sat and talked far into the morning.

Ayuel had some good news to share about their middle brother. Aleer had left Kakuma to study at Kampala International University in Uganda four years before Ayuel came to the United States. Ayuel had finally received a letter from him, saying he was still at the university studying law, was married and had two sons named for his brothers—Deng and Ayuel. At last, the three brothers made contact with each other and are happy in the knowledge that all are alive and well.

★

After five years in the United States, Ayuel and Beny were eligible for citizenship. They had jobs, were self-supporting, doing well in school and owned their own cars. Unfortunately, I was unable to attend either ceremony, but Gina accompanied Beny on December 8, 2006 to the Federal Courthouse in Kansas City. Sixty people, from forty-five different countries, were sworn in as new United States citizens. They had all passed the rigorous test on U. S. history, the Bill of Rights and the Constitution.

As a clerk called out each name, the candidate stood and stated his country of origin. The judge told the men and women how much he enjoyed doing this as a break from court cases. Then the clerk announced the names again for each one to come forward and receive his or her certificate. The new citizens, now eligible to vote, were referred to a desk where they could register. Someone was also available from the U. S. Post Office for those who wished to apply for a passport. Beny applied for his, as Ayuel would do later. Emotionally moved—as I was, though far away— Gina told me, "That was the most outstanding and amazing experience, and I will cherish forever that time with Beny." Beny and others she has befriended affectionately call her Gina Mama Kansas City.

On March 15, 2007, Ayuel experienced his ceremony of citizenship in a similarly moving way. They could now both go back to Africa without fear of being barred from re-entry to the United States. They longed to see their country again and reunite with friends and family members.

In mid-February, Beny left snow-covered Kansas City to fly to Atlanta and then to Paris where he missed his flight to Kenya. He was able to board a plane to Egypt and then to Khartoum, Sudan. "This is the place responsible for all the killing during my childhood," he thought as for the first time he set foot in that capital city. From there he flew to Nairobi, Kenya. He knew it would be an emotional greeting at the airport. He had not seen his Uncle Acuil since the time, at the age of nine, he chose to go with his father to see his brother Lueth in the cattle camp instead of into town with this uncle who had promised to buy him a shirt. That was when the Arabs had attacked the camp and he witnessed the horrors. After arriving in the United States, he sent his uncle money for much-needed eye surgery, which has proved to be successful.

And Mary Ajok, his childhood sweetheart? How would he feel? How would she react to seeing him again after a separation of thirteen years? She had left the Pochalla camp at age eleven with a small group, intending to go back to their hometown of Panrieng. Beny had heard no more about her until after coming to the United States. Then news came that she had made her way to Kakuma in 2001, only weeks after he had left. They had been in touch. He proposed marriage over the phone and hoped her mother and his uncle were in agreement.

When he got off the plane in Nairobi, Beny saw his Uncle Acuil and Mary A. waiting. With them stood a younger half-brother, Ayuong, whom Beny had never seen, as the boy had been born to one of his father's other wives after he'd left. Overcome with emotion, tears ran down Beny's face as he embraced them. Soon they were all crying with him.

Mary A. had come by bus from Kakuma and was staying with Uncle Acuil's family. Relatives of both families had agreed that the wedding should take place the next day. Marriage in Dinka culture is mandatory and part of becoming an adult. Beny was amazed at how tall and beautiful Mary A. had become. They were both overcome with delight to reunite —at long last— and become husband and wife.

Beny and Mary A. were married on February 14, 2007 in a traditional Dinka ceremony. Afterward, a large group of relatives and friends shared in the food and drink. His uncle then traveled to their hometown of Panrieng to arrange the bridewealth of cattle that would be paid to Mary A.'s family. Her mother, Beny's younger brother and sister and other relatives have moved back there. Another ceremony will take place in Panrieng before Mary A. comes to Kansas City. There, the cattle will be decorated with tassels and bells, led in a procession by young men singing. They will be met by young women also singing. Together they will participate in a ballet-type dance called *goor*. Cattle will be slaughtered for the meal and a feast prepared.

Ayuel left for his visit to Africa in May 2007 with Uganda as the first destination, where he would stay with his brother Aleer, his wife Anna and their two young sons. Unfortunately, he ran into flight delays in Newark,

New Jersey, where he lost two agonizing days, thinking he might never get to Africa. The day after his arrival, Aleer and thirty relatives—most of whom he had not seen since childhood—arranged a welcoming party for him, held in a large hall.

Ayuel and Deng had been paying Aleer's school fees since being in contact with him, but now, thankfully, the government of Southern Sudan is providing Aleer a full scholarship. Aleer also works at the university as chairman of the Sudanese Student Law Association.

After a joyful visit, Ayuel traveled on to his old refugee camp in Kakuma, Kenya, where he stayed with his uncle, Leek Deng, and family. They had organized another large welcoming party. The camp had changed since most of the leaders and best students had gone to live in other countries. It seemed conditions were poorer and less safe. Yet, this was the place where he'd spent ten years of his childhood, full of both sad and positive memories. It was a heartwarming reunion with the relatives and friends who'd remained.

*

Most of the young people highlighted in the book, who came to the United States, like Mel Deng and Gabriel Manyang, are in school and working. Ayuel's half brother Gutthier and friend Monica Bol, are still in Australia where they went on their own. Gutthier recently received his BA in International Relations from the University of Queensland. Anderia Mayom is now in the U. S. Army serving in Iraq, filling an important position as interpreter of Arabic.

Beny's friend Samuel Kiir is in Tennessee, but his wife Nyibol is still in Kenya, as is Mary A. The separation of husbands and wives is stressful, but for the women to immigrate here, they must show they will not be economically dependent on the State. The young men cannot support a family while still in school. Therefore, Beny's and Samuel's wives are both studying English so they will be able to hold jobs in the United States before long.

Sadly, Tiop—the man in Itang who encouraged Beny and Samuel to go to Kakuma where they could learn English—died of a heart attack the day Garang's helicopter crashed. Tiop had lost his leg fighting for the SPLA and told the boys that when his hero Dr. John died, he would die too.

Donayok, who led the group of seventeen across the Sudan to Ethiopia and was Ayuel's mentor through all their years as refugees in Africa, stayed in Kenya and married. In early 2007, Ayuel learned that while driving a company truck in rainy weather, Donayok's vehicle slid in the mud and turned over. He died instantly.

Manute Bol, the seven-foot-seven Washington Bullets basketball star— who came by plane with Bishop Taban to encourage the starving children in Pochalla, Sudan—moved to a suburb of Kansas City in July 2007. Bol had continued to work tirelessly for Sudanese causes and given away his millions to charity. He made many trips to visit the refugee camps. In 1995, Bol returned to his country expecting to be named Minister of Sport, but the position was denied to him because he refused to convert to Islam. The Sudanese government then revoked his visa. He was thus stranded there for nearly five years until Connecticut Senator Joe Lieberman and others were able to arrange his release so he could return to the United States. His fortune was gone.

In 2004, he was badly injured in an automobile accident. Friends and organizations pitched in and paid his hospital bills—just as he had helped so many others. Since Kansas City and the surrounding area had become a welcoming place for Sudanese in America, Bol chose to make his home there in the suburban town of Olathe, Kansas. Many Lost Boys had already moved there from their assigned cities, finding the people friendly and the jobs and educational opportunities plentiful.

Beny and Ayuel both came to Bol's welcoming party, organized by the Sudanese Church women. Ayuel introduced himself and welcomed Bol to the Kansas City area. Beny had an opportunity to stand up and publicly thank Bol for the time he came to Pochalla with food when they were starving. He acknowledged the roles of those who had helped bring about the Comprehensive Peace Agreement: Dr. Garang with guns, Manute Bol with his money and influence and the Sudanese Church women who sent food and clothing to Sudan.

Ayuel plans to graduate from Avila College in December 2008 with a B.A. in Business Administration and a minor in Political Science. He works two jobs with barely enough time to sleep. Beny studied Community

Health in Medical Terminology at Penn Valley and graduated with an Associate of Arts. He is now enrolled at the University of Missouri, Kansas City, working toward a BA in Pre-law, Criminal Justice and Criminology. He plans to graduate in 2009. Since 2005, Beny has been employed at DEMDACO—a gift and home deco industry—packing, filling orders and other assigned duties. He's planning for the time his wife Mary A. can come be with him in Kansas City. He also hopes to bring his younger brother Ayuong there and get him enrolled in school.

Beny and Ayuel have both done remarkably well, and I feel honored to be their friend. As they, along with the 3,800 other young people from far away Sudan, finish their education and rise in the world, I am confident of the good they will do for America and their country, because they are truly the "seeds of the new Sudan." Their contributions will surely make for a better, more peaceful world.

ENGLISH/DINKA TRANSLATIONS

1.	God	1.	Nhialic
2.	Heaven	2.	Pan-nhial
3.	Earth	3.	Piny
4.	Sun	4.	Akol
5.	Moon	5.	Pei
6.	Adam	6.	Garang
7.	Eve	7.	Abuk
8.	Woman	8.	Tik
9.	Man	9.	Moc
10.	Boy	10.	Dhol
11.	Girl	11.	Nya
12.	Child	12.	Meth
13.	Sit	13.	Nyuoc
14.	Stand	14.	Koc
15.	Run	15.	Kat
16.	House	16.	Hot
17.	Fire	17.	Mac
18.	Gun	18.	Dhang
19.	Help	19.	Kuony
20.	Law	20.	Luong
21.	Power	21.	Riel

22.	Cow	22.	Weng
23.	Goat	23.	Beu
24.	Sheep	24.	Amal
25.	Exhaust	25.	Dak
26.	Marry	26.	Thiek
27.	Rich	27.	Jeek
28.	Poor	28.	Ngong
29.	Chief	29.	Beny
30.	Drought	30.	Yaak
31.	Sick	31.	Tuany
32.	Disease	32.	Jok
33.	Evil	33.	Rieec
34.	Suffer	34.	Mam
35.	Hope	35.	Ngath
36.	Courage	36.	Rielpiou
37.	Peace	37.	Door
38.	Justice	38.	Dik
39.	War	39.	Tong
40.	Education	40.	Pioch
41.	Live	41.	Piir
42.	Death	42.	Thou
43.	Happiness	43.	Mietpiou
44.	Hunger	44.	Cok
45.	Walk	45.	Cath
46.	Journey	46.	Kueth
47.	Thirsty	47.	Yal
48.	Water	48.	Piu
49.	Lion	49.	Koor
50.	Hyenas	50.	Anguei
51.	Tiger	51.	Kuac
52.	River	52.	Kiir
53.	Insect	53.	Kuom
54.	Animal	54.	Lei
55.	Talk	55.	Jam

56.	Silence	56.	Mim
57.	Faith	57.	Gam
58.	Call	58.	Cot
59.	Remember	59.	Tak
60.	Father	60.	Baba
61.	Mother	61.	Mama
62.	Desert	62.	Toor
63.	Disaster	63.	Riak
64.	Write	64.	Gat
65.	Read	65.	Kuan
66.	Community	66.	Akutnhom
67.	Unity	67.	Mat
68.	Reconciliation	68.	Maat
69.	Freedom	69.	Nhomlau
70.	Build	70.	Yik
71.	Terror	71.	Anakoc
72.	Depress	72.	Tektak
73.	Family	73.	Kochku
74.	Parent	74.	Kochkun
75.	Person	75.	Ran
76.	People	76.	Koc
77.	Human	77.	Thaai
78.	Oppress	78.	Yang
79.	Security	79.	Tiit
80.	Advise	80.	Kuen
81.	Road	81.	Kuer
82.	Car	82.	Rai
83.	Friend	83.	Math
84.	Sleep	84.	Niin
85.	Swim	85.	Kuang
86.	Thank	86.	Liec
87.	Revenge	87.	Guor
88.	Forgive	88.	Pal
89.	Share	89.	Ruom

90.	Cry	90.	Dhieu
91.	Truth	91.	Yiech
92.	Hide	92.	Thian
93.	Laugh	93.	Dol
94.	Love	94.	Dhier
95.	Watch	95.	Tekayuol
96.	Look	96.	Ting
97.	Beauty	97.	Dhuong
98.	Salt	98.	Awai
99.	Light	99.	Her
100.	Compete	100.	Meen
101.	Rain	101.	Deng
102.	Book	102.	Athor
103.	Surprise	102.	Gai
104.	Song	104.	Dit
105.	Bird	105.	Dit
106.	Night	106.	Wakou
107.	Evening	107.	Thei
108.	Day	108.	Akol
109.	Dream	109.	Nyuth
110.	Cold	110.	Wiir
111.	Sweat	111.	Tuc
112.	Hot	112.	Leeth
113.	Food	113.	Kuin
114.	Eat	114.	Cam
115.	Play	115.	Thuec
116.	Fear	116.	Riech
117.	Brave	117.	Ngeny
118.	Camp	118.	Wut
119.	Worry	119.	Dier
120.	Cloud	120.	Luat
121.	Drown	121.	Muo
122.	Enemy	122.	Ranater
123.	Oil	123.	Miok

124.	Work	124.	Loi
125.	Cook	125.	That
126.	Star	126.	Chier
127.	Cloth	127.	Alath
128.	Shoe	128.	Waar
129.	Tree	129.	Tim
130.	Respect	130.	Atheek
131.	Alcohol	131.	Mou
132.	Sweet White Flour	132.	Papa

Dinka Months

1.	Akochthi	January
2.	Aduong	February
3.	Alekbor	March
4.	Akoldit	April
5.	Bildit	May
6.	Bilthi	June
7.	Lal	July
8.	Hor	August
9.	Kongak	September
10.	Nyeth	October
11.	Kol	November
12.	Akoch	December

ACCLAIM
FOR
COURAGEOUS
JOURNEY

"Ayuel Leek Deng and Beny Ngor Chol face incredible obstacles in this story of courage and unrelenting determination. *Courageous Journey* makes a powerful statement about the effects of today's most threatening issues—terrorism, religious conflict and ethnic hatred—on the most vulnerable among us."

—**Former U.S. President Jimmy Carter, Nobel Peace Prize winner**

"As one who worked with the so-called 'lost boys' in Kakuma in different capacities, I heartily endorse this very important book that will be read by many to understand the tragedies that faced these young men in Sudan resulting from civil war. The content reflects a true picture from my point of view."

—**Stephen Kajirwa Keverenge, Associate Community Services Officer— United Nations High Commission for Refugees**

"*Courageous Journey* portrays an incredible child's-eye view of the recent civil war in the Sudan. As two boys grow to manhood they struggle with their own anger and try to understand the cruelty by their own government. It is fascinating to watch their growth toward a sense of peace and reconciliation. Barbara Youree must be commended for producing such a remarkable profile of human suffering, perseverance and determination. It is a work which all concerned with the plight of the Sudanese must read."

—**Dr. Francis M. Deng, Director, Sudan Peace Support Project**

ABOUT THE AUTHORS

 **Ayuel Leek Deng** has completed his A.A.S. degree in Paralegal Technology from Penn Valley Community College in Kansas City, Missouri. He is studying for a B.S. in Political Science from Avila University in Kansas City, Missouri, which is the city where he lives as well.

Beny Ngor Chol was the Community-Based Rehabilitation Program manager/trainer for the International Rescue Committee in Africa. He has completed an A.S. degree from Penn Valley Community College and is studying for his B.A. at the University of Missouri in Kansas City, Missouri, which is also where he resides.

 **Barbara Youree** has taught English and French and is the author of four novels, six children's books and numerous magazine articles. She has an M.S. from Emporia State University in Emporia, Kansas and a B.A. from Carson-Newman College in Jefferson City, Tennessee. She makes her home in Rogers, Arkansas.

Beny and Ayuel signing the contract for *Courageous Journey*. Photo by Barbara Youree.